DOCTRINE AND ARGUMENT IN INDIAN PHILOSOPHY

INDIAN THOUGHT

Managing Editor
Purusottama Bilimoria (Deakin University)
Advisory Editors
J. N. Mohanty (Temple University)
Bimal K. Matilal (University of Oxford)
Consulting Board
Anindita N. Balslev (Århus University)
Sibajiban Bhattacharya (India)
D. P. Chattopadhyaya (India)
Eliot Deutsch (University of Hawaii)
Ramchandra Gandhi (Delhi)
Paul J. Griffiths (University of Notre Dame)
Gerald Larson (University of California)
Julius Lipner (University of Cambridge)
Sengaku Mayeda (University of Tokyo)
Karl H. Potter (University of Washington)
Mark Siderits (Illinois State University)
Ninian Smart (University of California)

VOLUME 4

DOCTRINE AND ARGUMENT IN INDIAN PHILOSOPHY

BY

NINIAN SMART

SECOND REVISED EDITION

E.J. BRILL
LEIDEN • NEW YORK • KÖLN
1992

First published 1964
Second revised edition 1992

The paper in this book meets the guidelines for permanence and durability of the Committee on Production Guidelines for Book Longevity of the Council on Library Resources.

Library of Congress Cataloging-in-Publication Data

Smart, Ninian, 1927-
Doctrine and argument in Indian philosophy / by Ninian Smart.
p. cm. — (Indian thought, ISSN 0924-8986 ; v. 4)
Includes bibliographical references and index.
1. Philosophy, Indic. I. Title. II. Series: Indian thought and culture ; v. 4.
B131.S62 1992
181'.4—dc20 92-10917
CIP

ISSN 0924-8986
ISBN 90 04 09479 2

PRINTED IN THE NETHERLANDS

For My Father

CONTENTS

PREFACE TO THE NEW EDITION

I have revised this book somewhat, through changing its format compared to the 1964 edition and through updating the bibliography, etc. I am most grateful to Purushottama Bilimoria for creating the occasion of a new edition, and to Mary Churchill, Cybelle Shattuck and Sara Duke for aid in preparing the manuscript.

Ninian Smart
University of California Santa Barbara,
March 1990.

INTRODUCTION

Western philosophers do not pay much attention to Indian thought. The reasons are many. For one thing, though there are histories of Indian philosophy written in European languages, notably Surendranath Dasgupta's excellently monumental *A History of Indian Philosophy*, they, and most other works on the subject, keep breaking into Sanskrit. This reduces their intelligibility. Then again, Indian philosophy is much bound up with theology(as indeed European philosophy has been, though less so of late); and Indian theology cannot be understood without both a sympathy for what Indian religions are getting at (I say *sympathy*, but not necessarily agreement), and some acquaintance with the historical background of the Vedic, Buddhist and other texts. Again, contemporary Indian historians of philosophy tend to ignore the topics which exercise European and American philosophers: there is rather little concern, in the Sub-continent, for Wittgenstein, Sartre and Quine. Further, there is the prevalent suspicion, among English-speaking philosophers, that the theological bent of much Indian metaphysics means that Indian argumentation is neither rigorous nor realistic. Finally, it is sometimes opined that philosophy is either an international activity where national roots are irrelevant or it is mere history of ideas, in which case it is only of incidental interest to the true philosopher. Such suspicions of Indian philosophy are not mitigated by the current Western enthusiasm for Oriental spirituality: travelling monks and yogis (though often innocent of pompous intentions) tend to speak of their 'philosophy' rather than of religion, partly because the latter term is loaded in a special way in its Western use. Thus they give the impression that spiritual uplift, rather than analytic exactness, is the chief characteristic of Indian philosophy.

These suspicions and difficulties are relevant to the purposes of this book. My aim is two-fold. In the first place, there is no escaping the fact that the main determinants of systematic metaphysics in India have been religious in character. Therefore I wish to illuminate the way in which these determinants have been operative. Put crudely, my main thesis on this point is that different patterns of religious experience and activity give rise to varying patterns of theology and philosophy, ranging from atheistic to theistic doctrines. In elaborating and sustaining this thesis I shall be attempting to bring out more clearly what has been partially and obscurely hinted at in some comparative studies. India has been a laboratory of religious doctrines, and therefore conditions are peculiarly propitious for the exercise which I have in mind. In this way, I hope that some light will be thrown not only on the general pattern of Indian thought, but also upon the general relations between doctrines and the religious life—and thus also upon the philosophy of religion.

My second aim, which will occupy the second part of the book, is to exhibit some of the patterns of argument on various philosophical topics which can be found in the history of Indian thought. The fact that the main determinants of the metaphysical systems have been religious does not at all entail that the arguments used in elaborating and defending them are mere window-dressing. It does not at all mean that the arguments are lacking in subtlety and intrinsic interest. My aim therefore is a clear, if by necessity highly selective, exposition of such philosophical arguments, so that Westerners with philosophical interests can have a reasonably accurate picture of how certain main issues have been treated in the Indian tradition. I have confined my exposition to metaphysical and epistemological topics, since these show most clearly the philosophical dimensions of the main systems: I have therefore, for the most part, neglected the philosophy of value (ethics, political philosophy and aesthetics), together with formal logic. As to the latter, it does not lie within my competence to give an account of traditional Indian formal logic which would be useful, interesting or exciting to mathematical logicians. The key issues which I have chosen (for they are ones which exhibit important features of Indian philosophical thinking) are these: arguments for the existence of God, and the powerful criticisms of them; discussions about the soul; epistemological questions; the nature of causation; and problems about induction and inference. As will be noticed, these topics not only overlap and interrelate, but also introduce some interesting side-issues. In short, I hope the reader will acquire some insight into, and taste for, the arguments which exercized traditional Indian philosophy.

To this end I use no Sanskrit or Pali expressions in the text. As remarked above, one of the troubles with histories of Indian philosophy is that they keep breaking into these languages. This of course can be justified: surely the serious student of Indian philosophy ought to be acquainted with the languages. It could also be argued that concepts cannot be divorced from the language in which they are expressed —and so translations of many key concepts are not genuinely possible. But these arguments do not weigh with me: for two reasons. First, there is no dearth of expositions which make use of Sanskrit. But my aim is to give Indian philosophy a wider philosophical public: and indeed if philosophy is to be truly international the specialist in languages, though important, is not the only person to be considered. Second, I am bold enough to try to solve the problem of translation, and in the following way. The problem amounts to this: that though it is possible to give English equivalents of the key expressions in Sanskrit, such as *ātman* or self, it would be misleading to use the English expression without qualification. These concepts tend to be ramified—to have roots in a whole set of assertions. Consequently, they differ in certain important respects from their English equivalents, which have other ramifications. About many concepts we can say (with apologies to Wordsworth)

> ...not in utter nakedness
> But trailing clouds of theory do they come.

Now to some extent, this is a problem which we come across *within* a language, and not just in the context of translation. Hume's use of 'impression' for instance has to be understood in the milieu of his philosophical position. So part of the solution of the problem consists simply in an exposition of the ramifications. The rest of the solution, which I have here adopted, consists in the use of two devices.

First, the English expressions which I use to translate key Sanskrit and Pāli terms will be standardized throughout my text. At its first appearance a term will be given its Sanskrit or Pāli equivalent. Thereafter the same English word (e.g. 'self', 'atom', etc.) will be used. Secondly, I include at the end a glossary, in which I discuss the translations, where necessary. This will involve mentioning Sanskrit and Pali expressions, but I aim to do it in such a manner that the issues involved will be quite intelligible to the ordinary reader.

There is, however, one minor qualification in regard to this procedure. I shall not entirely eschew the use of those very few Sanskrit words which have virtually become part of English—such as nirvana, karma, Vedānta, Yoga, the Buddha, etc.

To some degree, the concept of this book, as I have so far outlined it, is rather traditional. There has grown up a custom for people to write about Indian philosophy as a single unit. There are a number of weighty histories of Indian philosophy, aiming to be comprehensive in scope. There are other briefer expositions, such as Mysore Hiriyanna's excellent *Outlines* and *Essentials of Indian Philosophy.* These too aim to cover more or less the whole field of traditional thought. In plan, however, the present book more nearly corresponds to Giuseppe Tucci's *Storia della flosofia indiana,* the first part of which is an account of the various systems, and the second an exposition of the arguments on various philosophical topics. Nevertheless, he does not aim at an explanation of the different patterns of metaphysical belief, as I do, nor to desanskritize. However, of course, the present work is on a much more modest scale than Tucci's erudite volume.

One of the reasons why there is so great a tendency to take a holistic view of Indian philosophy is that the latter has, in the course of its evolution, crystallized into a number of schools. Consequently, to understand some of the arguments it is useful to know the doctrines of other schools that they were aimed *against.* Another reason for the holistic approach is that among the orthodox, that is the Hindu, schools, it became fashionable to hold the eirenic doctrine that they represented different emphases in the delineation of the same underlying truth. There were religious reasons for this pacific and in some respects very unphilosophical view. But it has given impetus to the quest for a comprehensive treatment of Indian philosophy as a whole. As we shall see, the eirenic doctrine is neither justifiable nor characteristic of Indian philosophy during its most argumentative and flourishing period.

Nevertheless, the holistic approach, which in a sense I here adopt, is convenient. First, in describing the main features of certain important metaphysical systems in the Indian tradition, I hope to throw light, as I have said, on the religious determinants of them. And second, without some historical background, it would be impossible to go on to expound the arguments on various topics which I undertake in the second part.

I have had to be selective, both in regard to the systems of which I treat, and in regard to the philosophical topics. As to the former, I have confined my exposition to what I consider to be the most important *traditional* schools. I have not ventured to describe what some modern Indian philosophers, such as Radhakrishnan and Aurobindo, have said, nor in general do I survey contemporary developments in Indian philosophy. The reasons for this are rather simple. First, people like Aurobindo and Radhakrishnan write in English, and there is therefore little call to expound them further. Second, some contemporary developments are genuinely international, in the sense that they consist in Indian philosophers engaging in discussion of current topics with their counterparts in other countries (for instance in the pages of the new *Indian Journal of Philosophy* edited by Professor James Swamidasan). It would be pointless to treat such discussions on national lines. Third, in so far as the 'big names' in modern Indian philosophy have had powerful religious interests, the treatment of Indian metaphysical systems in the first part of this book may serve to show clearly the background against which those religious interests are to be understood.

It would, however, be dreary for the reader if I were to repeat in great detail the whole history of Indian religious and philosophical thought, in the first part. I aim rather to give the minimum amount of historical detail as is compatible with the reasonable clarity of my exposition of the various schools and with my aim of showing their religious determinants. In this sense, the first part of the book, like the second, is more analytical than historical in intent.

It may also be mentioned here that some of my notes (few in number) are more in the nature of appendices dealing with certain important issues about my exposition, etc. This is especially true of notes I.2, I.3, III.i, VII.i and X.i.

Finally, in regard to the plan I have outlined, it is worth warning the reader that the first part of the book ought to be more controversial than the second. In the latter I am concerned to expound, rather than to evaluate, arguments. I leave it to the philosophical acumen of the reader to determine whether they are cogent and important. But in the first part, though I hope that my exposition of the various schools is sound, the general thesis about their religious determinants is my own, and not just history. I trust, therefore, that even if it turns out to be false, it will prove at least to be *interestingly* false.

Naturally, my exposition owes a very great deal to other people—to those who through their painstaking and original work have opened up Indian philosophy to the West and have recovered for modern India the details of her philosophical tradition: above all, to the great Surendranath Dasgupta. If I can be a useful intermediary between them and the reader, I shall be satisfied.

PART I

CHAPTER I
METAPHYSICAL SYSTEMS

An indication of the connection between philosophy and the religious traditions of India is the fact that the various schools came to be classified as orthodox *āstika* and unorthodox *nāstika.* Literally, the Sanskrit words used mean 'asserting that there is' and 'asserting that there is not' respectively, and by Western analogies one might expect the implication to be this—that the orthodox assert, and the unorthodox deny, the existence of God. However, one can be an orthodox Hindu and an atheist, and some of the traditional schools deny the existence of a Creator God. No: orthodoxy consists, not in subscribing to such a particular doctrinal belief, but rather in accepting the validity of the Hindu scriptures. It is one of the paradoxes of the tradition that extraordinarily diverse doctrinal interpretations of the scriptures have been formulated, so that both atheism and theism are given a scriptural basis. However—and here we meet a linguistic difficulty— atheism in the Indian context does not carry with it irreligiousness. Atheism involves disbelief in a Creator, but is quite compatible with belief in salvation—that is, with belief in the possibility of release *(mokṣa)* from the round of rebirth. Nor is it incompatible with prayer to the gods, conceived as beings who are inside, rather than transcendent to, the empirical cosmos. Nor, more generally, is it incompatible with the complex of socio-religious duties which encompass the daily life of the orthodox Hindu. Consequently, atheism in this context is not necessarily anti-religious or indifferent to religion. Thus in an important way orthodoxy goes together with, not so much correct belief, as right practice.

For this reason, it is well to remember that the denial of the existence of a supreme Ruler of the universe is, in the Indian context, not to be equated with that set of beliefs about the world and religion which goes under the name of 'atheism' in the West; and to signalize this difference, and to represent the Sanskrit concept, I shall henceforth use 'atheism' *(anīśvaravād)* to stand for the Indian denial of a Creator.

Nevertheless, there are important religious divergences between the Brāhmanical religion which counts itself as orthodox and those beliefs which it categorizes as unorthodox, namely Buddhism, Jainism, certain other sects, and the Cārvaka school (a form of materialism analogous in some respects to that of Lucretius). It is therefore not inconvenient to adopt the distinction. It also draws attention to the fact that Jainism and Buddhism not only reject the Hindu scriptures as authoritative, but possess substantial bodies of scripture of their own.

By consequence, the period immediately before, and during the sixth and fifth centuries B. C. E. was determinative for the Indian tradition. On the one hand, this was roughly the period of the completion of the classical Upaniṣads, that collection of writings which sought in various ways to penetrate to the real religious meaning of the sacrificial religion expressed in the much earlier Vedic hymns and in the elaborate ritualistic literature appended thereto in the intervening centuries. It is above all the teaching of the Upaniṣads which later religious thinkers tried to systematize. This whole corpus of literature, regarded as sacred, is the basic canon of Hinduism— though additions, notably the *Bhagavadgītā*, are sometimes made. It is to this corpus that the orthodox appeal. It is regarded as expressing the eternal truth, and this truth, because orally transmitted from indefinitely ancient times, is called 'what is heard', or as might be said in the West, it is the Word; but we can perhaps signify what is meant by thinking of it as revelation *(śruti)*, though without the Western implication that revelation is necessarily *God's* revealing of himself or of the divine truth. The period in question, then, marks the climax of the composition of this revelation. In the latter part of the sixth century, and the early part of the fifth, there occur, moreover, the lives of the great Teachers of Buddhism and of Jainism, the Buddha and Mahāvīra. The corpus of scriptures built up within these faiths looks back to the teachings of these men. Thus the period is critical in the formation of both orthodox revelation and unorthodox scriptures.

The centuries following this period not only saw the rise of different schools within Buddhism, but the progressive formulation of various strands of orthodox thought. This latter process issued in the six branches of orthodox philosophy, sometimes referred to as the six viewpoints *(darśana)*. This traditional classification, as we shall see, is not altogether a rational one; but it is useful here, in a preliminary way, to outline these systems. It will help us to delimit the scope of the present survey.

The six viewpoints have come to be coupled together in three pairs. The reasons for this will be explained shortly. The three pairs are: Sāṃkhya and Yoga; Vaiśeṣika and Nyāya; and Vedānta and Mīmāṃsā. The latter of each of these pairs is more a methodology than a metaphysical system, and this is one reason for the oddness of the traditional classification into six viewpoints. Thus Yoga is primarily a method of spiritual and physical training; Nyāya is primarily logic and the rules of argument; Mīmāṃsā is primarily a formalization of methods of scriptural interpretation. However, in the history of the evolution of the viewpoints there has occurred a coalescence of Sāṃkhya with Yoga and Vaiśeṣika with Nyāya. In each case the methodological enquiry has felt, as it were, the need for a 'theoretical' background, so that the exponent of Yoga uses Sāṃkhya metaphysics, with some adaptations; and likewise the Nyāya has taken over the world-picture presented by the Vaiśeṣika school. Mīmāṃsā, however, has not taken over Vedānta conceptions, but has a somewhat rudimentary metaphysics of its own. On the other hand, the Vedānta, literally the 'end of the scriptures'—that is, the complete point of the scriptures, —aims to formulate the essential orthodox religious metaphysics. But within the Vedānta there are importantly different schools. Consequently, this viewpoint alone should be broken into several alternative metaphysical systems.

Briefly, the viewpoints in their fully elaborated forms assert the following. Sāṃkhya holds that nature *prakṛti*, i.e. everything except souls (*puruṣa*) is a unitary entity which evolves *pariṇāma* into varying forms, including minds (here regarded as distinct from the underlying souls). Release comes for a soul, which is normally implicated in nature and thereby in the round of rebirth, through discrimination (*viveka*) of its essential distinctness from nature. The word *Sāṃkhya* literally means 'enumeration', and there is some obscurity as to the reason for this name for the viewpoint. But it doubtless refers to the enumeration of types of entity, or categories, employed by *Sāṃkhya* in its description of the forms of nature's evolution, etc. Because of its use of such distinctions, and to suggest also its central doctrine of the distinctness of the soul from nature, it will be convenient to refer to this system as Distinctionism.

Yoga (literally 'harnessing', i.e. of a person's mental and physical powers) has essentially the same metaphysics, but grafts on to distinctionism belief in a Lord *(īśvara)*, i.e. a divine Being who, though not in a full sense creator of the world, assists souls in their quest for spiritual perfection and insight. 'Yoga' is sufficiently familiar in English to require no translation. But it should be noted that the methods associated with Yoga are also used both inside and outside the Hindu tradition in connection with a religious quest often conceived very differently from the way Yoga as a system conceives it. When it is necessary to refer to this family of methods analogous to those of orthodox Yoga, I shall use the lower-case 'yoga'. In this sense, it is right and proper to speak of Buddhist yoga, for example. Flabby Westerners sometimes feel the need for the physical aspect of yoga, though doubtless they do not subscribe to Yoga.

Vaiśeṣika holds that everything except the eternal selves (*ātman*) is built up out of infinitesimally small atoms In its later form, the viewpoint is theistic: it is God who ultimately imparts motion and order to the atoms. The school gets its name from *viśeṣa*, or difference, a concept which plays an important part in its formulations. But for our purposes it can conveniently be referred to as atomism. The metaphysical differences of Nyāya from Atomism, being rather slight, need not concern us here: suffice it to remark that Nyāya means 'method of correct reasoning', and can therefore be suitably translated as Logic (of course in a broad sense of 'logic').

Mīmāṃsā literally means 'investigation', i.e. into the text of revelation, and concentrates upon rules for interpreting the scriptures as a system of injunctions, rather than statements, concerned with the performance of religious duties. Its ritualistic emphasis led to curious results. The scriptures were regarded as everlasting and having intrinsic authority. For this reason, the viewpoint, alone among orthodox schools, denies the successive dissolution and recreation of the cosmos. Such a 'pulsating' universe might seem to require the intervention of a Lord to recreate the scriptures; and the Mīmāṃsā is atheistic. Though gods within the cosmos are recognized, as they are referred to in the Vedic hymns, etc., the sacrificial ritual is considered efficacious in itself. Moreover, other viewpoints describe ultimate release as involving the disappearance of the eternal self from the sphere of empirical existence, this school, until a late period in its development, described emancipation as life in heaven *sagga*. It is to be noted that in Indian religious thought heavens and purgatories *niraya* are generally considered as virtually being compartments of the cosmos, so that release normally means going beyond heaven. This is in line with the doctrine of rebirth, which took such a firm grip on the Indian imagination. However, it is only in the Upaniṣads that belief in rebirth is introduced into the orthodox tradition. The Vedic hymns and the sacrificial works appended to them conceive of heaven, rather than release, as the supreme goal. Thus the Mīmāṃsā represents a conservative exposition of early Brāhmanical religion. Its philosophical interest mainly consists in its attempt to analyse scripture as a set of imperatives—an analysis which stimulated linguistic speculation in India—and in its anti-theistic arguments. In view of the scriptural interests of this viewpoint, we can conveniently refer to it as Exegesis *(Mīmāṃsā)*.

Vedānta (a word sufficiently well known in English-speaking circles to justify its retention here) has proliferated, as we remarked above, into a number of different metaphysical systems. Of these, that of the great Śaṅkara (prob. 788-820) is best known. It involves a rigorous interpretation of certain texts in the Upaniṣads which imply the oneness between the self and holy Power *(Brahman)* sustaining the cosmos. In Śaṅkara's interpretation this 'oneness' is numerical identity: there is not therefore a plurality of selves. Further, the world, conceived as a distinct reality, is illusory (*māyā*). There is only one Being, and release consists in realizing one's identity with that Being in inner, contemplative experience. Because of his identification of the self with the one holy Being, Śaṅkara's doctrine is known as Non-Dualism *(Advaita).*

At the other extreme of the Vedānta lies Madhva, four centuries later, who argued for a sharp distinction between the selves and the holy Being, and also between both and the material world. Among various intermediate positions, that of Rāmānuja (twelth century) is justly the most influential. He held that the self shares the divine nature and ultimately, in release, is united with God. These two systems are referred to as Dualism *(Dvaita)* and Qualified Non-Dualism *Viśiṣṭādvaita* respectively.

There are, in addition, some Hindu schools which lie outside the six viewpoints, notably the Śaiva Siddhānta, or 'Śaivite Doctrine'. It has resemblances to the Vedānta, especially in the forms propounded by Rāmānuja and Madhva. The evolution of Hinduism brought to the fore two great gods each regarded by their adherents as the supreme object of worship, namely Viṣṇu and Śiva. Around these figures there grew up a body of sacred literature distinct from revelation. One social reason for this was the exclusion of the lowest classes from participation in orthodox religion, and these semi-orthodox writings enshrined a type of religion which was open to the underprivileged. Naturally, the Śaivite writings gave rise to their own particular theology, and this was formalized principally, among others, by Meykaṇḍa, in the thirteenth century.

I have mentioned above three important unorthodox movements, Buddhism, Jainism and Materialism. The first of these derives, of course, from the teachings of the Buddha (?563—? 483 B.C.E.), though there is little doubt that he made use of elements of religious thought and tradition prior to his time. But the remarkable transformation of ideas and practices effected by him is testimony to his great originality and insight. Although he accepted the doctrine of rebirth, which indeed is central to orthodox formulations of Buddhism, he alone among religious teachers in India (excepting the Non-Dualistic Vedānta) denied the existence of a plurality of eternal selves. In this respect, the Buddha was close to the contemporary materialists. Moreover, the Buddha was agnostic about the existence of a Lord. His rejection of both the concept of a holy Power underlying or sustaining the cosmos and of the concept of an eternal self has sometimes proved puzzling to Western commentators, who have been tempted therefore to reinterpret Buddhist texts in a way which would reintroduce either individual selves or a supreme Self. However, there is no doubt at all that the non-self (*anattā*) doctrine is deeply entrenched in the Pāli canon, and that there is to be found there no doctrine of an absolute underlying or embracing phenomena: and it is one of the remarkable features of Buddhist history that no one has explicitly attempted to propound a self doctrine (though there have been movements in this direction, but no one has dared use the word 'self'). There is therefore over-whelming reason for attributing the non-self doctrine to the earliest tradition, and doubtless to the Buddha himself.

The rejection of a permanent entity underlying psychological and physical states meant that persons were assimilated in one important respect to the rest of nature. For the Buddha also insisted on the doctrine of impermanence *(anicca).* All entities are analysed into a succession of impermanent states. Permanent substances having been banished from his metaphysics, the Buddha reinterpreted the transcendent goal, nirvana, not as a substance, with which the saint *(arhat)* becomes identified, but rather as a state—a permanent state.

As regards rebirth, it was not open to the Buddhists to conceive of it as involving the migration of a permanent *(nicca)* self from one psycho-physical organism to another. Instead, the whole sequence of lives (which we can conveniently call the 'macro-individual') is regarded in much the way that Hume conceived the life of a single person (the 'micro-individual'). At death, unless the person is beyond the grip of craving *taṇhā*, and has thereby attained nirvana in this life, a fresh sequence of psychophysical events is set up.

These doctrines, considerably overlaid by scholastic distinctions, are preserved in the Pāli canon and in the teachings of Theravāda Buddhism today. This, the surviving school of the so-called Lesser Vehicle, claims to preserve original Buddhism in its purity. Hence the name 'Theravāda', the Doctrine of the Elders (hereafter referred to as the Elder Doctrine, School, etc.). Two other Lesser Vehicle schools we shall have occasion to mention; once important, they have now disappeared. These are the Personalists *(Pudgalavādins)*, who came nearer than any other Buddhists to rejecting the non-self doctrine, and the Realists *(Sarvāstivādins)*, who came nearer than others to rejecting the doctrine of universal impermanence.

But beyond the Realist movement (the *Sarvāstivāda*), there developed the Mahāyāna, or 'Greater Vehicle'. This doctrinal tendency derived basically from two sources—changes in popular religion and metaphysical speculation.

Theoretically, the Buddha, though above ordinary humans, was in no sense divine. Thus—even today—in Sri Lanka and other countries belonging to the Elder school, though there are temples, in which one can find the image of the Buddha, the action of ordinary folk in laying flowers before such statues is no more than the paying of respects to the deceased Teacher— vanished from human ken in his attainment of final nirvana. However, with the growth of Mahāyāna practices, there started a twin tendency to deify the Buddha and to concentrate upon the ideal of the Buddha-to-be (or Bodhisattva). This ideal derives mainly from the story of the Buddha himself—before his Enlightenment, he was tempted by Māra (the Buddhist equivalent of Satan) to vanish into final nirvana without communicating his spiritual discoveries to mankind. Rejecting this, the Buddha went on, for some forty-five years, to preach and to teach in North India. Thus there arose the notion that the Buddha sacrifices himself on behalf of mankind. In conjunction with this, there were elaborated stories about the previous lives of the Buddha, when he was Buddha-to-be, in which he displayed heroic self- sacrifice. Consequently, it came to be believed that the heroic activities of the Bodhisattva attracted an inexhaustible store of merit which could be transferred to otherwise unworthy persons, provided that they called on the name of the Buddha in faith.

In this way there came into existence the cult, not only of celestial Buddhas apart from the historical Buddha (who in any event was not considered as unique, but as a member of a sequence of great Teachers), but also of heavenly Bodhisattvas or Buddhas-to-be. In this way the so-called Greater Vehicle stressed the importance of sacrifice on behalf of others, the essence of Buddhist compassion, in contrast to the supposedly narrow goal of the Lesser Vehicle, whereby the saint concentrates on achieving his own individual nirvana. This indeed is why the 'Greater Vehicle' adopted that name, and 'Lesser Vehicle' was used as a term of opprobrium. In any case, by the Christian era there was a powerful development of religious tendencies whereby Buddhism was in some degree assimilated to Hinduism: the celestial Buddhas and Bodhisattvas corresponded to the gods.

At the same time, Buddhist metaphysicians went in an idealistic direction. Phenomena were regarded either as products of the mind, as in the *Vijñānavāda* School or Idealism, or as contradictory. In the latter case, it was thought necessary to postulate an Absolute, described as the Void *śūnya*: not only were phenomena thought of as void, being contradictory and insubstantial *(adravyatā)*, but ultimate reality likewise was considered void, as being indescribable. Such was (crudely) the doctrine of the so-called 'Middle School' (the *Mādhyamika*), often known as the *Śunyavāda* or Void Doctrine. These movements resulted in belief in an Absolute or ultimate reality, sustaining or constituting the essence of the world of phenomena. In religious terms, this was identified with nirvana and with the essential nature of the Buddhas. The combination of religious and philosophical developments became formalized in the so-called Three-Body (*trikāya*) doctrine (or 'three-aspect doctrine') about the Buddha. In his earthly form, he adopts the Transformation-Body *nirmānakāya*, i.e. his mundane form. As the celestial object of worship, the Buddha has an Enjoyment-Body *(saṃbhogakāya)*. Finally, the inner nature of all Buddhas is identical with nirvana and with the Absolute, and as such is called the Truth-Body *(dharmakāya)*. This elaboration of Mahāyāna doctrine represented, not merely a metaphysical change in comparison with early Buddhist beliefs, but a formalization of religious intuitions and strivings. From a faith in which worship in the proper sense was insignificant, Buddhism developed into one which had its analogies to theism.

Jainism, on the other hand, has over the centuries proved highly conservative. Like Distinctionism, it believes in innumerable eternal souls or life-monads *(jīva)*, normally implicated in the round of rebirth. Also, like Distinctionism it is atheistic. It also tends to be both legalistic and literalistic. Injury to life-monads is a damaging offense, in terms of the doctrine of karma, and it does not matter whether the offence is intentional or not. When a life-monad attains the equivalent of release, it ascends to the top of the cosmos and remains there immobile. Jainism, as well as its cosmological doctrines (which are of some interest), has grown a kind of philosophical relativism, of some attraction though apparently not fitting very closely the main tenets of the faith. Though it has split into two sects, the differences between them are of no great importance. Jainism has strong analogies both to Buddhism and to Distinctionism, and it is probable that all three represent in reasonably sophisticated form the religion of India before the Āryans, or at least one of the main forms thereof.

The third unorthodox school is that of Cārvāka, an anti-religious metaphysics, which can conveniently be called Materialism. It has had a fairly bad press over the centuries in India, but has obviously had some influence—to judge from the counter-arguments adduced against it. Certainly until the mediaeval period, it remained in some degree active. Denying God, rebirth, and the efficacy of ritual, it challenged orthodoxy as well as Buddhism and Jainism; but it was swamped eventually by religious metaphysics.

There were other unorthodox movements, but Buddhism, Jainism and Materialism are the chief ones. Thus, of the traditional lines of thought in India, i.e. the traditional viewpoints, together with variants (under the heading of Vedānta), there are basically the following: Distinctionism and Yoga; Logic-Atomism; Exegesis; Non-Dualism; Qualified Non-Dualism; Dualism; Śaivite Doctrine; Elder Doctrine; Personalism; Realism; Idealism; Voidism (*Mādhyamika*); Jainism; and Materialism. It may be suitable at this point to exhibit their relationship diagrammatically (See p. 17).

This chart exhibits, somewhat crudely by necessity, the three main background influences which have helped to form the religious and metaphysical beliefs of the main Indian tradition. It is interesting to note one or two features of the influences and continuities which the downward-pointing arrows signify. It is generally recognized—and certainly since the work of Heinrich Zimmer—that the complex of belief in eternal selves, rebirth and release or nirvana is non-Āryan. This complex, coupled with atheism or agnosticism about the existence of a Lord, is typical of unorthodox religion, except that Buddhism subtracted the selves. In this respect Buddhism displayed its relationship to Materialism—the only school really to deny the whole complex.

I have indicated on the chart that Materialism is an offshoot of 'protoscience'. The latter is a useful, though loose, expression for sceptical attitudes and speculations about nature. It would, however, be wrong to suppose that such attitudes and such speculations are absent from the Vedic writings and from orthodox systems other than Logic-Atomism. But the main emphasis of this viewpoint, even in later times when its theism became well elaborated, was not religious, and so, more than other schools, it has its origin in protoscience.

It is now time to move towards a fuller description of the principal viewpoints, before considering the nature of the religious factors which have determined their structure.

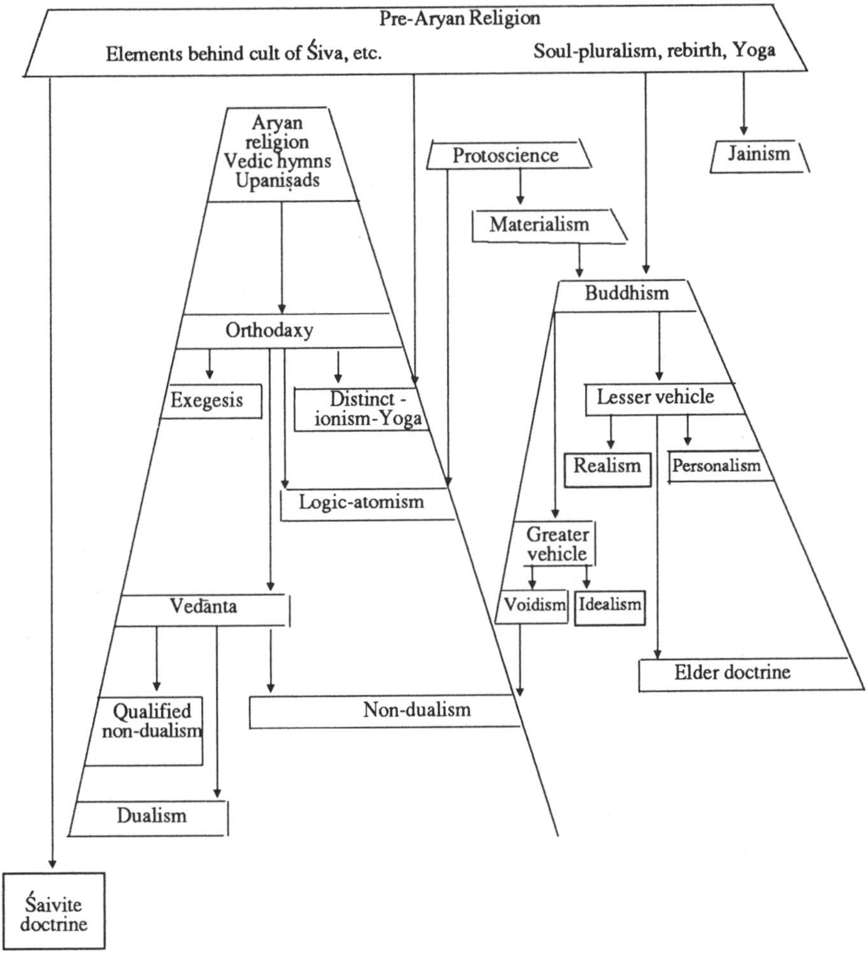

CHAPTER II
BUDDHIST METAPHYSICS

In view of the long and variegated development of Buddhism, and therefore also of its scriptures, it is not always easy to detect the original teachings of the Buddha himself. But there can be little doubt that the summary of the Buddhist outlook known as the Four Noble Truths represents something very early and probably traceable to the Enlightened One *(Buddha)* himself. According to this formula, life is permeated with suffering *(dukkha)*, the cause of which lies ultimately in craving, and so the cessation of craving will bring about a cessation of suffering: the way to bring about this cessation of craving is by treading the Noble Eightfold Path. A successful negotiation of this Path results in release from rebirth, or nirvana.

It is interesting that the way the Four Noble Truths are expressed corresponds to traditional Indian medical practice. The disease is diagnosed (it is suffering); its cause is outlined (it is craving); and it is asked whether the cause can be removed and a cure effected. The answer being in the affirmative, a course of treatment is prescribed. The medical flavour of the Buddha's teaching seems to indicate an attempt to apply protoscience to religious problems. It also is a sign of the pragmatism enshrined in much Buddhist thinking.

Nevertheless, the cure for human evils can only be properly understood against the background of a certain view of the cosmos. Not only is life seen to be permeated by suffering; but also, more metaphysically, the Buddha affirmed the twin doctrines of impermanence and non-self, i.e. he analysed substances into a succession of impermanent events or states, and likewise denied the existence of eternal selves underlying psychological states.

The latter doctrine, however, must be viewed in relation to rebirth. Thus the 'macro-individual' (see above) is virtually everlasting, and only ceases if he attains final nirvana. I say 'virtually everlasting', because the Buddha held that certain questions, including the question of whether or not the cosmos is finite in space and time, are undetermined *(avyākatāni)*, i.e. are wrongly put, and incapable of a meaningful answer. This, as we shall see, is highly relevant to a problem created by the non-self doctrine taken in conjunction with that of nirvana.

The concept of nirvana has proved puzzling to many commentators (especially Western ones) for a number of reasons. First, it is not always kept clearly in mind that there is a distinction to be drawn between nirvana as achieved by a saint in this life and final nirvana, when that particular macro-individual ceases. These two phases of nirvana are called 'nirvana with and without substrate'. It will perhaps be clearer for our purposes to dub them 'empirical' and 'transcendent' nirvana respectively. The achievement of the former (which leads on death to the attainment of transcendent nirvana) involves gaining peace *(santi)* and insight *(paññā)*, in which not only is craving destroyed, but the truth of the Buddha's teaching is seen existentially to be true.

A second reason for confusion about nirvana is that it is quite in accord with the Indian belief in rebirth not merely that one can be reborn in different states in this world (e.g. as an animal or in a different caste), but also in 'another' world—in a heaven or purgatory. Such places are thought of generally as other compartments of this cosmos. Hence, since nirvana means release from rebirth, it transcends even heavenly existence, and those, in the West, who have seen in nirvana a counterpart to the Christian conception of heavenly immortality have not taken into account the need for a clear way of distinguishing between the Christian heaven and the heavens of popular Indian religion. Moreover, the Christian concept involves individual survival, whereas nirvana, as we shall see, does not.

A third source of confusion is difficulty about the non-self doctrine. If there is no eternal self, then transcendent nirvana amounts to annihilation—and yet on the other hand the Buddha explicitly condemned belief in annihilation. However, there were, according to our evidence in the Pāli canon, two different forms of this belief. On the one hand, in line with Materialist views, some held that after death a person is finished, i.e. annihilationism here amounts to a rejection of the doctrine of rebirth. There are no difficulties about the Buddha's repudiation of this form of annihilationism—or rather, no difficulties that directly bear on the notion of nirvana. The second form of annihilationism involved the denial that after his decease, the Buddha or a Buddhist saint continued to exist. Here the situation is more complicated, since the question 'Does the Buddha or saint continue to exist after death?' was put by the Buddha in the category of undetermined questions. His reason for doing so is interesting, and very up-to-date in style.

He compared the question to 'Which direction does a flame go when it goes out?' In regard to the latter, it is neither right to say 'It goes North' nor 'It does not go North'. Actually, the Buddha's negations were more elaborate: he used the so-called four-cornered negation *(catuṣkoṭi)*—he denied 'It goes North', 'It does not go North', 'It both goes North and does not go North' and 'It neither goes North nor does not go North'. We shall have to discuss the full significance of this elaboration of negations later. But meanwhile, it is clear that the Buddha was meaning to bring out the point that the question 'Does a Buddha or saint survive his decease?' was unanswerable, because an improper or defective question.

The reason for this seems to be two-fold. First, as we have seen, the Buddha analysed the individual as a sequence of psycho-physical states. Rebirth consists in the setting up of a continuation of the sequence. It follows that when this sequence finishes, upon the death of an individual who has uprooted craving, it is no longer possible to refer to the individual—whether as surviving or not surviving. Thus the question 'Does the saint survive?' is analogous to 'Is the King of France bald?' But it is only *analogous* in type and not exactly similar. For it is only a contingent fact that a King of France does not exist, and the question about his baldness could, in other periods of history, be perfectly sensible. But the deceased saint is not just contingently not there to be referred to. The metaphysical scheme propounded by the Buddha rules out any such reference.

A second, but subsidiary reason, why the question is improper is practical. Probably, the Buddha objected to the doctrine of an eternal self not merely upon metaphysical grounds, but also because it encouraged a selfish attitude to salvation. The idea of an individual eternal self, such as is found in Jainism, Yoga and Distinctionism, conduces to desiring a sort of individual immortality, whereas the true saint desires neither to live nor not to live. But it would be wrong, as some commentators have done, to think that the Buddha's silence about nirvana is simply due to his pragmatism. It is quite clear from the way in which he treats the undetermined questions that they are improper in a deeper sense than that they are tactically unwise (if you want salvation). This is brought out by the fact that, at any rate according to the scriptural tradition, the topic of whether the self and body are identical or not is ruled out as improperly expressed—and yet the Buddha says that for the ordinary, uninstructed man it is better to think of the self as being constituted by the body. Thus he clearly distinguishes the absolutely correct way of looking at the matter (seeing why it is that certain questions do not arise) from such views as are a crude approximation useful for the business of becoming a better man. That is, he distinguishes the theoretical issue from the merely pragmatic one. In this connection it is worth stressing that there is a tendency in Indian spirituality to consider that ignorance *(avidyā)* rather than sin is what causes the trouble. By consequence, what brings a conversion to the right path is knowledge. Admittedly such knowledge involves, or usually involves, some immediate religious experience, and thus is not like scientific knowledge as it would be understood today. Nevertheless, a right view of the world is centrally important, and this should not be regarded as a mere engineering device for getting people to do the right thing. It is not therefore surprising that the beginning of the Eightfold Path is right view *(diṭṭhi)*. This concept rules out a merely pragmatic interpretation of the Buddha's teaching. The medical analogy is important here: though the main aim is cure of the disease, it is absolutely necessary for this that the diagnosis rests upon a true appraisal of the situation.

In the Elder tradition, and this probably in substance enshrines the original teaching of the Buddha, nirvana is not to be thought of as an Absolute underlying or constituting the essence of empirical reality—a divine Ground, as it were, sustaining the world. It is necessary to be reasonably clear about this, for two reasons. First, some Western commentators and some Hindu commentators have tried to assimilate the concept of nirvana to God and the divine Absolute respectively—that is, to assimilate Buddhism to their own forms of faith. Second, Buddhism itself, in its evolution into the Greater Vehicle, reformulated the doctrine of nirvana in an absolutistic direction. One need not deny that there are the seeds of this development in early Buddhism. Nevertheless, it would certainly be wrong to ascribe such a view to the Pāli scriptures.

Now admittedly there is some murkiness about the terms we have used above to express what nirvana is not, in the Pāli tradition: 'Absolute', 'Ground' and even 'God' are imprecise, ambiguous and abstract, partly because of the odd nature of talk about the transcendent. However, nirvana is not cause of the world, and is not a personal entity: thus it is, so far, most unlike God. It is not that which underlies, and so serves to explain the occurrence of, phenomena: it is not therefore like a divine Ground or Absolute. Nor does it represent the 'inner nature' of empirical reality. But we can put all this in another way, by pointing out that the conceptions of God or Ground are, generally speaking, formed against a certain view of the world, namely that the world is constituted by a complex of things or substances. The transcendent therefore is conceived as a transcendent substance. But since the Buddha's analysis of the world was rather that it is constituted by a complex of impermanent states *(dhamma)*, governed by causal laws, nirvana is conceived as a transcendent state, rather than a transcendent substance.

I have referred to attempts to interpret nirvana against a Christian or Hindu framework. This points to an important methodological principle, about which it is as well to be clear, since confusion about it in the realm of religious studies is common. It is vital to distinguish between the doctrinal interpretation put upon an event, religious experience, or complex of such, etc., by a religious tradition and the interpretation which might be put upon it by some other tradition. Naturally, the Christian, if he respects the insights of Buddhism, will want to see how far a Christian construction can be put upon certain Buddhist concepts. But it is essential to be clear about what is going on: otherwise alien thoughts are liable to be foisted upon another tradition and passed off as the 'real meaning' of that tradition. In brief, we must distinguish between auto-interpretation (how, e.g., the Buddhist interprets the data of the Buddhist tradition) and hetero-interpretation (how, e.g., a Hindu interprets the data of the Buddhist tradition). Thus our present remarks about nirvana are not meant to be remarks about the proper or improper modes of the hetero-interpretation of nirvana, but about the ways we must describe the concept of nirvana from the standpoint of Buddhist (and here, for the moment, the Elder) auto-interpretation of it. This is not to deny that thereafter a philosophical interpretation of the data can be fruitful.

There is another reason, perhaps, why it is necessary to resist equating transcendent nirvana, except in some places in the Mahāyāna, with a unitary substance or Absolute. As has been remarked earlier, there are strong resemblances between the mythological and other traditions of Jainism, Buddhism and Distinctionism. If this group represents, as we averred earlier, an important strand of non-Aryan religion, it would be wise to see the originality of the Buddha's teaching against this background (rather than, say, the Brahmanic background). This background is distinguished by its emphasis upon the existence of a plurality of souls, caught up in the round of rebirth and karma. The denial of the soul or self in Buddhism represents, then, an important departure from the non-Aryan background. But yet there remains in the Buddha's teachings a strong flavour of the pluralistic and individualistic views of the self and salvation.

Both from the motive of economy of thought and from that of pragmatism, the Buddha removed from his teachings the concept of an eternal self. With his emphasis on the causality involved in rebirth, he no doubt perceived that the concept of an underlying self, persisting from one birth to another, only helps to make rebirth intelligible at the metaphysical level (that is, if one feels that there must be a permanent substrate beneath the shifting phenomena of the macro-individual's life): but it still leaves the mechanism of rebirth—the causal laws involved—unexplained. Against a different view of the world, as a complex of events rather than of substances, it readily becomes apparent that the self can be dispensed with. All that is required for the doctrine of release is the individual's capacity for release. Thus in the Buddha's scheme of thought the possibility of nirvana takes the place of the self. Thus there is substituted for the doctrine of a plurality of selves or souls the doctrine of a plurality of individuals capable of attaining nirvana. Thus the concept of nirvana, in the Buddhist scheme, arises out of, though it transcends, a traditional soul-pluralism: and in this sense it has the flavour of pluralism, rather than that of Upaniṣadic monism.

There is a final important point to be made about nirvana. The Eightfold Path is the way to it: and to understand the goal it is necessary to understand the manner of gaining it. Now the Path is divided into three main sections. The first two stages, namely right view and right resolve concern the correct attitudes for embarking on, and conducting, the quest. The next three, namely right speech, right action and right mode of livelihood, concern the moral and social aspects of the Buddhist way of life. The last three stages, namely right effort, right awareness (*sati*) and right concentration *(samādhi),* concern the correct methods of interior self-training. In brief, the Path divides into commitment, morals and meditation. Now although the stages are not intended as a temporal sequence, the final group has place of honour. The contemplative life is the ultimate practical aim of Buddhism.

To overlook this, as some early Western commentators did, leads to viewing Buddhism simply as an ethical system. Part of the trouble arises from Occidental concepts of religion. It is usual to think of religion, in the West, as necessarily involving belief in God or gods. Since Elder Buddhism does not involve belief in God, and regards the gods as quite peripheral to its main spiritual interests, it is tempting to say that it is not a religion. Indeed, some Buddhists say this, to bring out clearly its agnosticism about a Creator. Yet it is equally necessary to bring out the difference between Buddhism and systems of belief which are non-religious (in the god-oriented sense of the term), such as Marxism, atheistic Existentialism, and the like. For Buddhism, even in its doctrinally austere Elder form, centrally involves a certain kind of *spiritual* practice, namely the contemplative life—which also figures in other religions. Thus we have two terminological choices: either consciously to use the word 'religion' so that it covers Buddhism, and thus cannot be defined by reference to belief in God or gods; or to invent some term to cover both 'religion' in the god-oriented sense and Buddhism. The former seems the rational choice, not merely because Buddhism in its later developments shows strong affinities to god-oriented religions, but also because, as we have noted, mysticism, i.e. the contemplative life, appears both at the heart of agnostic Buddhism and in some phases of god-oriented religion. Thus, in terms of the central concerns of religions, we can say that a religion displays either devotion to a personal God (or gods) or the contemplative life (whether interpreted as involving a relation to God, or the gods, or not), or both. This disjunctive definition will no doubt commend itself the more easily today, in view of Wittgenstein's doctrine of 'family-resemblance'. Then, taking up a usage proposed by Paul Tillich, we can refer to Marxism, humanism, etc., as 'quasi-religions'.[1]

Thus, in our sense of the word, Buddhism in all its phases, is definitely a religious system. But unlike the Semitic faiths (Judaism, Christianity and Islam) it starts from an interior mystical quest, rather than from the prophetic experience of a dynamic personal God. It is mysticism without God. It is contemplation-centred, and neglects prophecy: just as early Judaism and Islam were prophecy-centred and neglected mystical contemplation.

Unfortunately it is necessary here to make a further terminological point, since the manifold uses of the words 'mysticism', 'mystical', 'mystic' and so on have been a potent source of confusion in this area. Since a proper definition of mysticism is vitally necessary for my aim, later to be elaborated, of diagnosing the religious determinants of different systems of Indian metaphysics, this is a suitable juncture to clarify the matter. I shall use the words 'mysticism', etc., to refer to a certain form of spiritual life and to those involved in it. The form in question can be summed up as the contemplative life; and its representatives can be sampled as follow—by saying that Eckhart, St John of the Cross, Boehme, Plotinus, the Ṣūfis, the Buddha, yogis, Śaṅkara, Lao-Tze and Bodhidharma are mystics. Negatively, mysticism, in my sense, can be distinguished from prophecy, devotionalism and in general the vivid apprehension of the numinous; and mystics can be contrasted to Isaiah, Muhammad, St Paul (as on the Damascus Road), Luther and Wesley. The mystical experience generally accrues, where it accrues, upon a certain form of interior training, and differs usually from the spontaneous awareness of a dynamic and personal Other characteristic of prophetic and devotional experience. We can therefore make a (necessarily crude and rough) distinction between two types of religious experience—between the numinous and the mystical, or between the devotional and the contemplative. The former calls forth worship, adoration, self-abasement, a sense of sin or of religious inadequacy: the latter often, and especially in the Indian tradition, is unconnected with the religion of worship, and no need is there felt to identify the 'object' of contemplative experience with the Object of worship.

Thus it appears reprehensibly loose to use 'mystical' as meaning only any kind of direct experience of *God*. Moreover, it is unilluminating: for if there really is such a strong analogy between the experiences of Muhammad and of the Buddha, how is it that their respective teachings were so radically different? If there is a single form of religious experience, how is it that such different theologies are constructed upon it? Of course, the presupposition here that religious experiences are important determinants of theological systems may be questioned. Undoubtedly social and cultural factors are important. But these themselves include certain kinds of religious practice, such as sacrificial cults and yoga, with which certain forms of experience and modes of religious expression are characteristically associated. Thus it is wise to see religious experience in its practical setting. But this complex of experience and cult or path of training is certainly centrally relevant to explaining a theology. Hence the claim that there is some one form of religious experience still fails to illuminate the divergences of doctrine in the world, and in particular in India.

Still worse is it to use 'mystical' as an obscure contrast to 'rational'. It is true that metaphysical systems, such as that of Leibniz, may well be the consequence of reflection, rather than of some kind of religious experience: and it is true (indeed a central thesis of this book) that the shape of other systems can only be understood in relation to religious factors. But to say that some system is rational, as an evaluative judgment, does not at all entail that it is a consequence of metaphysical reflection about the world, as distinguished from starting from religious experience and the like. For it is a matter of debate, and it is not *a priori* obvious, that appeals to religious experience, revelation and so on are necessarily philosophical errors. Moreover, the loose contrast between 'rational' and 'mystical' tends to group together with mysticism proper the vapourings of seers and tyrants, such as Father Divine and Adolf Hitler. In brief, it is desirable to limit the use of 'mystical' and its cognates, and to refrain from giving it any evaluative overtones.

This clears the path for making a final general comment on the concept of nirvana. As we have seen, it normally could be said to involve a distinctively mystical experience (or experiences), accruing upon the practice of concentration. In view of this, some of the epithets ascribed to nirvana can be understood not merely in a metaphysical sense, but also as expressing something given to the saint or the Buddha in interior experience. Thus it is supreme tranquillity, which corresponds to the bliss reported by mystics in other traditions. It is the immortal or deathless; and the sense of transcending the temporal flow of events which constitutes the world-process, or cycle *(samsāra)* of existence, is not unrelated to the techniques used in Buddhist concentration, where the mind is successively withdrawn from perceptions and mental images, and thus from a perception of time. Similarly, nirvana is without empirical qualities or datumless, and this is an epithet used of a form of concentration. There seems little doubt then that we should interpret these terms against the background of meditation *(dhyāna)* and mystical states. This also helps to explain the fact that nirvana is often said to be ineffable and inconceivable. In one sense, of course, it would be false to call it inconceivable, since there is definitely a doctrine of nirvana in Buddhism, and consequently concepts are applied to it: for instance, it involves the cessation of rebirth. On the other hand, it is characteristic of mysticism to speak of the ineffability of the contemplative state. This occurs for at least three reasons. First, the knowledge that it brings is not arrived at by ratiocination. The pursuit of nirvana is not a merely intellectual or theoretical one. Second, 'ineffable', 'unspeakable' and related expressions are not always to be taken quite at their face value, but serve to intensify the expressive aspect of utterances concerning inner states, etc. For instance, unutterable pain is no more or less utterable than other pains, but it is *worse*. Third, the lack of mental images, or visions in the more obvious sense, and the lack of discursive thought involved in the pacification of the inner self mean that the mystical state cannot be described in the way more ordinary contents of the mind can be described. Thus I can say that the ship I imagine is blue, long, on a stormy sea; but such a description, in terms of perceptible qualities, etc., is impossible in regard to the contemplative state: nor can it be expressed in terms of the thoughts passing through the mind of the contemplative. For these reasons, then, we might expect a certain difficulty in giving clear expression to what nirvana amounts to. In so far as a certain sort of inner experience is relevant when ascribing the attainment of nirvana, the latter has some likeness to knowing what happiness is like—for a necessary condition of this is the experience of being happy.

So much then for the concept of nirvana in the Elder system and in early Buddhism. We shall see later that an identification of nirvana with the Absolute, together with certain other developments, characterized some of the Greater Vehicle teachings.

In view of the Buddhist emphasis on awareness and mental control, and in view also of the repudiation of the concept of a permanent self, it is not surprising that Buddhism attempts a detailed analysis of the psycho-physical make-up of the individual. It was not only necessary to insist upon a description of the person as constituted by a succession of impermanent states, but also to discriminate the different elements which, grouped together, form the individual. Characteristic, therefore, of Buddhism is the doctrine of groups *(khandha)*, that is to say categories of states or events which go to make up the individual. This breakdown of what constitutes the person has two functions—to exhibit the structure of the person (seeing that the easy way out, in terms of an essential self, is barred), and to serve as a model which will be the object of meditation for the adept, thereby enabling him to see that the unitary person does not exist, but is constituted by a complex of impersonal factors. In this way, it is hoped, the adept will learn to see himself not as 'I doing this' but as a complex of different elements operating in a certain way. That is—as with the concept of nirvana—the doctrine of groups has in Buddhism not only a theoretical interest, but also a practical aim. Here again we see the importance of the medical analogy, for in medicine the facts are investigated with certain objectives in mind.

According to the somewhat stylized doctrine of groups to be discovered in the Pāli canon, there are five categories of states which in combination constitute a person. These are: corporeal *(rūpa)* phenomena; feelings *(vedanā)*; cognitions *(saññā)*; active tendencies *(sankhārā)*; and consciousness *(vijñanā)*. These categories, because (*inter alia*) they to some extent fail to coincide with lines of division which Western philosophers are inclined to make, require some explanation. But first, a general and fundamental point. The groups are *classes* of states, and are not intended to refer to permanent entities the combination of which constitutes a person. Thus consciousness is a class of events or states of a certain sort, and not a unitary principle animating an individual. Thus the doctrine of groups indicates the double way in which Buddhism breaks down the common-sense belief in a persistent self: for not only is the individual analysed as a mere combination of states of different categories; but also the individual is fragmented in time into a succession of evanescent events. He is chopped up (as it were) both vertically and horizontally. The doctrine of groups performs the first operation: the doctrine of impermanence performs the second.

The first group mentioned above (namely corporeal phenomena) could more literally be translated 'form', or 'forms'. In ordinary language, the word signified things which have shape, or the shapes themselves. But in the special usage here in view it means (roughly) anything manifested in ordinary perceptual experience. This somewhat ambiguous account of its meaning is not without reason. Three types of entity count as corporeal phenomena: things which are perceived in the ordinary way (together with their properties, etc.), the underlying conditions which determine what is given in sense-experience, and what the Western philosopher would call 'sensations' (provided also that mental images are here included). To choose a modern example: tables, electrons and sensations would all count as belonging to the category of corporeal phenomena. Of course, it should be remembered that the doctrine of groups was enunciated with special reference to the individual living being, and in particular to the human person. Consequently, the electrons belonging to the table in front of me would not be part of me as an individual: but the electrons in my little finger would. It is of some interest that (and here Buddhism is characteristic of the Indian tradition) my sensations are counted as corporeal entities.

It may also be noted that the sense-organs are counted as six in number—the five senses usually recognized, plus the mind-organ *(manas)*, which functions in a triple way—it combines impressions derived from the five sense-organs (and thus is the *sensus communis*), while also more generally it abstracts from phenomena to form general ideas, etc. Further, it introspects feelings, active tendencies, etc. The expression 'mind-organ' will serve to bring out the difference in conception between this and the complex concept of 'mind' in English. It will be seen from the above, and also more generally from similar ideas to be found in other Indian systems, that the mind-organ is part of the corporeal phenomena which constitute the bodily aspect of the individual. Thus the so-called 'mind-body' problem needs to be stated in a very different way in the Indian context.

The category of feelings presents no great difficulty. Pleasant, un-pleasant and neutral feelings are distinguished. It is (in view of what is said below about active tendencies) useful to emphasize that feelings are, like 'passions' in its etymological sense, conceived as happening to the individual—he is so far passive.

The distinction between corporeal phenomena, which include sensations, and cognitions is not altogether an easy one to make. Sensations are events occurring 'in' the sense-organs, while cognitions are ocurrences whereby external or internal objects are discriminated on the basis of sensations. 'I have a blue sensation' would describe what occurs in me, while 'That is the sky' expresses my cognition. Since the mind-organ is one of the senses, cognitions include abstract judgements.

The category of active tendencies is in some respects puzzling, since the word used in Pāli and Sanskrit also means 'compound things' (as when it is said that 'All compound things are impermanent'). This latter sense arises because the expression literally means 'putting together', 'preparation' and hence 'what is put together'. But in the sense used in the doctrine of groups the composite aspect is relatively unimportant: rather it refers to impulses, volitions, dispositions, etc.—that is, the immediate determinants of a person's actions. Some translators have tried to bring in the composite and combining aspect of the term's meaning by speaking of 'mental coefficients'. But unfortunately this expression is meaningless in English. 'Active tendencies' shows that the factors falling under this group are manifestations of preformed dispositions, as well as decisions and immediate intentions, etc. But although the compound aspect is relatively unimportant, it has had its influence upon Buddhist thinking on this score—so that the active tendencies have been regarded as the group which organizes the individual into a whole.

The final group, consciousness or conscious events, is in some passages looked on as the most important, in that it is said to be the support of the other groups. In ordinary language, the word meant 'discrimination', 'skill', 'intelligence'; but in the context of the doctrine of groups it comes to mean pure consciousness as the factor which as it were plays upon the data supplied by the external and internal world and thereby makes it proper to speak of individual experience. For this reason, the series of conscious events can be highly misleading, from the Buddhist point of view. For it is the existence of consciousness which above all leads the individual to think of himself as a personal being, having a certain identity in virtue of the unity of his experience. But according to Buddhist doctrine, consciousness is a series of discrete events or states, and belongs to no one. It belongs to no one, because the concept of a unitary self is ruled out. The individual is merely a combination of groups.

A very early simile no doubt represents the Buddha's 'original gospel' in regard to the individual. Just as a chariot is so-called because a number of different parts have been assembled in a certain manner, so that there is no underlying something, distinct from the parts, which is the 'essential' chariot, so likewise the individual is just a combination of the groups. And just as 'chariot' is just a conventional expression we apply to the combination of chariot-parts, so 'I' is just a conventional expression for the complex of groups. The illusion of a self is partly a bewitchment produced by language.

It will thus be seen that the Buddhist doctrine cuts against not only the notion of a permanent soul as propounded by Distinctionism, Jainism, etc., but also against the common-sense view of individuality. It attempts to destroy not only a metaphysical and religious doctrine, but the ordinary man's feeling of states and things as belonging to himself. Thus in practice the prospective saint must try to abandon all talk of 'me' and 'mine', or if that proves to be impossible, to regard 'me' and 'mine' as mere conventional labels.

If the doctrines of nirvana and non-self are at the heart of the Buddha's teaching, so likewise is the doctrine of origination *(pratītyasamutpāda)*. It was part of the Buddha's attitude that all states have causes, so that in particular the existence of suffering requires explanation. The formula of origination attempts to give such an explanation. The fully-elaborated formula found in some passages in the scriptures shows signs of having been the result of additions over a longish period, and it does not hang together very well. It can be stated either in forward or reverse order: the latter beginning with the condition, namely decay and death, which requires explanation. In its full form, it runs as follows.

Decay and death would not happen if there were no birth, so the latter is the condition of the former. But what is the cause of birth? The process of existence *(bhava)*, i.e. in particular the process of rebirth. The cause of this in turn is attachment *(upādāna)*. Attachment arises from craving (which we discussed earlier in relation to the Four Noble Truths). But a precondition of craving is feelings (one of the groups, it will be recalled). But feelings arise from sense-contacts *(phassa)*. (This is in line with the belief that the birthplace of mental events lies in the sensations and sense-organs; and with the Buddhist emphasis on the need, if one wishes to attain peace, which involves a stilling of feelings, to turn away from the phenomenal world.) Sense-contacts in turn originate from the sense-fields *(āyatana)* (which include the sense-objects, sensations and sense-organs, among which it will be remembered is counted the mind-organ). But a condition of the functioning of the sense-fields is the existence of the psycho-physical *(nāmarūpa)* complex. The psycho-physical complex could not be said to exist without consciousness. But the determining cause of the arising of consciousness (e.g. in the foetus) is karma, and more particularly the active tendencies which express the operation of karma in the sequence of lives. The active tendencies in turn only are operative because of the individual's lack of spiritual insight (for otherwise he would have vanished at nirvana) and this lack of insight is called ignorance. In brief the sequence goes as follows: death and decay, existence-process, attachment, craving; feelings, sense- contacts, sense-fields, psycho-physical complex, consciousness; active tendencies, ignorance.

It will be noted that I have punctuated the series in three groups. The initial four members of the sequence probably correspond to the primitive doctrine of origination, and represent an elucidation of the first two Noble Truths. The next five members probably are tacked on as an analysis of the conditions which underlie the existence of craving in the individual. This part of the sequence would no doubt hold, or be thought to hold, independently of belief in rebirth. The last two members of the sequence return to the problem of how rebirth operates, and in particular how consciousness arises, since it is the stream of conscious events which provides the immediate link between one life and the next. Since it is the active tendencies which bring about actions, and actions generate karma (karma literally means 'action' or 'law of action'), they bring about the continuation of the life-series. Finally ignorance is added as the necessary condition of active tendencies as generative of karma. It will be observed, then, that some of the links in the chain refer to the process of rebirth, and so can be given a temporal relationship, while others either are analytic or state necessary conditions which cannot be temporally ordered. It is not as if in the beginning there was ignorance, then disembodied active tendencies, then, disembodied consciousness, etc. The puzzlement occasioned by the doctrine of origination partly arises because some links in the chain are related horizontally, in time, and others vertically. Partly, too, the trouble is that the doctrine is an amalgam which has been put together over a longish period (as we saw).

In any event, the series is not (as some others in the Indian tradition are) to be taken as tracing causes back to a first principle underlying the evolution of the cosmos. This fact connects with Buddha's multiple negations, mentioned earlier, about certain questions—the undetermined questions, those which are to be 'set aside' as unanswerable. Not only is the question of the persistence of the Buddha or saint after attaining transcendent nirvana unanswerable, but also the questions as to whether the world is finite or not in space and time. Thus the question of whether there is a First Cause is to be set aside. Neither is it correct to affirm an eternal principle underlying the empirical world nor to deny it, nor both nor neither. It is somewhat hard to discover the targets the Buddha had in mind in employing such an elaborate form of negation, the so-called four-cornered negation. The scriptures and commentators themselves give different interpretations. But the possibilities seem to be as follows.

First (as we saw regarding his negations about the survival of a Buddha after nirvana), the question is meaningless or inapplicable in terms of the Buddha's metaphysical system. Second, there is scriptural evidence that some recluses at the time of the Buddha affirmed such peculiar conjunctions of propositions as the following: 'There is another world; there is not; there both is and is not; there neither is nor is not'. These were castigated as 'eel-wrigglers', who shied away from committing any error in their replies to questions by giving all possible answers. (Contradictions seem a rather inadequate way of doing this! But it ties in with later theories that in matters of faith everyone is somehow right.) The Buddha's fourfold negation could then be interpreted as a repudiation of 'eel-wriggling'. Third, the Buddha may have meant that questions about the world are simply not conducive to salvation, and it is better to refrain from speculations. Fourth, the Buddha may have wished to indicate that silence about ultimate reality is the only possible course.

As we have seen, there is good ground, regarding the non-self doctrine, for affirming the first of these interpretations. Likewise, regarding the eternity and infinity of the cosmos, there may be good ground for supposing that the Buddha, or at least early Buddhism, in propounding a doctrine of universal causation, saw that the series of causes could be traced back indefinitely in time, but any supposed First Cause would itself require explanation. This indeed is the treatment according to Brahmā, the Creator God in the scriptures. At the beginning of a world-cycle, he is the first being to become manifest, and wrongly supposes that he is Creator, because he perceives other beings coming into existence after him: *post me, propter me*, he thinks. But he himself only arises because of prior karmic conditions—and so on. Any God must have phenomenal properties of some kind to be active and creative; but all phenomenal properties arise from some prior cause. It may well be, then, that the Buddha regarded it as impossible either to set a limit to the spatio-temporal complex of events which constitutes the cosmos or to affirm (beyond all possible experience) that the complex is actually infinite.

The second interpretation, the 'anti-eel-wriggler' one, is not incompatible with the above: and may also reflect the Buddha's repudiation of radical scepticism, such as was current in his day. The Materialists rejected inference, partly in order to combat religious inferences to the transcendent, to invisible karma, and so on. Now while the Buddha's teachings are in a sense empiricist and anti-speculative, for he claimed that his knowledge of causation and of nirvana itself was based upon experience, so that in some respects he is on the side of scepticism (especially in its anti-orthodox form), he nevertheless *did* wish to assert that there is a transcendent state and thus a mode of release. In brief, he adopted a middle position between materialistic scepticism and dogmatic religion.

The third interpretation, the pragmatic one, ascribes to the Buddha a rather poor sense of psychology, as though people would refrain from investigating questions which were meaningful and apparently of great importance for the formation of a *Weltanschauung* merely because they were told that it was bad for them. Again, the Buddha seems to have steered a middle course. The speculative questions were not conducive to salvation mainly because they were unanswerable or involved going beyond what could be founded upon experience. Speculative views are a 'jungle' and a 'snare', not because time taken off doing cosmology would be better spent meditating, but because while they pretended to be a framework for the religious life, they were not founded upon the central data of the contemplative life.

The fourth interpretation has, as we saw earlier in discussing the ineffability of nirvana, some force; and it is not inconsistent with the first. In short, the Buddha seems to have perceived that it is necessary to give a minimal doctrinal interpretation to the experience of nirvana.

However, as we shall see, the Void School of the Mahāyāna, gave a somewhat different interpretation to the fourfold negations, namely a dialectical one. That is, the negations indicate that all views about reality are contradictory, while the positive teachings of the Buddha, e.g. about the groups (as part of his non-self doctrine), are intended as a thesis which has be transcended.

But although the Buddha preserved a sort of silence about what transcends the empirical world, and thus gives a minimal doctrinal interpretation of nirvana, Buddhism traditionally involves a rich and striking cosmology. The cycle of existence, i.e. the world-process, is depicted as immense in space and time. It includes an indefinite number of world-systems, like that of the earth with its sun, moon, etc. (Modern Buddhists interpret this in line with modern astronomy as a virtual infinity of galaxies, though early Indian mythological cosmology regarded the earth as flat: the Buddhists conceived it as floating in space *(ākāśa)* which was not just a system of locations, but a kind of ethereal substance. These world-systems evolve over immense stretches of time, and eventually collapse—individually, they 'pulsate', somewhat analogously to the modern theory of a 'pulsating' universe. As an instance of the way Buddhist writings pile on the figures, we may note that 1,000 world-systems constitute one 'small chiliocosm', 1,000 'small chiliocosms' make up a 'middle chiliocosm', and 1,000 'middle chiliocosms' constitute a 'great chiliocosm'. But in addition Buddhist mythological cosmology conceives different planes *(loka)* of existence.

Not only does a world-system contain its heavens and hells, but the universe is regarded as theoretically divisible in to three planes: first, the sensual *(kāmaloka)* plane, which includes beings, such as humans and animals, which are fully corporeal, i.e. constituted by elements perceptible by the five senses; second, there is the corporeal plane, which includes those gods who are conceived as being visible and audible, but not tangible, etc.; and finally, there is a more refined sphere, the incorporeal *(arūpa)* plane, which includes beings who have a mental, but not a physical, life. The system of heavens cuts across the last two planes: the lower heavens belong to the corporeal plane, the four highest heavens to the incorporeal. Two features of this picture of the world are of special interest. First, nirvana lies 'beyond' even the incorporeal sphere: even in the latter there is impermanence, Thus even a refined picture of heaven is to be distinguished from the transcendent state of nirvana.

Second, the theory of the planes of existence ties up with Buddhist contemplative practices, and in particular with the meditations, a series of stages of contemplation centrally important in Buddhist self-training.

The first four meditations involve concentrating upon some object, such as a blue flower, seeing it in isolation from its environment, treating it as a mere sense-datum and thereby attaining a kind of 'pure', unconceptualized awareness. But though this procedure brings about tranquillity, there remains a tenuous link, via the sense-datum, with the corporeal plane. The higher stages of meditation are called incorporeal, and involve using formulae for guiding the adept. The repetition of these formulae both helps to induce, and to express, the states of mind that are reached. Thus first the meditator thinks 'It is all infinite space', thereby emptying his mind of all images or corporeal entities. Then 'It is all infinite consciousness' in which even the tenuous concept of locomotion through empty space is banished. Then 'There is nothing', in which even the concept of subjective experience is removed. Previous stages are hereby replaced, as it were, by a blank. But even here effort is required, together with some kind of tenuous awareness that the imaginative content of the mind is a blank. There is, then, some kind of judgment or perception. In the final stage the adept needs to pass into the state of 'neither-cognition-nor-non-cognition'.

In the course of all this the adept is supposed to attain considerable lucidity of consciousness and a stilling of feelings. The practice of such meditations was not confined to Buddhists, but was found among other yogis—though there is evidence that they did not include the last stage, which was held to be peculiar to Buddhist yoga. It should not be thought that nirvana consists in attaining the series of meditations (indeed this was condemned as a heresy). But they, and some other meditations, are central to Buddhist yoga. That nirvana does not consist in the attainment of the meditations appears to follow from certain considerations. First, the meditations must be co-ordinated to the proper following of the Buddhist Path. Second, and connectedly, the meditations must lead to a proper awareness of the Buddhist truth—and in particular to an experiential knowledge of the nature of the world and of nirvana. Thus, insight must be gained, and this is intentionally defined by reference to specifically Buddhist concepts (and not just any old yoga theory). Third, transcendent nirvana involves the cutting off of rebirth, and so cannot be simply defined by reference to meditative experience.

We may note how the meditations are co-ordinated to the three planes of existence. By considering, in the early stages, a sense-datum, the adept rises (as it were) beyond the sensual plane to the pure corporeal plane. In the next three stages, he acquires (as it were) the properties of the datumless incorporeal plane. Finally, in being beyond cognition and non-cognition, he rehearses within himself the nature of transcendent nirvana, which lies even beyond the incorporeal plane. Thus there is some integration between mystical experience and the mythological cosmology of Buddhism. It is now necessary to survey the ways in which Buddhist metaphysics developed.

The main feature of Buddhist history was, as we have seen, the gradual divide between the two great wings of Buddhism, the so-called Lesser and Greater Vehicles. The former is today represented by one surviving school, that of the Elders; but there is a fair amount of literary evidence about earlier schools, though the relation between them and the developing Mahāyāna remains somewhat obscure. It is sufficient for our purposes to mention only the Realist and Personalist schools, since they indicate some of the difficulties presented by the Buddhist metaphysical scheme and thereby help to show the kind of Philosophical development culminating in the full-blown Mahāyāna.

The doctrines of impermanence and non-self created problems partly because they cut at common-sense ideas, and partly because, interpreted in a certain way, they could seriously affect basic religious teachings. Thus speculation about the doctrine of impermanence led to a theory that all states (or rather all conditioned states) are momentary, *khaṇika*. In brief, the doctrine that what common sense would regard as at least relatively permanent things are complexes of short-lived states was taken to the extreme of considering reality as broken up into a swarm of atomic instants. This created difficulties about perception, since sensations do not appear to be broken up into instants. What then was the relation between the event-states which give rise to sensations and the sensations themselves? Further, the doctrine of momentariness presented problems about causation. There was no general *metaphysical* problem here, in so far as Buddhism had no great difficulty in conceiving of causation as a correlation of events, rather than as involving an 'inner' or necessary relation between cause and effect. But Buddhist psychology, as co-ordinated to the doctrine of karma, appeared to imply that present acts have psychological effects in the rather distant future: moreover the concept of active tendencies implied that prior dispositions become manifested on particular occasions. All this meant that Buddhist psychology made use of (or at least seemed to make use of) the concept of 'action at a distance in time'. The idea of momentariness made this hard to understand.

Whether or not the fully-fledged version of this idea can be traced as far back as the early period during which the Realist school had its rise, some such problems as those outlined above were likely to be presented by the doctrine of impermanence. The Realists provided a sort of solution. This was made especially urgent because of the danger that the doctrines of karma and nirvana might be undermined. The status of the Buddha likewise might have been affected. All this was liable to happen in the following ways. As seen above, karma appears to require action at a temporal distance, and without karma the religious problem of how to attain release would disappear. Moreover, in so far as moral good and evil were conceived as bearing good and evil fruits for the individual, a disregard of the ethical side of Buddhism might have been held to accrue upon the destruction of the karma-concept. Then again, if the saint upon attaining empirical nirvana can no longer fall from grace and would therefore inevitably decease into transcendent nirvana, an explanation is wanted of how a momentary event (the attainment of empirical nirvana) can have this effect stretching over quite a period of time, till his decease. Finally, the problem of perception could easily create a tendency to philosophical idealism—as indeed happened in the Mahāyāna. Such a view of the illusory nature of the world as conceived by common sense could bring with it a belief in the Buddha as a mere manifestation of the Absolute within the illusory world. This tendency was already appearing among early Buddhist schools, notably among the so-called Transcendentalists *(lokottaravādin)*, who held that the Buddha is essentially a transcendent being, who merely assumed a human guise as a device to teach men. Thus the trend towards a divinization of the Buddha was accompanied by a docetic view of the historical Buddha. Apart from the fact that such an attitude was liable to issue in unorthodoxy, for the actual teachings of the Buddha could be to some degree neglected as themselves part of the illusion, there were ethical dangers involved—so thought the Realists. For if the Buddha were not truly human, there could be no assurance that ordinary mortals could imitate his ideal conduct.

It will be perceived, then, that there were religious motives, as well as any strictly philosophical ones, for the Realist suspicion of an extreme application of the doctrine of impermanence. The name of the school, here translated as Realist, signifies 'the doctrine that everything exists', and this title is to be interpreted in two ways, so far as we can gather from our sources. On the one hand, the Realists affirmed the real existence of the various elementary states, complexes of which go to make up things and persons. Second, they also held that both past and future states genuinely exist. On the first point, it should be understood that in one way the Realists were orthodox in denying the real existence of certain sorts of entity, such as the self. Indeed, all complex substances are only real in so far as they are congeries of real states, but the treatment of them as things and persons is due to convention, i.e. to the way we use words. On the second point, the Realists argued that there could be no causal efficacy if the past was held to be non-existent. Their principal difficulty was in formulating a way of asserting that past states exist without implying that in some sense they are everlasting: this would fall foul of the doctrine of impermanence as usually interpreted. As we shall see later, the concept of momentary events raised certain problems for the analysis of causation which provided the Voidists with an opportunity to argue that the notion of causation itself is contradictory.

If the Realists attempted to resist certain inferences which might be drawn from the doctrine of impermanence, the Personalists tried to formulate a solution to certain difficulties in the non-self doctrine. For example, it was argued that moral responsibility presupposes an agent who performs deeds (and without such a concept the notion of karma as operating justly would break down). Similarly, cognitive experiences imply an active subject. Likewise, compassion and benevolence would be pointless unless there were subjects at whom such attitudes could be directed. It is therefore necessary to hold that there is a person *(pudgala)* or agent who 'supports' the groups. This, so far, has a strong analogy to the Logic-Atomists' belief in a self: but in accordance with Buddhist doctrine, the Personalists held that the person is not eternal, but is manifested through a succession of short-lived states. Even so, the underlying person in a sense persists, in distinction from the groups: and therefore was combated by the other Buddhist schools. Yet it is interesting to observe that, despite analogies to the self doctrine, the Personalists studiously avoided the word 'self'. This is an indication of the centrality of the non-self teaching in the early Buddhist tradition.

The metaphysical speculations of these schools paved the way, in a sense, for the emergence of Greater Vehicle absolutism. The most impressive version of this was the Void School. As we have seen, philosophical developments in the Mahāyāna accompanied religious changes—the cult of Buddhas-to-be and of Buddhas and the belief that Buddhahood was a universal destiny. Thus the Void doctrine cannot be considered apart from these new directions of Buddhist practice. But the difficulties which Realism and Personalism attempted to meet presented Greater Vehicle metaphysicians with an opportunity to bring a dialectical critique to bear on all common-sense beliefs and thus to evolve out of agnosticism an ineffable Absolute, the Void.

For example, the Voidists criticized different theories about causality. The Distinctionists held that in essence the effect is identical with its cause, so that causal changes are just a transformation of a single underlying substance. This was criticized as involving a contradition, for change implies that the effect has different characteristics from the cause, and in this case it is not identical with it. On the other hand, Buddhists held that cause and effect have no inner or essential connection. But the Voidists argued that then there is no reason why a cause should produce a particular effect rather than anything else. In the third place, the schools could attempt to combine the two views of causality, but this would only shift the point of contradiction. Finally, one could hold that all events are random. But this would either be a mere dogma, or it would require evidential support. But the latter suggestion itself involves contradicting the thesis. Thus the different views of causation all, according to the Voidists, collapse. Similar kinds of criticism were directed at other concepts.

The essence of the Voidist dialectic could be boiled down to this: the concept of relation is self-contractory. Since the empirical world, both as described in Buddhism, through the doctrine of origination, and as seen in ordinary experience, is comprised of things or states in relation to one another, any view about the world will involve a contradition. *Relation* is a contradictory concept since a real relation between entities implies that they have an inner connection and so are in a sense identical: but it also implies that there are two terms, and thus the entities have to be different.

This critique of all views could be given some scriptural backing. The Buddha claimed to be free from views, i.e. from theories. Moreover the four-cornered negations could be generalized, so that the Buddha could be represented as denying all theses about ultimate reality, together with their contradictories, as well as combinations of theses and the dogmatic rejection of all theses. Consequently, the Buddha's teaching could be seen as a critical process, culminating in a transcendence of all doctrines about the world. This critical process results in a perception that all things are insubstantial or void.

Nevertheless, Voidism does, paradoxically, have what is in effect a view about ultimate reality. All empirical phenomena are insubstantial, because relative; but yet their inner nature can be said to be constituted by Voidness *(śūnyatā)*. Thus the world seen from the standpoint of discursive reason and perception is unreal, and in its place one must substitute an apprehension of the Void. This, admittedly very thinly described, functions in the system as a sort of Absolute. Thus the Void or Suchness (as it is sometimes referred to) is, in effect, Ultimate reality.

It relation to the traditional concepts of Buddhism, the Void plays a number of roles. First, it correlates with the voidness of inner states which is one of the marks of Buddhist contemplation. Second, the apprehension of the Void becomes equivalent to the attainment of nirvana. Since the experience of mystical apprehension is non-dual, there is no distinction now between the contemplative and the Void; and since also, in the Greater Vehicle, the quest for nirvana is seen as the quest for Buddhahood, the apprehension of the Void is equivalent to Buddhahood. The Buddha's essential nature is the Void. In brief, the Buddha becomes a manifestation of the Absolute: Absolute equals nirvana equals Buddhahood. This links up with the Three-Body formulation described in the previous chapter. The Absolute (equated with the Truth-Body of the Buddha) phenomenalizes itself as the celestial Lord and on earth as the historical Buddha.

It will be observed that the destruction of reason is here (as in some Christian views) a preparation for the acceptance of revelation. Nothing can be asserted about the Absolute or about ultimate reality, beyond the claim that there is somehow an unknown X. But happily this unknown X phenomenalizes itself in the shape of the Buddha-Lord. This enables the Buddha mysteriously to guide the faithful onwards along the Path until the adept can at last realize in direct experience the voidness of things and indeed the Void itself.

There is a further equation in the Void doctrine (and sometimes elsewhere in the Greater Vehicle)—an equation which at first sight causes extreme puzzlement. It is this: that nirvana equals the cycle of existence. Nirvana and the empirical world are identical. This should indeed cause puzzlement, since (in the Elder doctrine and elsewhere) nirvana is a transcendent state, and this means that it is distinct from the empirical world. And does not nirvana consist in release from the cycle of existence and from the process of rebirth? It therefore must seem an extraordinary paradox to affirm that after all nirvana and the empirical world are identical. But the paradox follows from the main position of Voidism. For the distinction between the Absolute and empirical phenomena is not an ontological one, but epistemological. That is, the common-sense viewpoint takes the world to be real and substantial, whereas in its 'inner nature' it is void. In other words, the Absolute is phenomena seen from a higher point of view. It follows that nirvana, identified with the Absolute, and the cycle of existence are one. This leads to the further paradox that there is no real release: merely a change in the saint's experience and attitudes.

The mention of a 'higher point of view' reveals a feature of Voidist absolutism which indeed is clearly necessary—namely a doctrine of two levels of truth. Thus ordinary *(vyāvahārika)* truth, covering the facts which are yielded by perception, etc., is distinguished from higher truth, *(paramārtha)* which is discovered in spiritual experience as accruing upon going through the voidist dialectic. Consequently, though phenomena are in their inner essence regarded (from the standpoint of higher truth) as contradictory, it is legitimate to assert ordinary facts about the world (from the standpoint of ordinary truth). Thus from one standpoint states of affairs are illusory: but from the other they are not. Indeed, and to avoid the kind of vacuity which statements like 'All perceptions are illusory' risk, since 'illusory' needs its contrast with 'veridical', the Voidist system distinguishes between ordinary facts and perceptual (and other) illusions—all within the realm of ordinary truth and falsity. Thus the notion that all phenomena are illusory does not entail a confusion between true and false propositions at the level of the ordinary, and must be understood by reference to the standpoint of higher, truth.

It may be noted that the Voidist dialectic sets great emphasis, paradoxically, on intellectual processes as a means of spiritual enlightenment. For the process of the dialectic, whereby through intellectual operations we come to see the bankruptcy of reason, prepares the way for the non-dual *(advaya)* experience of the Void. Thus Voidism represents a kind of intellectual yoga. In many phases of Indian religion, there is some contrast drawn between intellectual and experiential self-training, between spiritual enlightenment through knowledge and that which comes through yoga and direct experience. But further investigation of the contrast shows that it is an expression merely of different emphases. That is, there are two sides to mystical experience—the theoretical or doctrinal structure built round the contemplative path and the inner experience accruing upon the treading of the path which verifies the doctrinal scheme. For example, in the case of Buddhist nirvana, insight involves not only seeing that the Buddhist view of reality is true, but also seeing this in inner experience. It follows that there are, from the standpoint of the contemplative life, twin dangers to be avoided—that of detaching the intellectual structure from religious experience and thus having a merely formal view of the truth; and that of detaching experience from the intellectual structure, and thus destroying the notion of truth in religion and substituting for it the bare acquisition of a certain mental state. Given that the mystical experience is regarded (as indeed it is in most of the Indian tradition) as cognitive, the two sides of religion must be held together. Thus in the Indian tradition, 'knowledge', understood as having to do with ultimate reality, must always be interpreted as presupposing that there can be a contemplative intuition of the truth; while intuitive experience in turn presupposes some background of doctrine which is the setting for the yogic quest. Hence the Voidist dialectic, though it is intellectualist in appearance and method, must not be misunderstood as being just a philosophical exercise, but is supposed to have experiential fruition. There is some analogy with the Platonic dialectic, in so far as the latter culminates in an ineffable acquaintance with the Good.

All this is relevant to the genesis of the last Buddhist school which we shall here discuss, viz. the Idealist school that adhered to the doctrine of consciousness-only, i.e. the Absolute is constituted by pure consciousness. The school was also referred to as the Yoga-Practitioners *(Yogācārin)*:

for whereas the emphasis in the Void school was on insight or wisdom, the emphasis among the Idealists was upon the practice of yoga. But as we have seen this was only a difference of emphasis, and the two schools rarely clashed with one another. However, it turned out that though both are similar in referring to an Absolute and in treating phenomena as illusory, their doctrines of the Absolute diverged. For the voidists, the Absolute is at best tenuously describable, namely as the Void, and otherwise is an unknown X; but the psychological interests of the Yoga-Practitioners led them to describe the Absolute in terms of consciousness.

The school held, in line with something which goes back far in Buddhism, possibly to its origin, that objects are linguistic constructs. That is, our treatment of an individual as a separate whole or substance depends upon the bewitchment of language, which in giving names to objects leads us to project on to the world the conventions of human speech. But whereas in the Elder doctrine, this conventionality applies to substances *(dravya)*, while the states or events which substances have to be broken up into are real enough, in the Idealist school all concepts of the world of phenomena set over against the percipient have to be destroyed. Thus the subject-object distinction is itself merely a projection of conventional language. Consequently, it is seen that the world is at most a flow of experiences. The relation between this denial of the subject-object relation and the contemplative treatment of sense-data in the stages of meditation described earlier is close.

Further reflection, according to the Idealists, leads us to perceive that the 'inner nature' of the world must be consciousness or thought alone. Consequently, release from the cycle of existence—from the empirical world—comes from attaining to the non-dual experience of pure consciousness in which all the false constructs of thought are banished.

There is, of course, some problem as to how these false constructs got there in the first place; how is it that the experiences of the individual arise? The Idealists held that underlying the ordinary experiences of the individual is the so-called store-consciousness *(ālayavijñāna)* (sometimes compared to the unconscious in modern psychological theory). This store-consciousness is that source and repository of traces. These persist to form the conscious states of the individual: and thus the school gives a more generalized interpretation to the operation of karma. Thus the emergence of the groups is referred back to the underlying store-consciousness. It is worth noting that the Idealists substitute another expression for consciousness in the doctrine of groups. This is to avoid the confusion which would arise from the use of the same term for the Absolute and for one of the elements of individuality. It is also worth noting that since (still in accordance with Buddhist orthodoxy) the Idealists analyse the conscious individual in terms of the groups, the store-consciousness, which underlies the individual, and is not part of what constitutes the individual, cannot be considered as the name for an entity peculiar to any individual. Thus it corresponds (very roughtly) more to Jung's collective unconscious than to Freud's concept. Or—to put the situation in another way—the question of number does not enter when we are dealing with what lies beyond the plurality of particular individuals. (There remains, of course, a difficulty for any theory of the absolute as to how this 'single' entity breaks up into, or somehow generates, the many individuals of ordinary experience: and to hold that the plurality of individuals rests upon an illusion removes the difficulty at the expense of seeing it appear at another level.)

So much, most briefly, for the Idealist school. It will be observed that its emphasis upon the notion of consciousness, in comparison with the concept of the Void in the Voidist school, is related to the difference of emphasis mentioned above. For the Voidist the Absolute transcends reason: for the Idealist it transcends ordinary conscious-states. Thus for the former, the technique of attaining the transcendent is the use of the dialectic: for the latter the technique is the use of the methods of yoga, i.e. the control of consciousness.

It will be necessary later to attempt a more detailed analysis of the determinants of Buddhist metaphysics. But as a preliminary outline, we can say this: the correlation between the growth of Greater Vehicle absolutism and the development of the cult of Buddhas-to-be and of devotionalism *(bhaktimārga)* may not be entirely fortuitous. For whereas in the Elder doctrine, the transcendent is conceived as a state, the Greater Vehicle schools we have discussed treat the transcendent, in effect, as a kind of substance. This enables them to conceive the more easily of the Buddha as a manifestation of a 'hidden' ultimate reality. Hence, absolutist metaphysics dovetails with the Three-Body doctrine, which is a formal expression of different elements in the developed religion of the Mahāyāna. It remains true that in Voidism and Idealism devotional, *bhakti*, religion still takes second place. That is, the cult of quasi-divine Buddhas is subordinated to the ultimate mystical experience of non-duality. Only in some later and more Eastern phases of the Greater Vehicle does devotional religion become paramount, so that faith in the Buddha is the sufficient condition of salvation, and the concept of nirvana as the goal fades into second place (a trend, in the Pure Land school, which paradoxically brings Buddhism close to theism). Nevertheless, devotionalism plays a powerful role in the phase of the Mahāyāna which we are principally considering. The Three-Body formulation both gives it a place and puts it in its place. Likewise, the two-truth theory of Voidist absolutism allows the florid expression of devotional religion at the lower level of truth while at the same time subordinating it to the higher truth of mystical experience. As we shall observe in later discussions, a greater deal of Indian metaphysics and theology turns on the relative emphasis given in a system to devotional and mystical religion. We could put the situation crudely, in the case of Buddhism, by means of the following equations:

2 x meditative mysticism + 0 x devotionalism = Elder doctrine
2 x m.m. + 1 x d. = Voidism / Idealism
1 x m.m. + 2 x d. = Pure Land quasi-theism.

It may be noted that the idealism of the Absolutist schools can be seen partly as exhibiting some devaluation of ordinary concepts, including those that serve to express the devotional religion which especially appeals to those immersed in the affairs of the world. But at the same time, idealism presents a *picture* which is in line with a way of imagining the relation between the transcendent and the empirical typical of theism and other forms of devotional religion. For in theism there is the picture that the world, as it were, forms a screen behind which lives divinity. He is concealed, until such time as (through his own initiative —hence doctrines of grace) he chooses to manifest himself to men: he is concealed unless self-revealed. This 'screen-picture' is also suggested by Idealism, for the illusions of ordinary knowledge cover up ultimate reality. This may serve to show why Absolutism (which already has made concessions, so to speak, to devotionalism) contrasts to impermanent states a kind of permanent substance (even if it be only thinly describable). For there are two sorts of contrast that can be made here: either to set over against the impermanent states a permanent state, as in Elder metaphysics; or to see the impermanent states as contrasted to a permanent underlying substance. This latter contrast is imaginatively affiliated to the 'screen-picture'.

There are certain other, and perhaps paradoxical, generalities to be asserted about Idealism. The Lesser Vehicle insists upon the reality of the impermanent states: and one oinner reason for this may be the importance placed by the Buddha upon the ethical side of the path. There is an evident tendency among those forms of mysticism which strongly express the illusoriness of the world to consider moral activity as of quite secondary importance. Yet in the case of Buddhism this represents a paradox. For the adherents of the Greater Vehicle criticized the Lesser sharply for its self-centredness and lack of universal compassion—the point being that the ideal of the saint who gains his own release was thought, by the Greater Vehicle, to be selfish in essence. The ideal of the self-sacrificing Buddha-to-be, on the other hand, encouraged altruism and universal compassion. Thus the axiom 'Doctrines of illusion and moral concern do not blend easily' seems in need of revision. But the situation in the Greater Vehicle can be explained as follows. The introduction of devotionalism tended towards religious universalism. No longer is Buddhism *primarily* the faith of monks and nuns. Real participation in its higher fruits is increasingly open to the layman. Thus the path of the Buddha-to-be is substituted for that of the in-turning saint. But though devotionalism, and thereby the imitation of the object of devotion, are ultimately swallowed up in the non-dual experience, where the empirical world vanishes (so to speak), the latter experience provided, as we saw earlier, the basis for the identification of the Buddha with ultimate reality. Moreover, the quest for that experience is identical with the quest for Buddhahood. It follows that the devotee, in worshipping the Buddha, is worshipping his own future state. Thus, the imitation of Buddhas-to-be is not merely a matter of being Buddha-like (as the Christian might be Christ-like), but of the devotee's recognition of his own potential Buddhahood.

Briefly, then, the Lesser Vehicle represents an elaboration of a faith centered on mysticism, but without God; in the Greater Vehicle, there remains the mysticism, but its goal is interpreted in such a way that the Absolute which can be realized in contemplative experience also manifests to human imagination in the form of a divine Buddha (or rather of countless such Buddhas, united however in their Truth-Body). It is mysticism with God; but God remains secondary, as does devotion.

CHAPTER III
JAIN METAPHYSICS

Buddhism, as was remarked earlier, has affinities with Jainism, Distinctionism and Materialism. The rather conservative and unspeculative religion of the Jains has a mythological and legendary heritage which has remarkable affinities to that of Buddhism: and consequently there is good ground for supposing that they stem from a similar tradition in archaic times. But Jainism retains many more archaic properties. Though the last great teacher, Vardhamāna (often entitled Mahāvīra) was a contemporary of the Buddha's and had a not dissimilar career, there is reason to suppose that he was merely restoring and amplifying an existing religion; while the Buddha, though drawing on a like background of religious ideas and customs, was (it seems) much more of an innovator, and therefore can justly be described as the 'founder' of Buddhism; this description would scarcely apply, as Jain tradition indeed insists, to Vardhamāna. At least one of his legendary twenty-three predecessors, the 'Ford-makers' who enable the faithful to cross the stream of rebirth to the other side, is most probably an actual historical figure, preceding Vardhamāna by about two centuries.

Though only now having about four million adherents, Jainism has had an influence out of proportion to its present numbers, partly because of the prosperity of the community, partly because of being more numerous in mediaeval times and partly because of its special contribution to the Indian heritage, namely the doctrine of non-injury *(ahiṃsā)* or non-violence, which was in recent times given a social and political application by Gandhi.

The central feature of Jainism, apart from the doctrines of karma, rebirth and the possibility of release, is its cosmology, which was elaborated in some detail, is probably quite ancient and is given practical significance by being a topic of meditation for the adherent. The cosmos, according to the Jain view, is everlasting and uncreated. The latter point follows from the atheistic nature of the Jain system. In the cosmos are to be discovered two kinds of entities—souls or life-monads *(jīvas),* and non-living *(ajīva)* matter. The former are infinite in number, and possess the essential properties of omniscience and blissfulness. (The property of omniscience, as we shall see, affected Jain theories of perception: perceptions being rather the occasion of the manifestation of knowledge than the source of knowledge.) These properties are obscured through the entanglement of the life-monads in non-living matter, and in particular through the functioning of karma. The latter was conceived by the Jains as being a subtle material force. The life-monads implicated in the round of rebirth are weighed down by this karmic force. Upon release, they rise to the top of the cosmos, where they exist, quiescent and motionless, enjoying their essential omniscience and bliss.

Why the top of the cosmos? In accordance with certain archaic elements in the Jain system, it pictures the cosmos as roughly having the shape of a gigantic man or woman. The world inhabited by men is like a great disc, corresponding to the waist of the cosmic man. The continents are thought to be arranged concentrically and divided from each other by circular oceans. Below the world disc, there are seven levels, each including a million purgatories. Above the disc there is a like series of heavens, with the gods distributed hierarchically within them. Right on top of these heavens, and corresponding to the top of the cosmic man's head, is the summit of the cosmos, whither the liberated life-monads ascend. Surrounding the whole 'man' there are three layers of air, and then infinite space.

The dimensions of this cosmos are huge. Its height is calculated as being 14 major units of length. Each of these is computed as being the distance covered in six months by a being travelling at 2 million miles per micro-second or smallest unit of time. In time, the cosmos is, as we have seen, infinite; but the passage of history is cyclical—each aeon commences with a Golden Age, when men are of enormous size and Methuselah-like in lifespan and miraculous trees supply all their needs. Thus government and property are unnecessary. But decline always sets in: the present time is one, for instance, when the world is rapidly going down-hill (hence the small numbers of Jains). Gradually the religion will die out, until it is restored in the next aeon. Buddhism, it should be noted, has a not dissimilar view of human history and the state of true religion.

The above cosmology created certain problems: though motion characterizes the contents of the cosmos, the liberated life- monads at the summit of the cosmos are supposed to be motionless; and again, the cosmos as a whole should disintegrate if it be supposed that things might fly off into the surrounding infinite space. Both these problems are solved, according to the Jains, by the use of certain concepts of space. Space may be conceived either as a medium of motion or as a system of locations. The Jains hold therefore that there can be space in the second sense which does not contain the medium of motion. Only where the latter extends is motion possible. Indeed, to complicate matters slightly they postulate also a medium of rest. Thus there is a triple distinction: local space *(ākāśa)*; motion-medium *(dharma)*; and rest-medium *(adharma)*. Thus infinite local space surrounding the cosmos does not contain the motion-medium, and hence there is no chance of things flying off into infinite space. Similarly, it is held that at the summit of the cosmos there is rest-medium, but not motion-medium, and consequently the liberated life-monads remain motionless.

It may be noted that the great teachers of Jainism, the Ford-makers, *Tīrthaṃkara*, to whom we referred earlier, figure, in the development of the religion, increasingly as objects of a temple cult. *Mutatis mutandis*, a Jain temple is not unlike a Hindu one. One might therefore be excused for conceiving of the Ford-makers as gods analogous to those in Hinduism. But the doctrine of the motionlessness of the liberated implies that the Ford-makers are utterly beyond any kind of transaction with the rest of the cosmos. Thus they are not beings who have creative capacities, or ability to intervene in answer to prayer, and the like. Though conceived differently from the Buddhas of the Elder School, they likewise have disappeared from human ken. Hence, the cult of Jainism still leaves its essential character unaffected—namely an atheistic system which allows the Indian gods a place in the hierarchy of intra-cosmic heavens. Both Buddhism and Jainism transcend polytheism, by exalting above the gods the idea of a liberation which has nothing to do with God or gods. Both can therefore be dubbed 'transpolytheistic atheism'.[1]

Not only is the Jain cosmos infinite in time and surrounded by infinite space, but it contains an infinity of life-monads. These are classified in accordance with the number of sense-organs they possess. Men, gods and the inhabitants of the purgatories have the usual five senses plus the mind-organ, conceived as a material entity. The higher animals have the five senses, but no mind-organ. Lower animals have a decreasing number of sense-organs. Thus worms have only touch and taste. Lower down still, plants and the atomic elements (of fire, earth, air and water) have primitive souls, with only the sense of touch. Finally, there are even more microsopic life-monads, which do not individually possess organs, but clustering together share the capacities for respiration and nutrition. They are infinitesimally small, and the cosmos is jam-packed with them. Generally speaking, the law of karma applies only to the hierarchy of beings between these animalcules and the liberated life-monads. The latter have left the realm of karma, the former have not yet entered upon the karmic cycle. But from time to time animalcules 'rise', as it were, and transmigrate through the cycle of animal life. Thus they make up for the souls who go out of ordinary existence into the state of perfection. They form an inexhaustible source of fresh transmigrating life-monads.

I have referred to life-monads as being microscopic, etc. Despite the sharp divide which is made in Jainism between life-monads and non-living matter, the souls are conceived in a somewhat materialistic manner. They expand and contract to fill the bodies with which they are clothed. An image used in this connection is that of light which pervades larger and smaller volumes in accordance with the position of the obstructions surrounding a light-source. Further, life-monads have an intrinsic direction of motion, namely upwards. Karma is therefore thought of as weighing them down. Once therefore a life-monad's clinging karma has been annihilated, it will rise automatically to the summit of the cosmos. Thus the religious problem of Jainism is: how to annihilate karma.

In this matter, Jainism is both more legalistic and austere than Buddhism. Legalistic: because the taking of life (for example) has evil karmic effects irrespectively of the intentions of the agent. For this reason, the way to liberation is one of most extreme austerity. Only by refraining from ordinary pursuits and by mortifying the flesh can the monk hope to gain perfect release. Since taking life is the chief infringment of the duty of non-injury, the ultimate ideal for the monk—when he has reached the stage of spiritual development which makes it possible—is suicide by starvation. In this, the monk follows Vardhamāna. But though there is greater emphasis in Jainism upon asceticism than in Buddhism, the use of meditations akin to those of Buddhist yoga is also central to the quest.

Since release from rebirth involves, according to Jainism, the attainment of perfect knowledge—and thus the claim is made that the Ford-makers, for instance, are omniscient—a distinction is made between empirical and higher perception. This higher and omniscient knowledge is a property of the life-monad in the liberated state; but it is normally obscured by karmic matter. Thus when karma is annihilated omniscience becomes actually manifested in the soul. It follows that empirical knowledge is part due to the operation of karma. However, it is not supposed that empirical knowledge is basically illusory, as some other viewpoints hold. Rather, an ordinary perception is a glimpse of the truth: though only the saint can hope to have complete knowledge of the whole structure of the cosmos. Consequently, every perception is a partial, but only a partial, manifestation of what in principle is known by the life-monad. Jainism is realistic; and never developes, as did Buddhism, a form of philosophical idealism. Nevertheless, grafted on to the above beliefs, it possesses a doctrine of perspectives *(naya)* and of relativism *(syādvāda)* which were to be given an interpretation implying religious tolerance.

According to the theory of perspectives, any object can be considered from a number of points of view. This is in line with the notion that empirical perception is only partial. Thus, in considering an object, it is possible to see it in a number of perspectives. These are categorized as seven. First, one can consider the object without distinguishing its specific or generic properties. Second, one can look at the object as exhibiting its generic properties (e.g. one can consider a car simply from the perspective of being an instance of a car). Third, one can note its individual properties, not bothering about its generic ones) e.g. one adverts to, say, the registration number, etc.). Fourth, one may consider its immediate contemporary character, without thought of its past history or future (e.g. without thought of its previous owner, etc.). Fifth, one can consider the object in relation to the conventional meaning of the word or words used to classify it (e.g. one reflects, confronted by a car, on the ordinary usage of 'car' and 'automobile', etc.). In this way, one notes how the words correctly *refer* to the object under consideration. Sixth, one may contemplate the various nuances of the different words which correctly refer to the object (e.g. as between 'car' and 'automobile')—and in this way one adverts to the *meanings* of the expressions which in this case correctly *refer*. Finally, one may consider the correspondence between these meanings and aspects of the object under consideration.

This rather formal classification of perspectives indicates that Jainism holds a correspondence theory of truth, namely that judgments are true when they correspond to features of the world. Hence the preoccupation in the last three of the above perspectives with the relation between language and objects. Judgments are expressed in language, and therefore it is important to see in detail the relationship between expressions and the aspects of things to which they refer.

There is a further sevenfold classification which is of interest in this connection: it is the doctrine which we have dubbed relativism. According to this, judgments about an entity fall under seven forms. These are as follows. (1) 'Could be it is'; (2) 'Could be it is not'; (3) 'Could be it is and it is not'; (4) 'Could be it is inexpressible'; (5) 'Could be it is and is inexpressible'; (6) 'Could be it is not and is inexpressible'; (7) 'Could be it is and is not and is inexpressible'. The first thing to note in this peculiar scheme of judgments is that each judgment is prefaced by the words 'could be'. Indeed the doctrine's official title should literally be translated 'could-be-ism' or 'perhapsism'. This form of words is designed to indicate that dogmatic judgments are out of place. The danger of simply asserting a proposition is that the hearer will not see the assertion in its right context, one namely where the assertion is qualified by reference to a particular aspect of the object under consideration, and does not apply outside this reference. Or in brief, only in limited contexts are assertions true. It should also be noted about the scheme that the verb 'to be' can be used both in its existential and copulative sense.

The scheme could be exemplified as follows. One may perceive an orchid. Then the judgment 'Could be this orchid exists' applies; or (provided one recalls the whole context) one can simply say 'This orchid exists'. But this judgment is not explicit enough, for it fails to bring out the fact that only by a process of making distinctions can we assert particular judgments. That is, in so far as we treat the individual entity under consideration as an instance of an orchid, we are treating it as a non-instance of something else, e.g. a rainbow. Thus we are also bound to assert 'In respect of being a rainbow, it is not' (judgment (2) above). Thirdly, we can combine the two previous assertions, and affirm (3). Judgment (4) is more obscure, but is grounded on a number of considerations. One is this: under (1) and (2) one can show in what respect the positive assertion holds, and in what respect the negative. One can then simply combine the propositions under form (3). But if one asks: 'In what respect is this both an orchid and not a number?' there is no answer, so that there is a way in which the entity is indescribable. According to Jain linguistic theory, there is a one-one relation between linguistic expressions and meanings (a word having more than one meaning counts as more than one word). It follows that there is no intermediate expression between any two basic expressions which can express the respect in which they both apply to the same entity. Thus existence and non-existence cannot be *simultaneously* predicated of the same entity. Finally, there remain (5), (6) and (7), which result from combining a selection of judgments (1) to (4).

It will be noted that there is a strong resemblance between this Jain doctrine and the multiple negation and classification of undetermined questions in Buddhism. There is evidence that both the Jain and Buddhist teaching in this matter, together with that of early Indian scepticism drew upon a common intellectual fund. But the aim of the Jain doctrine is not that of sustaining a form of scepticism which leaves room for an ineffable higher truth, in the manner of the Voidist school. Rather its object is in part to accept one of the grounds of scepticism while retaining a positive doctrine about the world. The fact that apparently contradictory assertions can be made about an entity, that it is and is not, is not made the basis of the view that nothing can be said about the world; but is taken to show first that we must consider in relation to what an assertion is being made (in short, we must see its context), and second that ordinary knowledge is partial. But its partiality, though it leaves room for saying that in some unknown respects individual entities are indescribable, does not affect its validity within the limits prescribed by the context. Further, both the classification of judgments and the doctrine of perspectives serve to underline the Jain view that no entity is isolated, but that the cosmos is an organic whole. Thus the archaic picture of the cosmos as being like a gigantic man or woman has the metaphysical justification that entities are not to be viewed in isolation from one another: every apparently non-relative affirmation implicitly involves assertions about relations. Finally, the two 'sevenfold' doctrines were given a wider interpretation, in the direction of expressing doctrinal tolerance in respect of other faiths. Thus relativism was applied to the Jain system itself. In some respects, Jainism is true; but there could be others in which other religions are so. The Jains here made use of a simile, both to exhibit what was meant by relativism and to show what religious truth is like. A number of blind men hold on to different parts of an elephant; but each gives a different report of the object—while of course all along it is the same object. Likewise, different faiths are but partial expressions of the highest truth. It does not, of course, need much perspicuity to see both that it is natural to hold some such view in a society where different religions live together over long periods, as in India, and that it must involve a doctrinal contradiction—unless the respect in which non-Jain religions are true is indescribable.

The archaic and conservative nature of Jainism did not, as it turned out, allow of much development within the metaphysical views expressing the religion. Indeed, the only major schism within the faith had to do with certain ritual or ethical matters (principally the issue of nudism, i.e. whether monks should adopt this, the limit of simplicity and independence of material goods); while the major teachings about the world and indeed about the right way of life remained largely unchanged over more than 2,500 years. In comparison with Buddhism, Jainism is tremendously austere; but like Buddhism it essentially involves the quest for mystical release. This, however, is considerably overlaid by a preoccupation with karma. As we saw, karma is a subtle material force inevitably generated by entanglement in ordinary pursuits. Thus Jainism could be described as being a religion of genuine mysticism, but one where an extreme emphasis upon a rather detailed morality, seen in the light of karma, means that self-mortification comes to be regarded as the primary means of release.

CHAPTER IV
MATERIALISM AND EXEGESIS

In the sixth century B.C.E. and onwards, there is no doubt that materialistic doctrines flourished. The writings of other schools, such as the Buddhist scriptures, amply testify to this trend, though it is not always clear how far there were different schools comprised under the various names used of the Materialists: there is reference to the Cārvāka school, called after its founder or supposed founder; to unorthodoxy which did not merely deny the validity of Brāhmanic revelation, but also denied the existence of a future life, etc.; to naturalism *(svabhāvavāda)*; and to materialism in the sense of denying the existence of a transcendent realm beyond this world. It is probable that in a period of speculative ferment, a number of tendencies combined into the system which bears Cārvāka's name. The first of these was anti-Vedic and, more generally, anti-religious; there was no dearth, it seems, of people and arguments seeking to undermine the theological beliefs of the period. Second, there was naturalistic speculation about the physical world, which sought to explain all phenomena in terms of the four elements. Such physical materialism assisted anti-religious arguments by forming the basis for a denial of the eternal self. Third, philosophical scepticism, though it did not marry too easily with physical materialism, could be used as a blanket support for common-sense anti-religious arguments. Part of the difficulty in describing early Indian Materialism is that we have to rely almost entirely on accounts of the Materialist position supplied by its opponents; and then again, though there is some textual material from a much later period, the fact that by the middle ages Materialism virtually disappeared from the Indian scene makes it hard to reconstruct the ongoing anti-religious tradition.

However, something can be said about the three tendencies mentioned above. First of all, there is ample evidence (and even within the Upaniṣads) of anti-religious feelings and arguments in ancient India. Some of these were directed against the validity of revelation. For instance, it was held that some of the rites prescribed by scripture were barbarous, and so contrary to ordinary moral beliefs. Again, Materialism tended to disregard the value of verbal testimony, (*śabda*), since statements about reality should be based upon observation. Consequently, the acceptance of testimony can only be justified on the ground that testimony itself is based on perception: but this makes testimony otiose. This attitude is undoubtedly affected by the consideration that acceptance of testimony would in practice imply willingness to accept scriptural revelation, a form of verbal testimony. Further, particular arguments were adduced against the contents of revelation. For example, belief in heaven was criticized on the ground that if people have such a future life, and if they love their families, why is it that they never return from the heavenly realm to visit them? Likewise, there were criticisms of the doctrine of rebirth, on the ground that we have no memory of previous lives, etc. In brief, the Materialists levelled common-sense objections against the assumptions of both orthodox and unorthodox faith.

The criticisms of heaven and like concepts were connected with the second tendency noted above, namely the attempt to frame a genuinely materialistic picture of reality. Thus, things and events in the world could be explained, according to Materialism, in terms of the four elements, of earth, water, fire and air. Naturally, this presented a problem in regard to the nature of consciousness. Here the Materialists used the analogy of the intoxicating properties of liquor. These properties arise from a certain mixture of the ingredients; and likewise consciousness arises given a certain combination of material elements, such as is found in certain organic bodies. We shall have occasion later to consider in further detail the Materialist arguments against the eternal self. It can be seen, then, that part of the Materialist movement is constituted by a protoscientific attempt to account, in a relatively simple manner, for the varied phenomena encountered in the world.

The third tendency was epistemological. As we have noted, the Materialists rejected verbal testimony as an independent source of knowledge. Similarly, there were anti-religious motives for being suspicion of inference as a means of knowledge. For it was partly on *anumāna*, the basis of inference, that theological speculation attempted to show the existence of a divine Being and of an eternal self. Some of the sceptical arguments against inference were rather subtle, as we shall see in the second part of this book, and reminiscent of some modern discussions of verification and induction. It is probable that the Materialists, properly so-called, made use of considerations advanced by philosophical sceptics and agnostics who were not genuinely Materialists. For this reason, there was some inconsistency in the Cārvāka attack on inferential knowledge, since the doctrine of four elements itself is in some degree speculative and therefore scarcely something yielded by pure observation. Thus later Materialism modified its scepticism about inference, allowing that inference from perception to conclusions about what is in principle perceptible is legitimate. However, it may be noted that Materialists rejected the atomic theory of other schools, since atoms as usually conceived lay inevitably beyond the possibility of perception.

It also appears that the form of multiple negation used by the Buddha in connection with the undetermined questions (discussed in Chapter II) owes something to the philosophical sceptics from whom Materialism borrowed its rejection of inference.

The paucity of evidence about the degree to which Materialism was a systematized doctrine makes the attempt to expound its tenets inevitably disappointing. It is fortunate therefore that a fair number of Materialist *arguments* have been preserved in the works of their opponents, and we shall have occasion to examine some of these in the second part of the book.

It is of some interest to contrast what we know of Materialism with the most curious and (in some ways) most archaic of the orthodox viewpoints, namely Exegesis Mīmāṃsā. For it happened that a concentration upon Vedic ritualism, in order to reduce the scriptural teachings to a clear order, led to a virtual scepticism about some aspects of religion and religious speculation. As has been pointed out in Chapter I, Exegesis, until a late period in its development, conceived of heaven, rather than a pure state of release, as the spiritual goal. This indicates its early fidelity to the position of the Vedic hymns, and to Āryan faith, which did not originally incorporate the notions of rebirth and release which were so to dominate later Indian religion. Yet in another way, Exegesis appears to move far from those Vedic writings. By focusing its attention on ritual, the school tended to neglect the structure of belief expressed in revelation. In the course of its history Exegesis elaborated the thesis that the texts of revelation must be interpreted solely as *injunctions*. It is of course clear that in so far as scriptures are binding as to ritual, they will be prescribing what ought to be done, rather than describing what is the case. The Exegetes showed considerable ingenuity in treating all the sentences of the Veda as being essentially imperative. This meant, among other things, that hymns addressed to the gods were not interpreted as making statements about them, but rather as just expressing the context or nature of the particular sacrifices with which the hymns are associated. Since Vedic remarks about sacrifices are injunctions, all Vedic remarks are thereby interpreted as injunctions. Furthermore, the concentration on ritual led to the belief that ritual is effective quite irrespectively of the operation of the gods. The power implicit in the sacrifice is sufficient to bring about the beneficial results the sacrificer looks to. Thus the Veda is now thought of neither as containing assertions about the gods nor as ascribing religious potency to them. They become virtually otiose in the Exegete system.

The autonomy of the sacrifice and of revelation itself led the Exegetes to resist any concept of a divine Creator. The scriptures, if they were created by a Lord, would derive their authority from him (as the Logic-Atomist school indeed held): but the Exegetes considered that revelation is self-authenticating. Moreover, if the usual Indian belief in a 'pulsating' cosmos were entertained, the scriptures would have to be refashioned in each epoch by God. So Exegesis denies the 'pulsating' character of the cosmos, but holds it to be everlasting in a formed condition. The Veda is likewise everlasting.

Though the denial of God and of periodic cosmic chaos involves Exegesis in a *Weltanschauung*, the general tenour of Exegete though is that factual knowledge is only necessary, in the context of religious truth, in order that we may the better understand the scriptural injunctions.

Religious 'truth' is essentially a set of imperatives. Thus in general Exegesis sets itself against the varied forms of theological speculation in the Indian tradition.

The doctrine of the eternity and self-authentication of revelation is the most extreme expression of the fundamentalist attitude to be found in world religions. It had, however, a useful effect, in so far as it stimulated debate about the nature of language. The position of Exegesis about language, and in particular about the Sanskrit language as the sacred tongue of Brāhmanism, is that words do not acquire their meanings by convention (though an exception is made about the reference of personal names). The meaning of a word is an intrinsic power which it possesses—so that an account of meaning certainly need not involve reference to the understanding of communications by hearers. But even this thesis was not sufficient for the purposes of Exegesis, ever ready to defend the validity and eternity of revelation. Language exists as a separate entity, which becoms manifest when actually used by people: thus it could be held that there is (so to say) an invisible scriptural language, the formulae of which become manifested when used in ceremonial, etc. Thus language is, in a sense, a transcendent system of expressions, which are made evident in an empirical way by humans who use them. It therefore became, on this basis, easy for Exegesis to claim that revelation exists in an essentially everlasting manner, even though it is only manifested in the particular circumstances of early Indian history. As we have seen, this view of language created discussion; and indeed one of the more interesting aspects of Indian traditional philosophy is linguistic speculation. It happened both that language was a central religious issue, and that grammatical analysis reached an extraordinarily advanced stage in India early on.

Because of its interest in the methodology of scriptural interpretation, Exegesis paid special attention to epistemology, and we shall in the latter part of the book have occasion to examine some of its doctrines on this matter in relation to the continuing debate in traditional Indian philosophy about the number, nature and validity of the so-called sources or bases of knowledge, *pramāṇa*.

As Exegesis developed, it tended to involve itself in discussions with other schools, and so to evolve views about matter and the self akin to those held elsewhere. Thus the eternity of the self is affirmed; though the grounds for believing in such an entity have a characteristic emphasis in the school. The necessity of a permanent entity underlying the states of the psycho-physical organism (which are accounted for by a general atomic theory) is that volitions presuppose a continuing agent. This is of course in line with the Exegete stress on the imperatival nature of religious 'truth'. The self, furthermore, was held to be omnipresent, as it is absurd to speak of it as localized, even though each self is conjoined to, and expresses itself through, a localizable organism. Since, however, this omnipresent self needs to be associated with a psycho-physical complex to perform any acts and to acquire knowledge, in the state of release it is absolutely quiescent: it is in a condition of pure potentiality. It may be noted, though, that the development of this view (somewhat similar to that of Distinctionism), the Exegetic school has substituted for the strictly Vedic, or early Vedic, belief in salvation as heavenly existence a concept which is close to the characteristic ideas of the non-Āryan tradition.

Briefly, one could characterize Exegesis as the result of a split in religious thinking—a split between the *reference* of religious activities (e.g. the gods or God) and those activities themselves. Exegesis belongs essentially to those forms of religion which centre upon the numinous experience and sacramental activities: it has no interest in contemplation and mysticism. And yet by a strange paradox, it loses all concern for the 'objects' of worship and sacrifice. It abandons the gods, virtually, and yet not by way of substituting one God or the Absolute of Brahmanism. Instead it substitutes for the gods only ritual power—it is solely through the right performance of religious duties that salvation accrues. It is as though a Christian were to become an atheist, and yet believe in the independent efficacy of the sacraments.

CHAPTER V

DISTINCTIONISM AND YOGA

It is somewhat hard to determine the origins of the Distinctionist *(Sāṃkhya)* and Yoga systems. In their classical forms they were closely associated, the former serving as the metaphysical basis for the mainly practical interests of the latter—even though the latter did add on to the atheistic Distinctionism the doctrine of a personal Lord as object of meditation. There are elements of Distinctionist thought present in the Upaniṣads, and more notably in the *Gītā*. In particular, these elements occur in two Upaniṣads which have a theistic tendency; and the *Gītā* too, of course, teaches a personal Lord. Also, it is notable that the Vaiṣṇavite schools of the mediaeval period make use of Distinctionist ideas, especially those of a cosmological nature. For these reasons, there has been mooted the thesis that the original Distinctionism, now lost to view, was theistic. But there are strong indications that this is not so. In view of the general resemblance of Distinctionism to Jain and Buddhist ideas, pointed out by Heinrich Zimmer, and in view of the agreed atheistic character of classical Distinctionism, it is not surprising that Śaṅkara should have referred to Distinctionism as semi-nihilistic, with the implication that it was not at one time recognized as an orthodox school. In short, there is a strong presumption that the viewpoint had its origins outside the Brahmanical tradition. The fact that its ideas were made use of by theists and by the Upaniṣadic authors is no more an indication of its theistic character in origin than is the use of yogic concepts in the same works a sign that yogic methods were typical of early Brahmanism. The reverse appears true: that yogic practices, later to be formulated in classical Yoga and given a metaphysical backcloth by Distinctionism, were developed in a general tradition if anything hostile, like Jainism and early Buddhism, to theism.

Our concern, however, is primarily with the classical formulations of the doctrines of the two viewpoints. In effect the two can be treated together: for the chief divergence between them, namely that Yoga includes belief in a Lord, appears to be more a late recognition of what had come to be Yogic practice, i.e. the meditation on the Lord as an aid towards release, than a feature which lent a totally new dynamic to the Yoga viewpoint. It is in the nature of an extra tacked on.

As we have seen in an earlier chapter, the principal feature of Distinctionism is its view of reality as consisting on the one hand of a unitary nature which evolves into the world as manifested through our senses and on the other hand in an infinity of distinct souls. As in other viewpoints, most of what the Western metaphysician would tend to classify under the head of mind, as distinguished from matter, is considered to be part of the natural or material world. Indeed the soul as such is inactive, and it is only through its combination with various mental elements, together with a body, that it acquires the characteristics normally associated with consciousness. The inclusion under the head of nature of mental elements serves to explain some of the peculiar features of the doctrine of evolution of nature propounded in this viewpoint. It may be noted, incidentally, that the active character of nature and the passive character of souls may well reflect the feminine gender of the word for the former and the masculine gender of the word for 'soul' (for the Western idea of the relative activeness of the male and female tend to be reversed in the Indian tradition); this in turn may reflect an archaic anthropomorphization of nature, somewhat in line with the anthropomorphic way in which the universe is sometimes depicted in Jain cosmology. In any event, the active character of nature helped to suggest, what we find in classical Distinctionism, the idea that nature has an inherent teleology whereby its subserves, in the last resort, the best interests of souls.

The evolution of nature must be seen against the background of the typical, and well-nigh universal, Indian concept of the 'pulsating' universe. After a period of quiescence, during which nature is in a virtually undifferentiated state, certain internal forces, hitherto in a state of equilibrium, lose this balance, and gradually nature is transformed into its present state. These forces enter into a lot of traditional Indian thought about cosmology, and are the three so-called qualities or strands *guṇa*—entities which have a partly psychological and partly physical character. When the strand-substances are in a state of mutually balanced tension, so that there is no change in the situation, nature is, as we have seen, in equilibrium. The disturbance of the equilibrium being responsible for the manifestation of determinate things, it was not thought unreasonable to explain psychological and other phenomena in terms of the relative proportions of the strand-substances. Indeed, the doctrine of strand-substances formed the basis of the traditional Indian theory of temperaments.

These strand-substances were categorized respectively as the brightness *sattva*-strand, the force *rajas*-strand and the mass *tamas*-strand. The first has the properties of lucidity and adaptability, and forms the basis, among other things, of the higher mental functions. The second is volatile and imparts energy. The third is dull and sluggish, and forms the substance of heavy and dense material objects. It is easy to see that analogies can be drawn between lucidity, energy and density as manifested at the physical level and types of psychological disposition. Moreover, of course, as we shall see more clearly in the description of the process of evolution, it is somewhat misleading in regard to Distinctionism to draw any sharp line between the mental and the physical.

However, the evolution of nature was not merely conceived as the consequence of the disturbance of an original equilibrium, but was described in terms of a series of principles successively manifested in the process. This progressive manifestation of principles, however, should be pictured as an increasing differentiation of nature, and not as a localized evolution of new factors.

The general pattern of the evolutionary process is this. The brightness-strand in the initial stage of disequilibrium becomes predominant. But when the strand-substances are not held in balanced tension with one another, they have a tendency to become increasingly differentiated. This leaves room where one of the other strand-substances becomes predominant, and so in turn *it* becomes more differentiated. Thus indeterminate nature polarizes into different sorts of entities: and the interplay between these in turn produces further types of entity.

The first stage of the process is that whereby the preponderance of brightness-substance causes a differentiation of the intellects *(buddhi)* associated previously (i.e. before the period of world dissolution *(praḷaya)* out of which the cosmos is supposed, according to the theory, to be moving) with the various souls which are still in a state of bondage. Thus there is generated an infinite number of intellects, conceived as being composed of the purest natural substance.

The differentiation of brightness-substance releases the energy of the force-strand, which has the effect of giving a boost to the differentiating tendencies in the other strands: this produces on the one hand a further particularizing of the intellects, and on the other hand, a release of the hitherto constrained (because weaker, since brightness-substance first achieved preponderance in the initial disequilibrium) mass-strand. Nature henceforth pursues, as it were, two parallel lines of evolution, corresponding roughly to the mental and physical. The stage of differentiation of the brightness-strand, after the evolution of intellects, is now this: that there manifests itself the individuating factor *(ahaṃkāra)*, whereby there is self- consciousness on the part of the intellects. There is then a further development whereby the self-conscious intellects acquire sense and other faculties: the five senses, plus five active faculties (of speech, handling, locomotion, waste-ejection and generation) and the mind-organ, serving as a *sensus communis.*

The other line of evolution, resulting from the progressive distillation of mass-stuff, begins with the differentiation of an inner material substratum *(bhūtādi)*, corresponding to the individuating factor of consciousness in so far as it provides the ultimate basis for discriminating individual material entities, since it is divisible, i.e. it possesses quantitative properties, but no others. The interplay of force-substance upon this brings into being certain types of subtle matter, corresponding to the qualities perceived by the five senses. These potentials *(tanmātra)* are not themselves perceptible, and can only give rise to sensations when they have been combined in various ways into atoms. This latter indeed is the last and final stage of the evolution of matter. The potentials (sound, touch, colour, taste and smell potentials) are accounted for in an ingenious way. The first to emerge from the substratum is the sound-potential, also described as the space-potential (since space is the medium of sound).

The combination of this with a quantum of mass-stuff out of the substratum gives rise to the next potential, and so on with the others.

It is likewise in terms of combination that the atoms are accounted for. They are the space atoms, air atoms, fire atoms, water atoms and earth atoms. The first are formed by a combination of the space-potentials with the remaining mass-substances in the substratum. The space-atoms have the property of penetrability, so that now the material world is pervaded by space in a form which makes motion possible. The combination of touch- and sound-potentials gives rise to the air atoms; of the colour-, touch- and taste-potentials to the earth atoms. It may be noted that this account gives a rough classification of the substances accessible to different numbers of the senses (thus air can be felt as pressure and heard, water can be seen, touched, heard and tasted, etc.).

As has been remarked, this marks the conclusion of the evolutionary process whereby different sorts of substance are distilled out of undifferentiated nature. Macroscopic entities such as trees and mountains are simply conglomerations of atoms and do not possess any further properties not found in the atoms, potentials, etc. The whole account, it can easily be seen, involves a symmetry between the two lines of evolution, for the psychical organs that are evolved out of the intellect and brightness line of development are matched in the mass-strand line of development by the production of the capacities in matter to give rise to the relevant sense-data. Thus information gathered by the intellect is a reflection of the outside world.

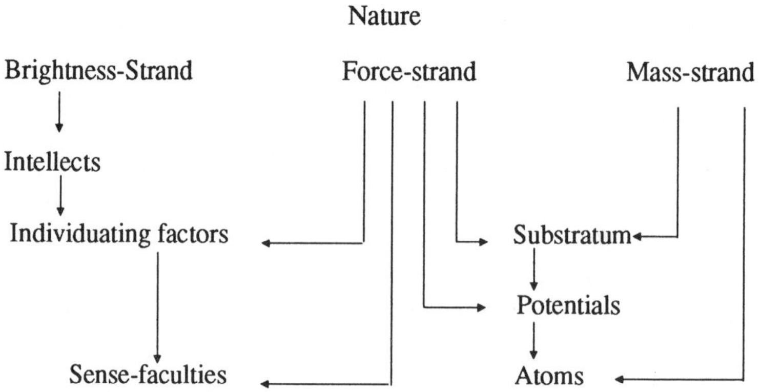

The somewhat complex nature of the above theory of the evolution of the various elements in the world can be represented by a diagram, as follows:

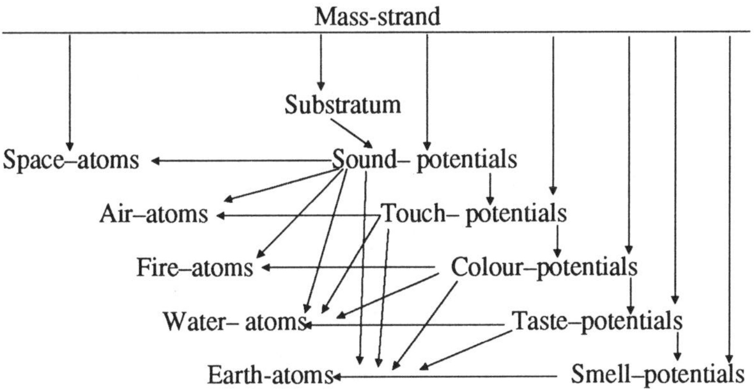

The genesis of the potentials and atoms can be represented in more detail as follows:

It may be asked what such a complex, but archaic-looking cosmology adds up to. It expresses a number of different motifs which are interwoven. First, but perhaps not most important, it has its protoscientific aspect—here is an attempt to give an explanation of the phenomena of the visible world in terms of an underlying unitary substance (nature) which evolves according to its own laws, through the disturbance of an original equilibrium. The concept of the three strands allows the Distinctionist to explain the manifestation of phenomena by reference to a rudimentary dynamics. At the same time there is a clear attempt to show that apparent novelties in the evolutionary process are simply the working out of what was implicit in the unitary nature to start with. Thus although atomism is made use of in the final stages, the atoms themselves are not basic substances, but are distillations out of a single underlying something. Second, the cosmological scheme as evinced in this evolutionary account of the transformation of entities out of nature attempts to explain how it is we can have knowledge of the external world, by supposing that matter evolves (and matter, we must remember, here includes the mental side) on parallel and mutually adapted lines out of the same underlying something. This opens the way for a type of correspondence theory of perception. Third, the whole scheme provides a way of accounting for phenomena which does not need the intervention of a Lord and creator. However, in more than one way it implies that nature contains an inherent teleology, despite the apparently dynamical mode of description of the various phases of natural development. Not only is there an apparent teleology in the way the outer and inner worlds are mutually adaptive, but more importantly, the whole of this process is supposed to be subservient to the long-term interests of the souls. For the souls, in becoming associated with matter (the intellects serving, so to say, as the junction-points), are gradually taught by natural processes that empirical existence is sorrowful and eventually they acquire, without being forced, a distaste for life which is the beginning of their road towards release—in which the souls become entirely detached from nature, and exist in a blankly satisfactory state, impervious now to sorrow and pain, even if also devoid of bliss and pleasure. Thus it was a common criticism of the Distinctionist system that it posited an inherent teleology in nature, though nature was unconscious: would it not be more reasonable to believe in a Lord who guides the whole process? By externalizing the teleology in this way, theistic schools, notably the Vaiṣṇavite ones, were enabled to use Distinctionist cosmology as a supplement to their doctrines about the transcendent world.

The manner in which souls become conjoined to intellects and thereby to the rest of their psycho-physical organisms—a conjunction which is responsible for their tribulations, since in a released state there are none such—is obscure, if we are looking to the origins of this situation. Indeed, from the Distinctionist viewpoint, as in some other systems, there is no question of talking of origins. The process of rebirth is beginningless: all we can say is that souls find themselves in a condition of bondage, though they have the chance of escaping therefrom. But the existence of the possibility of escape does not entail a primordial state when souls were free, only at some point to undergo a 'Fall'. True, they happily undergo a period of quiescence during the dissolution of the cosmos, when they have a rest (as it were) from the bombardments of experience. But otherwise from time immemorial and incalculable they exist in the state of bondage. The problem is one of release *de novo*, not of the restoration of a primeval well-being. Thus, from the Distinctionist point of view, we cannot ask: 'How did the souls come to be associated with intellects and the rest?' We have rather to ask: 'What is the *nature* of the association between souls and intellects and the rest?'

Although we have referred to intellects, the individuating factors, etc., as representing the mental side of reality, the Distinctionists nevertheless hold that without the existence of transcendent souls there would be no consciousness. It is the souls which, so to say, illumine the intellects and the rest. Hence, for experiences as we ordinarily understand them two conditions are necessary—the soul and the psycho-physical organism. In all this, the intellect has a bridging role. Because of the great refinement of the matter of which it is composed (it is of course an evolute of pure brightness-substance) it is well adapted to be the medium of consciousness. It is like some translucent material through which the soul shines. But this is what creates the soul's strange predicament. For the individual person, being aware of his inner states, is deceived by the translucency of his own intellect, and confuses it with his essential self. He sees through a glass too brightly. In identifying the soul with the (admittedly refined) matter of his intellect he is in a state of ignorance. It is this ignorant identification of one's essential self with the psycho-physical organism which is the root of the sorrow and tribulation one undergoes in the almost ceaseless round of reincarnation.

Consequently, the problem of release is the problem as to how a clear awareness of the distinctness of the soul from the psycho-physical organism can be achieved. More particularly, since the doctrine of rebirth accustoms the ordinary man not to identify himself with the present body, the problem is to see the distinction between the soul and the mind. Thus it is not just *soma sema,* as in Orphism, but more perilously *psyche sema.* The seeing of the difference is called discrimination in Distinctionism. In principle it is a form of knowledge: and some texts speak as if it is sufficient to have mastered the metaphysics of Distinctionism to be assured of release. But this impression is misleading: for as elsewhere in the Indian tradition, knowledge is not just theoretical in flavour, but must be endowed with existential impact. This means in effect that metaphysics acquires its meditative side. Self-training and the pondering of the propositions enunciated by the system in a special way are the means of acquiring this discrimination. It is not therefore surprising that Distinctionism should be so closely associated with the Yoga school, which has formulated the methods of outer and inner control with the express intent of acquiring that interior vision and equanimity which will free men from the round of rebirth.

Before going on in more detail to consider the Yogic methods of contemplation, it is worth while making a further point about the Distinctionist concept of the soul. Unlike the Jains, who were content to make the life-monad a spatial entity capable of contraction and expansion, the Distinctionists regard the soul as all-pervasive. This is a way of denying them finite location and dimensions. The reasons for this thesis are not far to find—the space-atoms, which provide places for the various objects manifested in nature, are as we saw, part of the material world, which is held to be, by the Distinctionists, in radical contrast with souls. Nevertheless, souls are individually in conjunction with organisms which *are* spatio-temporal. This is because individual intellects mirror 'their' souls. Now one might suppose, from this account, that Distinctionism might have posited just one soul, mirrored in different ways by the various intellects (this would bring it close to Śaṅkara's Non-Dualism). For there is some difficulty in individuating souls who all have the same nature (consciousness) and who all, as it were, occupy the same place, being all-pervasive. However, it is argued that there are innumerable souls, on the ground that what happens to one does not happen to the others—which ought to happen if they were all one. For instance, the release of one soul does not entail the release of all. This is detectably so, since one can discriminate those who have attained release in the manner prescribed by Distinctionism, and one can observe that other beings retain consciousness, which *ex hypothesi* is due to the conjuction of the soul's luminosity with the translucent medium of the various intellects. It may be noted, incidentally, that the nature of the soul, as constituted by consciousness, in a pure and non-discursive and non-imaginative form, gives the state of release a somewhat negative aspect. Bliss and sorrow being contingent upon association with the natural world, the liberated soul has no further particular experiences: for this reason its disappearnace from the scene is scarcely distinguishable from annihilation. This state of release is described as isolation *(kaivalya)* in both the Distinctionist and Yoga viewpoints.

We have seen that the root of men's troubles is the false identification of the intellect with the soul. It is therefore the aim of the Yoga technique to bring about a purification of the intellect which will prevent its further making this error. This can only be achieved properly if the old habits of mind are destroyed. for a merely temporary conviction of the distinction between soul and intellect is insufficient, since a falling-away will leave the individual still in a state of bondage. Herein, Yoga adheres to the ideal of living release *(jīvanmukti)* which is found elsewhere, though not universally by any means, in the Indian tradition: i.e. the concept of one who has attained the assurance of release when he comes to die, and meanwhile lives on, exhausting the karma that has already ripened and so must take its effect, but not creating new karma to implicate him in a further life. As the potter's wheel, when the potter has finished his task, goes on spinning a while, but will come to a halt—so the living released one carries on quietly until death.

It is therefore necessary, according to Yoga, to still the dispositions which exist in a person in order that he may be assured that his discrimination of the distinction between his soul and his mind is genuine and permanent. Thus Yoga does not merely involve the higher stages of concentration, but various disciplines which help to tame desire, remove impurities and bring self-sufficiency. The analogy between the form of the Yogic path and that of Buddhism is quite close. Thus the Yogin must practise virtue as an integral part of his training: thus, he must practise non-injury, truthfulness, honesty over property, sexual continence and the repudiation of unnecessary articles and enjoyments. In addition, he must cultivate certain moral attitudes, such as benevolence towards all beings, and modes of cultivating these through meditation are laid down. In these ways, the Yogi will gain indifference to worldly things.

As a further part of his training (and here the emphasis is rather different in Yoga than in Buddhism) he should indulge in breathing exercises, together with the practising of certain rather complicated physical postures. These help to give him complete mastery over his body, so that normal physiological processes can be virtually stilled, if necessary, as an aid to the quietude needed for contemplation.

The higher stages of meditation can supervene once the Yogin has attained this detachment and mastery. In later Yoga it became common to meditate upon the Lord, conceived as the one soul which, in its splendour, had never been implicated in ignorance and the round of rebirth. This was considered to be a useful means of helping the Yogin towards his release. But the classical forms of concentration are designed to produce a state of consciousness which has no object whatsoever (not even the Lord or some such exalted being). Thus successively the adept rises from concentrating upon selected objects, such as the potentials, which he can fix firmly before his mind, to the exclusion of other objects, to the contemplation of more refined and abstract objects, such as the blissful quality of one's intellect, and the existence of substance in abstraction from all qualities. As in Buddhist meditation, even these rather tenuous contents of the mind are finally to be superseded by a state of objectless concentration. With the final purification of the intellect in this manner there dawns an existential knowledge of the distinctness of it from the soul, and the adept is ripe for release. This knowledge dawns thus, because there are no more contents of the intellect which can be falsely superimposed on, or attributed to, the underlying soul. In this way, the Yogi is beyond sorrow, and his psycho-physical organism, and in particular his mind or intellect, will vanish away at his death.

An interesting feature of the Distinctionist-Yoga doctrine of release—and a further indication of its original unorthodoxy to which we referred earlier—is this. Feeling-states are regarded as produced by nature, and are not intrinsic to souls (indeed the theory of strands as a basis for temperaments is part of this thesis). Thus even the Yogin must put away bliss. With it, there is, moreover, attendant its dark opposite, suffering. Likewise, it is held, the performance of ordinary religious duties, such as the Vedic sacrifices, will not being release or emancipation. For their aim is either the favour of the gods or, more importantly, happiness in the life to come. But the pursuit of such an aim only binds one further to the ṛound of sorrow, by implicating oneself in worldly concerns. Hence even apparently otherworldly interests are worldly. Like Buddhism and Jainism, Distinctionism-Yoga does not deny, but nevertheless firmly transcends, the cult of the gods. Although in its later mediaeval developments Yoga became increasingly theistic, under the influence of surrounding trends, the practice of meditation upon the Lord in classical Yoga is not predicated on the principle that through prayer favours may be showered on the individual, but rather, as we have seen, on the idea that contemplation of the Lord brings before the adept the splendour of a soul never implicated in the round of rebirth, and this ideal will serve to inspire the Yogin in his work of self-discipline. Moreover, in release the Yogin's soul is, as we have seen, totally isolated. There is no question here of a transcendent enjoyment of relationship with the supreme Being, as in the properly theistic schools.

The main structure of Distinctionist cosmology was designed, among other things, to trace the various manifestations of the observable world back to a unitary source. This aim was reinforced by the Distinctionist doctrine of causation, which came to be the pattern whereby causation was treated in some other systems. It is the identity theory *satkāryavāda*, namely that the effect is identical with the cause, being a transformation of the latter, or the realization of what was potential in the former. This theory contrasts with that entertained by the Buddhists and Logic-Atomists, namely the non- identity theory, *(asatkāryavāda)*, which implies that there is no inner or necessary connection between cause and effect. These two represent the principle theories in the tradition; though we shall have occasion to examine a third view, viz. the appearance-theory, *(vivartavāda)*, which is peculiar to Śaṅkara's school and goes with his doctrine of the illusoriness of empirical reality—it implies that apparent changes in the world do not entail real change to the underlying substance, i.e. to the Absolute. The Distinctionist theory not only involved that effects are merely the manifestations of what was inherent in the causes, but also was given the interpretation that the potentialities within objects had an inherent tendency towards self-actualization. In this way natural laws came to be regarded as a limitation or canalization of forces: the potentialities would otherwise be breaking out, so to say, in all directions. Conversely, the production of artifacts, for example, was thought as the removal of certain barriers inhibiting the realization of the objects' potentialities. But although the limitation of one object, or set of objects, by others induces a relative stability in the system of nature—the achievement of local equilibrium—, overall the picture is one of continuous change, until at the end of an epoch nature winds herself up again into a quiescent state of world-dissolution. The continuous changes are, as it were, the incessant vibrations of nature in a phase of disequilibrium. Thus though Distinctionism is keen to stress the ever-changing aspect of the world, as are the Buddhists, the changes are (unlike the Buddhist view) changes in a single dynamic, but permanent, substance.

We have noted one application of the Distinctionist concept of potentiality, namely the evolution of the various sense-potentials. These, combined with units of the mass-substance, are transformed into atoms which mediate sense-data to the conscious individual. The knowledge which is gained through perception is in part the result of the synthesizing work of the mind-organ (interestingly enough, and by contrast with the soul, regarded as atomic). But more particularly the operations of the intellect on the materials supplied by the senses is dependent upon the illuminative power of the soul. Speaking here of the 'materials' supplied by the senses is no metaphor: for the experiences of a person are indeed subtle forms of material events (subtle, because of the preponderance of the brightness-substance). Thus external happenings imprint themselves, via the senses, and the mind-organ, on the intellect. These images are then illuminated by the soul. Consequently, the Distinctionists picture perception, etc., as a series of copies of external things. The mind is, as it were, a television screen in which the soul acts as scanner and thereby brings consciousness of the picture. It itself, however, can never be scanned, but its existence is known by inference. Nevertheless, as we have seen, the Yogin is supposed to be able to achieve a state in which in effect he realizes in experience the nature of the soul, for his mind, in its quiescent purity, conforms to the pattern of pure consciousness.

So much briefly for a description of the chief features of these closely associated systems. Taken in its atheistic form, it bears a considerable resemblance to Buddhism and to Jainism, though the differences too should not be ignored. But in these different schools there is an insistence on the sorrows of a real world, a plurality of beings seeking release, and the virtual disappearance of liberated souls from the scene. Sacrificial works and worship are of little or no avail, or indeed are a hindrance, in the path tosalvation. All stress a form of self-discipline for attaining release, culminating in a contemplative knowledge of reality and purity of consciousness. The development, however, of belief in a Lord does not essentially, except in some manifestations of its later mediaeval history, affect the structure and aims of the Yoga system. It no doubt, as we have remarked, represents a theoretical concession to what had become existing practice, namely meditation on god as part of the yogic exercises. The other main difference betwen Yoga and Distinctionism—the stress on physical and mental methods of self-control and meditation in the latter school—also is in a way marginal, for, as we saw, the discrimination of the intellect from the soul, which brings release according to Distinctionism, has to have the right existential character and is not mere 'book' knowledge. In so far as metaphysics here has become detached from meditative practice, this merely represents an exaggeration of one side of a polarity. It must be repeatedly insisted that the conceptual content of a path of release and its practical aspect are two sides, nearly always in India, of a single quest. The metaphysics of Distinctionism provides the conceptual ambience in which the Yogin trains himself, and full discrimination needs training, just as meditation needs a rationale and truth-content.

Naturally enough, Distinctionism is not solely a system of soul-pluralism adapted to the tenour of early Indian mysticism. Its cosmology has its independent interest: and of course the viewpoint in defending itself and criticizing others, provided its share of arguments on metaphysical themes to the Indian stock. But these are relegated to the second part of this book.

CHAPTER VI
LOGIC - ATOMISM

The coalescence of the schools of Logic and Atomism has a certain oddity: for the former is in essence a methodology of argument, and the latter is a fairly elaborate systematization of protoscientific and philosophical ideas. There is no intrinsic reason why dialectical expertise or the theory of inference should go together with a certain view of the world; and it perhaps seems strange that orthodox logicians should find themselves committed to a *Weltanschauung*. Admittedly we discovered a similar metaphysics-methodology coalition in the case of Distinctionism and Yoga; but since the former expresses the sort of soul-pluralism which typified Indian mysticism of the earliest period, the coalition is easily intelligible. However, certain features of Logic, especially its theory of inference, which was oriented towards inductive inference, fit in with the protoscientific concerns of Atomism.

It is my intention here to outline the principal doctrines of the two schools once they had become conjoined. I shall leave a consideration of the logical theories of the Logic school until the second part of the book, as part of a more general view of disputes and theses about inference, etc.

The basis of Atomism, as our name for it implies, is a theory of atoms as constituting the fundamental structure of material reality, though selves in addition are held to exist, and these are non-atomic, but all-pervading. Indeed the main ideas of Logic-Atomist cosmology are remarkably close to the concepts in the Distinctionist system, if we cut out of the latter the notion of nature and its evolutes down as far as the potentials. For Logic-Atomism likewise held that there are five elements, i.e. earth, water, air and fire, together with space. However, the last was conceived as all-pervasive, and was not given an atomic constitution, as in Distinctionism. The elements of earth, etc., were, of course, atoms of these different types. Like space and selves, they were eternal: perishable things being combinations of the atoms.

The way in which atoms combined presented a certain problem for the Atomists, since they were considered to be of infinitesimal magnitude. A question therefore arose as to how by the addition of infinitesimals a macroscopic entity could be produced. Difficulties over this were used, as we shall see in Chapter XI, as the basis for an argument to God's existence. But briefly, the attempted solution of the problem at the physical level was this. It was argued that when two infinitesimal atoms combine into a dyad there is a quantum jump, and the new sub-molecule has a minute *(hrasva)* magnitude (the minute was conceived as a tiny quantum which was, curiously as we shall see, held to be *sui generis*). Dyads then combine into molecules: three dyads constitute such a molecule, and there is another jump in magnitude to a gross *(mahat)* quantum. The addition of gross quanta accounts for the magnitudes of macroscopic objects: unlike infinitesimals and minute quanta, they can be simply added to one another to form the magnitudes of larger bodies. Now the first of these quantum jumps is intelligible enough—in the sense that the transition from infinitesimal to finite magnitudes however tiny represents a puzzle. But why the second, seemingly unnecessary quantum jump to the triads? The explanation appears to be that the Atomists argued that a multiplication of minute quanta ought to yield, not larger, but smaller units. But *ex hypothesi* the minute is the smallest finite magnitude. Therefore a simple combination of minute entities was insufficient; what was needed was a further quantum jump to the gross. This line of reasoning is based on the idea that the minute should be represented by a fraction less than a whole number, so that multiplication yields the result indicated above.

More generally, there was difficulty with the concept of number in this connection. It was held that only unity is an intrinsic property of substances. It follows that the number of a plurality of objects is not inherent in them, but is, as it were, imposed upon them by the mind—in particular by the process of connective understanding *(apekṣābuddhi.)* Now every phenomenon has a cause, and therefore it is necessary to ask what causes the emergence of the finite quanta of the dyads and triads. Different thinkers in the Logic-Atomism school at different periods gave diverse answers. On the one hand, it was simply held that atoms have a natural tendency to combine, and an invariable result of this is the phenomenon of the quantum jump—it is sufficient that there should be this invariable concomitance. On the other hand, it was argued that the additional factor (apart from combination) which helped to account for the novelty of the minute and gross quanta was number. Or rather it was *their* number—e.g. the duality of the dyadically combined atoms, etc. But as we have seen, number above one was regarded as mind-dependent. Hence (and we shall come back to this in Chapter XI) there was a reason for postulating an extra-cosmic Mind to account for the initial combinations of atoms.

Admittedly there is something rather untidy about simply introducing a quantum jump to account for the transition from the infinitesimals to finite magnitudes, but there is no theoretical objection to the procedure from the standpoint of the Logic-Atomism theory of causation. In contrast with the identity theory espoused by Distinctionism, the Atomists held the non-identity theory, i.e that the effect is not pre-existent in the cause. Causation occurs when a certain combination of conditions is followed (in accordance with a law of invariable concomitance) by a determinate effect. Thus in principle a set of conditions could be followed by any effect whatsoever: so there is no bar on genuine novelty arising from a set of conditions. Thus there is no theoretical bar, in Logic-Atomism on simply postulating the quantum jump. What, however, is tricky in the situation is that whereas other causal phenomena are explained on the basis of a concomitance which is observable, experience being the test of what in fact is caused by what, the states of molecular and submolecular combinations rest on inference. This type of inference to the unseen can be called transphenomenal *(sāmānyatodṛṣṭa)* inference (an example of its use in Logic-Atomism is the inference to the existence of other selves).

A further general feature of the atomic theory was an apparent disinclination on the part of the Atomists to hold that the idiosyncrasies of macroscopic things and events could be accounted for simply by reference to differences in the number, arrangement and type (i.e. earth, fire, etc.) of the atoms. For this reason, they introduced a category of 'kinkiness', as one might call it, to explain the idiosyncratic: atoms themselves, as well as possessing universal characteristics, such as fieriness, have their own indescribable particularities, *viśeṣa* (there is some similarity here, but only some, to Madhva's doctrine of relative particulars, *viśeṣa,* as described below, Chapter IX). The Sanskrit name of the Atomist school *(vaiśeṣika)* is indeed derived from the term here translated 'particularity'.

This feature of the system illustrates the manner in which Atomism, though going beyond common-sense ideas in postulating an atomic theory, also wished to synthesize this theory with an attempt to categorize the phenomena, etc., of ordinary experience from a commonsense point of view. That is, Atomism held, in conjunction with its atomism, a theory of categories *(padārtha)*, such as substance, quality, etc., which were supposedly derived from, or presupposed in, ordinary knowledge and language. Particularity was held to be one of these categories.

The most basic of these is substance, i.e. that in which the properties, etc., belonging to the other categories inhere. (A minor qualification is needed here in that inherence *(samavāya)* itself is regarded as a category and is the relation whereby substance and properties, etc., are held together. But the category of inherence itself presupposes substance, even if properly speaking it does not inhere in it.) The second category after substance is that of quality or property *(guṇa)*—but as we shall see it includes what would more naturally be called relations. First of all, there are five kinds of sense-properties, Second, there is the property of number. As we observed earlier, oneness is inherent in substances: and duality and plurality are due to the percipient's connective understanding. Thus number, apart from oneness, is constituted by a very complex relation between a set of objects of a simlar type and the observer or observers. By 'number' here is meant, of course, the number belonging to a set of concrete objects. Third, but distinguished from number, there is the 'property' of measure or magnitude (as appertaining to atoms, for example: as we have seen, there are three types, each *sui generis,* of magnitudes). Fourth, there is the property of separateness *(pṛthakaṭva)*, whereby one substance is distinguished as separate from another. Fifth, there is conjunction *(saṃyoga)*, whereby two separate substances are in close relation to one another: but being separate, the two substances are not in necessary relation to one another. This has its opposite in the relation of disjunction *(vibhāga)*, through which substances do not belong to the same set or area. Further, there are the properties of long and short distance in time and space, giving rise to the perceptions of long and short duration, etc. finally, as regards physical objects, there are the properties of heaviness, velocity, etc., regarded as potentialities of the substances in question (motion *karma* is counted as a separate category from property). The Logic-Atomists go on to list a further set of properties which pertain only to selves (such as sorrow, volitional activity, knowledge, etc.). In addition, governing both selves and the cosmic order is unseen force *(adṛṣṭa)*, which arranges the destiny of living beings, etc. This last item is perhaps an archaic one which does not ride easily with the attempted rationalism of atomic theory. Principally it has the function of explaining (if so dark a concept is at all explanatory) the working of karma.(It should be noted that the actual term *karma* in the Sanskrit is employed by the Atomists to refer to motion, our next category. Thus the unseen is in effect the equivalent of karma in other systems, even though the movement of magnets, for example, is ascribed to this force—again a case where atomism has not been fully integrated with pre-existing concepts).

The next category is, as we have said, motion, divided into kinds according to its directions. The reason for this latter is that the Logic-Atomists distinguish two sorts of space. One is the medium of sound, and is the type to which we referred earlier. Space as having to do with the location of objects, is directional space *(dik)*, a concept which allows us to refer to one object as to the right of another, etc. Since the directions are regarded as absolute (upward, downward, etc.) rather than relative and reversible, likewise motion came to be classified as upward, downward, etc. This corresponds to the way in which heaviness is made an absolute property of bodies, and means the potentiality towards going downwards towards the earth.

The fourth category is universality *(sāmānya)*. Universals inhere in different substances, so that we perceive the same colour, etc., in one thing as another. Up to now, the categories have fitted well enough with the requirements of atomic theory. Given that atoms have specific properties, and that they are in motion, it seems that the first three categories apply in a fairly straightforward way. The introduction, however, of the category of universal implies that macroscopic entities exhibit universals such as tree-ness which are not shared by atoms. This inhibits a full account of macroscopic properties in terms of the combination of atoms, etc.

Nevertheless, as we have seen, the doctrine of the non-identity of cause and effect allows the emergence of such new properties out of the interplay and combinations of microscopic entities. But the introduction of the category, together with that of particularity to which reference was made earlier, exhibits the way in which Atomism tries to synthesize atomism with abstractions out of common sense.

The sixth and last category is that of inherence, to which also we have previously referred. Its main point is to show recognition of the special relation which a property has to the substance in which it resides. However, Logic-Atomism, by recognizing macroscopic entities as genuine substances was faced with the problem of how this notion was to be co-ordinated to the doctrine of atoms as underlying or constituting these substances. Hence, the notion of inherence was extended to apply to the cause-effect relations. Thus the atoms as causes, by their combination, of macroscopic effects could be considered to be inseparably *(apṛthaksiddhi)* united and so, as it were, the theoretically independent atom-substances were bound together in the unities constituting macroscopic substances.

The inseparability of cause and effect does not, however, modify the empiricist view of causation in Logic-Atomism. In principle, as we have seen, anything can give rise to anything else. It is therefore a matter of experience to discover the actual laws of nature. This means that certain techniques of induction have to be formulated. The aim is to discover, about a particular class of effect, what its invariable antecedents are. This is done by the method of agreement and difference. But it is not sufficient that a class of effects must have unvarying antecedents: it has too to be shown that they are *immediate*. This obviates difficulties about a sunrise being the cause of next day's sunrise, and expresses the principle that there is no causal action-at-a-distance. In addition, certain entities are regarded as general and non-specific conditions of causal operation—directional space, time and the unseen force which determines the destiny of living beings, etc. In the theistic version of Logic-Atomism, the activity of the Lord is also regarded as such a general condition of causality. Directional space and time are clear; important conditions from the Logic-Atomist viewpoint, since essentially all changes are due to the motion of atoms and molecules. A special part here (though Logic and Atomism differ somewhat as to the details of this process) is played by heat atoms, which break up combinations of atoms and change their properties. They propagate themselves rectilinearly and move at the highest possible speed (the speed of light is, so to say, the theoretical limit of velocity). No doubt the key part played by the heat - or fire- atoms was suggested to the Atomist speculators partly by the way in which light emanates from a source, and partly by the way in which heat transforms substances, e.g. in cooking. By consequence, some Atomists held that the sun, as the source of heat, is ultimately responsible for all terrestrial changes.

So far we have mainly been treating of the Logic-Atomist doctrines about physical objects. But as we have seen, in addition to the atomic substances which go to make up the physical world, Atomism argued, in common with most other Indian systems, to the existence of an eternal self presupposed by the operations of a conscious psycho-physical organism. Again, as in most other systems, the body, the sense-organs and the mind-organ (as the *sensus communis* and having certain other functions) are all material entities, built up out of atoms or (in the case of the mind, itself atomic). The self is regarded as essentially qualityless, but knowledge *(vidyā)* can inhere in it, together with the various kinds of consciousness and activity. All this occurs when a combination of conditions of the right sort is present. But in a state of release from all such conditions, the self is inert and unconscious, and it is only by a sort of charity that such a state is described as one of bliss: it is bliss because of the absence of sorrow that empirical experience invariably brings, but in no positive sense is it joyful. It is virtually equivalent to the annihilation of what is ordinarily meant by the self. However, the Logic-Atomists do not hold, as do the Distinctionists, that intellectual and conscious states are wrongly confused with the self. They really do inhere in the self. But eventually, in release, the self will no longer have these properties.

The all-pervasiveness of the self makes some breach in the principle of no causality-at-a-distance. As we have seen, causal links are strictly between immediately preceding and immediately succeeding events, states, etc. Normally also spatial contiguity is a necessary condition of applying the notion of cause and effect. However, with the doctrine of rebirth, it is possible for a new life to start spatially distant from where the old one ends (though still contiguous in time). Thus the all-pervasiveness of the self, as well as expressing the transcendent character (and so non-spatiality) of the self, assists in making reincarnation intelligible.

Since the sense-organs, etc., are material, perception, according to the Logic-Atomists, involves direct contact between the object perceived and the perceiving organism. The object sets in train a causal sequence ending in the mind of the percipient, and this sequence is continuous, so that the mind is in contact with the object. Except, therefore, in so far as mental functions, including perception, are held to presuppose the existence of an immaterial self, the general account of perception is, as sometimes elsewhere in the Indian tradition, materialistic.

There is one other respect, apart from the doctrine of selves, in which the metaphysical scheme of Logic-Atomism deviates from materialism and strict atomism—namely in its belief in a Lord accessible to the processes of inference from the physical world, who governs and controls the cosmos and the destiny of the selves. There is reason to suppose that this was not an original feature of Atomism, though the growth of Logic out of the dialectical needs of those called upon to defend orthodoxy may serve in some degree to explain how the synthetic system came to possess such a belief. But it is interesting that the reliance upon inference, i.e. upon natural theology, to establish the existence of the Lord meant that revelation was invoked only indirectly. For the validity of revelation was held to depend, not upon its intrinsic veracity, but upon its being the utterance of an omniscient Being whose existence could be independently argued. Thus Logic-Atomism preserved something of a rationalist air.

Some of the interest of the school lies in its particular doctrines about inference and epistemology, which will be discussed in the second part of this book. As a system, the viewpoint represents an elaboration of a certain kind of protoscience: and it is somewhat hard to take at face value its conformist claim to represent a path of salvation. Though such a claim became almost *de rigueur* in the Indian tradition, it is not easy to detect, in Logic-Atomism, the more direct interests of religious experience and practice which help to determine so strongly the shapes of many other of the Indian schools. That is to say, it does not have an inner religious logic, so to say, which determines its main structure; and the religious elements are almost certainly by way of an extraneous addition to an otherwise rationalistic system (I am not here, of course, meaning to pass truth- or value-judgments on religious or other metaphysical schemes). Nevertheless, the Logic-Atomists show a certain kinship with Distinctionism and unorthodox schools in their view that empirical existence is essentially sorrowful and that the chief end of human beings should be to attain release from this painful round. It is possible therefore that like Distinctionism and Materialism it had its ultimate origins in the ferment of atheistic religion and speculation that characterized part at least of the unorthodox aspect of early Indian culture. It is perhaps, then, still another testimony to the capacity for orthodox Hinduism to absorb all kinds of diverse movements. By the mediaeval period, certainly it was not merely orthodox, but theistic, and the treatise by Udayana which sets forth the principal arguments for the existence of God is looked upon as the main classic of Indian natural theology.

In regard to the Logic-Atomist doctrines about the physical world, we can sum up by saying that it is a blend of physical theory of (within the limits of protoscience) an ingenious kind with an analysis of the metaphysical ideas which seem to be implicit in a common-sense view of the world. In appealing to the ordinary man's view, the view-point was led to incorporate the beliefs in rebirth and (via the notion of the unseen force controlling the destiny of living beings) karma. It was only the Materialist and allied thinkers who challenged this otherwise all-pervasive doctrine. It was one of the items in the system which limited the full application of atomist theory.

CHAPTER VII
NON-DUALISM

The character of the viewpoints we have so far considered might well surprise anyone who was convinced that the heart of Hinduism is some kind of monism or pantheism. Belief in God is undoubtedly weakly represented in these systems; and one reason may well be (as we have argued) the generally unorthodox provenance of these schools (though paradoxically the arch-conservative Exegesis conspires also to be atheistic). With Śaṅkara we enter a very different atmosphere, though it is one which reflects the metaphysical and religious ideas of the Upaniṣads, and those too of the Mahāyāna Absolutists. Śaṅkara's metaphysics is *par excellence* the theology of modern Hinduism as presented to the West; and is the most vigorous and dominant doctrine among Hindu intellectuals.

The system proceeds from a very simple assumption—and one which has some scriptural backing. This is the thesis that there is complete identity between the self and the one Power sustaining the cosmos. It follows that the apparent multiplicity of selves is an illusion; and by extension, the whole variegation of empirical existence is likewise illusory. There is, then, only one Reality, and everything else, in so far as it gives the impression of being a substantial and independent reality, is productive of a kind of bewitchment of the mind. The Power alone exists: or in different terms the Self alone exists—and empirical existence is an insubstantial appearance. Once this has been realized existentially, there is release.

Śaṅkara does not proceed, as Nāgārjuna did, by trying to show the contradictoriness of common-sense notions about the world and thus to establish the doctrine of an Absolute in a dialectical manner. Rather, he is content to argue two things—that his interpretation of revelation is the correct one and that this solution is not contradicted by experience. Thus his method is apologetic in essence, and his standpoint is theological. Nevertheless, the system he enunciated has a certain bold simplicity which partly accounts for its grip on the Indian imagination. Dialectical methods, moreover, were developed in later Non Dualism.

In accordance with the traditional characterization of the Power, Śaṅkara describes the Absolute as consisting in being, consciousness and bliss. The first two of these elements are specially important (the blissfulness of the Self is mainly an expression of the joy and painlessness of release). First, then, the Absolute consists in being. Śaṅkara argues that in perception one is aware of an object which, so to say, gives off an appearance. But if there is but one reality the particular appearances of things at the empirical level are in the nature of an illusion. Consequently, on the one hand experience indicates an underlying something, but on the other hand is shot through with illusion. The reality underlying appearances can so far only be signified by the most abstract concept, that of pure being. The qualities which, in ordinary experience, we attribute to the Absolute, are therefore a projection *(adhyāsa)*.

To illustrate this, Śaṅkara uses the example of perceptual error. If we see a rope, but mistake it for a snake, two propositions are true. First, there is something of which we are aware; and second, the property which we ascribe to it does not in fact belong to it. Likewise, in experience we are genuinely aware of something, namely the underlying pure being; but we ascribe properties to it which it does not possess. But it should be noted that Śaṅkara distinguishes between genuine and illusory perceptions at the level of empirical experience. It is by analogy with ordinary illusion that we can say that the whole world as ordinarily understood is an illusion. This itself depends upon an analogy of experience. The experience of release, when one realizes one's essential identity with the one Reality, stands to veridical perception as the latter does to being hallucinated, etc. Thus Śaṅkara is able to argue that there is a basis in experience for the contrast between the Absolute and the grand illusion. But this also implies that the full understanding of his system, and its conclusive 'verification' comes through the non-dualistic realization of identity between Self and holy Power. Thus knowledge, at the higher level of metaphysical truth, is not theoretical; but it is essentially contemplative or mystical.

The analogy of illusion carries the clear implication that it is necessary to distinguish between two levels or spheres of truth: on the one hand the higher truth, which refers to the world as illusion, from the standpoint of the Absolute, and on the other ordinary truth, comprising the true assertions that can be made from the standpoint of common sense. All appearances are illusory, but some are more illusory than others (at the ordinary level). This is one of the features that Śaṅkara's system shares with Voidism. The two-level concept allows Śaṅkara to interpret different passages in the scriptures at different levels, thus bringing a very considerable consistency into his exegesis. It also enables him to affirm cosmological and other doctrines about empirical reality without abandoning the higher claim that empirical existence is illusory. To this we shall return.

Meanwhile, having looked at the Absolute as consisting of pure being, let us consider it as consciousness. The two sides of the Power-Self equation correspond to the two approaches, via being and via consciousness. In identifying ultimate reality with the Self, Śaṅkara is committed to characterizing it as in some sense having consciousness. If you look in an 'outward' direction, you can conceive the Power as pure being underlying appearances; if you look 'inwards', you can conceive it as the Self underlying ordinary psychological states. Now of course the concept of a transcendent ego is common enough in the Indian tradition. What distinguishes Śaṅkara from all others who hold that the concept applies (or rather from all those who hold this and are not Non-Dualists) is that he affirms that there is only one Self, not a plurality of selves. This Self is manifested as the inner witness *(sākṣī)* which, so to say, illuminates the myriad psycho-physical organisms with consciousness. But by this very fact it is wrongly taken by individuals to be broken up into a multiplicity of selves. Persons wrongly identify the one Self with their own egos; and this is a second aspect of the grand illusion.

The effective denial, by Śaṅkara, of a plurality of selves brings him closer than anyone else to the Buddhist viewpoint. All other Hindu schools mean by the self doctrine the thesis that individuals possess eternal souls which are individual. But Śaṅkara's position entails that individuality only properly pertains to the transmigrating self. This was one of the reasons why he was described as a crypto-Buddhist.

If we look at the illusion from the standpoint of the Self, it is the product of ignorance, as contrasted with the true knowledge gained in contemplative experience of the identity of the underlying Self with the underlying Power. The Self is, through association with the myriad psycho-physical organisms, veiled by ignorance: just as the association of pure being with innumerable appearances produces the illusion. However, Śaṅkara does not—from the standpoint of higher knowledge—claim that the illusion was *brought into being* by the Absolute, or that the Self brings ignorance into being. The situation is beginningless, and Śaṅkara's doctrines, at this level, are simply meant as a correct analysis of the state of affairs, rather than an explanation of how things came to be thus. Consequently, questions about the origin of the illusion are unanswerable, and the nature of illusion (floating as it were between existence and non-existence) is indefinable *(anirvacanīya)*. Thus from the higher standpoint, the empirical world is a surd. But this should occasion no surprise, since notions like explanation, which enter into the attempt to understand phenomena, are necessarily limited to the empirical and illusory world.

However, it follows from this that some sort of explanation can be given at the common-sense level. It is true that as such the illusion cannot be explained, since illusion is a concept of the higher level; but the empirical existence of the cosmos can be explained, as due to the creative activity of a Lord. Thus natural theology, inappropriate at the higher level, reappears at the lower. The Lord is the holy Power as seen from the standpoint of the ordinary worshipper, immersed in ordinary experience. By consequence, Śaṅkara formulates a double-decker theory of the holy Power: the supreme Power is qualityless *(nirguṇa)* (it is *pure* being, *pure* consciousness, *pure* bliss), but there is a lower manifestation of it, possessing personal characteristics, etc., and this being is the Lord and creator of the world.

This synthesis between Absolutism and theism, with theism of course very much in second place, is made easier for Śaṅkara by the history of the term here translated as illusion. In the period preceding

Śaṅkara, among the Buddhist metaphysicians, the term definitely meant 'illusion', as though men, in being deceived by appearances, were subject to conjuring trick. But in its earlier and more orthodox applications, the term meant 'creative power' *(māyā)* or 'creative substance'—the capacity of God to produce magical transformations of matter and thereby bring the visible cosmos into being, or the material he used in this process of transformation. The hint of magic in this idea of course accounts for the development of the sense of 'illusion': God is the great illusionist, we might say. But the association of the word with the creative energy of God made it easier for Śaṅkara to present a picture of the Power underlying the illusion as also being (from the standpoint of this world) the Lord of the cosmos. In any event, Śaṅkara succeeded in expressing a view about religion, as well as about existence as a whole, which had different levels. This is one reason for his remarkable contemporary influence, since this key idea (elaborated into many levels if necessary) is well adapted to modern Hinduism's claims to be in the forefront of the development of a synthesis between the various faiths of the world. For clearly, if we can arrange otherwise conflicting doctrines in a hierarchy of levels of truth, two ends are achieved: first to remove contradictions in the idea of a synthesis between faiths and second to indicate what manifestations of religion are higher (thus giving a clear procedure to Hindu apologetics).

The nearness of Śaṅkara to Buddhist doctrines about the self and his undoubted indebtedness to the Mahāyāna Absolutists made him appear unorthodox to some. This appearance was reinforced by his treatment of revelation. As we have seen, his exegesis made use of the two-level principle. This was applied by consigning the so-called works, *karma*-portion of scriptures (i.e. those passages dealing with the requirements of Vedic religion, moral duties, etc.) to the level of ordinary truth. The references to the Power as a personal Lord, etc., were also so consigned. Only those texts affirming the identity of the Power and the Self, and cognate ideas, belonged to the higher level. All this looked like saying that Brāhmanical orthodoxy was only a means to a higher end. Śaṅkara was, it seemed, transcending Hinduism as it had been understood. However, the impression of Śaṅkara's neglect of lower-level religion is misleading. Not only was he much concerned to reform religion, and spent a considerable amount of energy doing this, partly through the establishment of monasteries; but also he was a devotional hymn writer of some power. For him, the Lord appeared as Śiva or as other gods: and the devotionalism of the mediaeval period found ready expression in his writings. Nevertheless, it remains clear that though not neglecting the religion of ritual and worship to which he was heir, he insisted that ultimately one must go beyond it. That is, transcendence rather than mere negation or neglect of devotionalism and traditional ritual was his aim. Devotionalism and piety were the way through, and by treading this path one could ascend to the higher reaches of intuitive realization, in contemplative experience, of the Absolute. To this point we shall return later.

The position of the Lord can be further brought out by a brief account of Śaṅkara's cosmology. In its general outline, it has some analogy with the Distinctionist viewpoint. Of course, for Śaṅkara, there could be no self-subsistent nature which evolves itself out into the varied phenomena with which we are directly acquainted. But the illusion-substance, through and on which, from the empirical standpoint, the Lord acts, takes the place of nature. The notion of the three strands or qualities (see above, p. 66) is made use of, and varying combinations of these account for the various entities manifested in the illusion-substance. The term used for strand also signifies qualities *(saguṇa)*: and when the Lord is described as qualified, in distinction from the Power conceived at the higher level, which is qualityless, partial reference is being made to the doctrine of the strands. For the Lord is (as in Qualified Non-Dualism) both efficient and material cause—producing the world, so to say, out of his own substance. This makes it clearer that by being Creator the Lord is much implicated in the world. Or to put the matter another way, by creating *(sṛṣṭi)* the illusion, the Lord himself is infected with illusion.

However, the crucial problem for Non-Dualism is how the one Self appears to be associated with a multiplicity of empirical egos. The Non-Dualist attempt to explain this involves two phases. First, it has to be shown that the Self exists in some sense 'in' empirical individuals. Second, some analogy has to be produced to indicate that no contradiction is implied by the doctrine of one Self in many life-monads. Having thus given a coherent account of the actual situation, the problem of how the Self *comes to be* associated with the life-monads can be allowed to evaporate. For, as we have seen, the existence of ignorance and illusion is a beginningless fact of life: the problem is not how they came to be associated, but only the problem of how they can be dissociated.

In regard to the first phase, Śaṅkara (harking back to an argument in the Upaniṣads) claims that we are introspectively, through an immediate intuition, aware of an 'I' which is prior to all particular contents of consciousness: a subject which is never itself the object of discriminated experience and which is therefore of the nature of pure consciousness. Only in the non-dualistic *(advaita)* contemplative state is one able to attain to such pure consciousness without any overlay of discriminative experience. Moreover, we can be assured that our awareness of a pure subject underlying psychological phenomena is not mistaken, since the statement 'I doubt the existence of the self' itself presupposes the doubting I. But further, if the self has no features, being pure consciousness, one cannot individuate one self from another, i.e. there is one Self only.

The second phase consists in the search for suitable analogies. The Self somehow manifests itself as the underlying witness in a myriad of empirical life-monads: it appears refracted by the limiting conditions *(upādhi)* which constitute each empirical ego. But is this possible without its being broken up, so to speak, into fragments and thereby becoming many? One analogy used here is that of space. We can speak of the space contained in a jug, for example; but this does not entail that there are many spaces—space remains a single whole, and it is only from a certain point of view that we can regard the space as limited by the jug. Thus Śaṅkara held that it was possible to operate with the concept of the egos as limiting conditions projected upon the Self, without running into the contradiction that the Self is really a lot of selves. Another analogy, less satisfactory, used by some Non-Dualists was that of reflection *(pratibimba)*. Just as the sun, for example, is reflected in thousands of puddles, and yet remains the same sun, so the Self can be reflected in a host of life-monads while remaining single. However, the analogy of reflection did not serve the Non-Dualist purpose too well, and indeed was made use of by the Dualists and others—for one can distinguish between the reflections and the source of those reflections, whereas the whole logic of the Śaṅkarite position was to affirm the identity of the Self in all individuals.

We have seen that, provided he can make sense of the relation between the Self and the empirical life-monads, Śaṅkara scarcely feels called upon to answer the question of the *origin* of the association. But it is of course vitally necessary for him to say something about the possibility of dissociation. That is, the whole aim of his doctrines is to point the way to release. This is partly a matter, to be sure, of recommending the right form of spiritual exercises. But these in turn are co-ordinated to matters of doctrine. In common with many other Indian systems, knowledge is held to be the key to release. By knowing one's true nature one is saved (conversely, the source of our troubles is not original sin, but original ignorance, veiling us from reality). Now clearly, the knowledge required is that one's Self is identical with the Absolute—is the sole Being. As we have seen, the nature of the Self is pure consciousness. Thus the practical problem is the attainment of an existential awareness of that pure consciousness, in the context of faith in Non-Dualist doctrine. Consequently, the path must involve not only the prior conformity to Vedic duties, devotionalism and ordinary religion,[1] but must culminate in reflection upon the true purport of revelation (i.e. upon the identity of the Self with the one Power), accompanied by meditation and concentration, in the manner of yoga. The attainment of higher consciousness in the right conceptual ambience, will bring intuitive knowledge of the higher truth, and thereby release.

But there is something of a paradox here. For release does not here mean that one *becomes* the holy Power, that one is thereby *united* with ultimate reality: for the whole doctrine of Śaṅkara entails that one is already identical with ultimate reality—beginninglessly so, or more correctly, timelessly so. There is no question of a change in one's status (from the higher-level point of view). Nevertheless, there is release considered in relation to the empirical ego. For upon the supervening of the intuitive insight which is the goal of the saint, there is removed the possibility of further rebirth. These particular limiting conditions which contained the Self will vanish away. In the meantime the saint goes on living, in the state of living-release. He will have seen through empirical existence, to its essential illusoriness, and he will remain unmoved by the temptations and sorrows of this world—the bliss of the Self glowing brightly in him. Thus to say that the existence of the limiting conditions which obscure the true nature of the Self is due to primordial ignorance is in effect just the converse of the claim that through spiritual knowledge those conditions will disappear.

We have already noted some of the similarities between the Mahāyāna schools and Non-Dualism. Both are designed to point the enquirer towards a certain kind of experience—the contemplative intuition of identity with ultimate reality. But both also incorporate the religion of devotion into the scheme of salvation, via the concept of a personal Lord who is a lower manifestation of the Absolute. The differences between dŚaṅkara and these Mahāyāna doctrines are largely a matter of emphasis and of background. For, of course, Non-Dualism is orthodox and thus appeals to Vedic revelation, while the Mahāyāna does not. But even this is less of a gap than at first sight appears, since the ultimate import of revelation is the non-dual experience. As for emphasis: Śaṅkara's description of the Power as pure being, and the ground of the illusion, implies in a strong way that the Power is an eternal substance. On the other hand, the Voidist doctrine avoids speaking of the Void as a substance, since it starts from a critique of, among other things, the concept of a permanent substance. Nevertheless, by the use of a substantival expression, the Absolute being described as Suchness *(tathatā)*, Voidness, etc, and by its identification with the Truth-Body of the Buddhas, the flavour of Voidism (and the same is still more obvious in the cases of Buddhist Idealism) is very similar to that of Non-Dualism: admittedly *the Void* is a much more shadowy concept than the Self. But it is not misleading to use the substantival-sounding 'Absolute' as a label for it.

However, because of the Vedic tradition, Śaṅkara's notion of the Lord is that of a transcendent creator; while the Buddhist metaphysicians were content to identify the Lord with the Buddha as he appears to the faithful. The Buddhist tradition excluded a genuine creator, even though celestial Buddhas could create their own 'Buddha-fields' or sub-universes. Moreover, of course, the particular duties of the Hindu follower of Śaṅkara would differ greatly from those of the unorthodox. But the correspondences in structure between the two forms of Absolutism are nevertheless striking; and as we shall argue later, are essentially due to the same underlying religious motivations.

As we shall observe, the success of Non-Dualism determined in some measure the type of philosophical dispute which engaged metaphysicians during the mediaeval period. For example, it became necessary for other orthodox schools to argue for the validity of common-sense knowledge against the doctrine of illusionism. This was one of the many respects in which Non-Dualism exhibited its power over the later Indian imagination. It was also another instance of the kind of issue which had its religious as well as its purely metaphysical or epistemological side. For theism, in expressing a distinction between the soul and God and (by reflection) between the world and God had some interest in maintaining the reality of the world of ordinary experience. For a distinction between the Lord and the cosmos presupposes the reality of both parties. Moreover, despite the antinomianism always liable to characterize any form of extreme devotionalism, the attitudes of worship and devotion tend to be more closely integrated with the ordinary moral duties of the layman than does the path of inner contemplation and this doubtless strengthens the sense of the value of the cosmos. This in turn bears on its reality; since so frequently in metaphysics and religion judgments about value are intertwined with judgments about reality. It is perchance no accident that the Sanskrit term for *being* is also used as a term of appraisal. In any event, there seems little doubt that realism is cherished, in the context of religious speculations, by theism—certainly in the Indian tradition. But it is true that the atheistic (as opposed to Absolutistic) systems are realistic also. It is Absolutistic mysticism, for reasons which we shall analyse later, that characteristically runs to idealism.

CHAPTER VIII
QUALIFIED NON-DUALISM

Although the general sort of position which came to be elaborated in detail by Rāmānuja and others after him was probably in existence before Śaṅkara, and certainly of course reflects religious tendencies present in Vaiṣṇavism, Rāmānuja's Qualified Non-Dualism represents a reaction to Śaṅkara's metaphysics. As we shall see, this reaction is at least in part a consequence of genuine religious differences between Rāmānuja and Śaṅkara. It is partly also due to the philosophical difficulties implicit in a theory of the illusoriness of the world. Since, however, the religious divergence was crucial, it is important to note that Rāmānuja wished to show that there was some kind of distinction between the self and ultimate reality—between the self and the holy Power. Such a distinction makes sense of devotionalism in a way in which the Non-Dualism of Śaṅkara does not. On the other hand, Rāmānuja was not insensible to the monistic import of certain passages in revelation. Moreover, the famous text 'That art thou' and its analogues suggested some sort of identity or close similarity between the self and the holy Power. Thus his system was conceived as one in which distinctions between the material world, selves and the Lord were maintained in one way; and yet at the same time the three categories were seen as some kind of unity. This task was achieved in an ingenious manner, in which Rāmānuja replaced Śaṅkara's idealism with a form of realism, and qualified his Non-Dualism. The system thus excogitated was further developed and clarified by Rāmānuja's successors (notably Veṅkaṭanātha): and the following account draws not only on Rāmānuja's own explicit teachings, but also on these elaborations.

Given that Rāmānuja and his successors were committed to a (formally at least) absolutist position, i.e. the view that the holy Power embraces everything, including both God qua transcendent being and the cosmos inhabited by persons possessing selves; and given too that they rejected the Non-Dualist theory of illusion, and so were landed with saying that the world of change is real;—given these conditions, they required to find some analogy which could explain how there can be an identity in difference. Some metaphysicians simply affirmed that such identity-in-difference exists, a 'solution' not acceptable to Rāmānuja, as it appeared to involve saying (and theologians both East and West are sometimes inclined to do this) that there is something contradictory in the concept of God or the Power—but never mind, the truths of revelation are beyond human comprehension. Such an espousal of contradiction is, to put no finer point on it, scarcely philosophical. Thus the Rāmānujists hoped to show that a sensible account could be given of how the Absolute embraces both the changeless and the changeable.

Rāmānuja approached this problem through an analysis of the relation between the self and the body, and there is a considerable discussion in the literature designed to arrive at a definition of 'body' which will not only accord with observed facts and usage, but also provide a correct account of the relation between the Lord and the world (including individual selves). The definition arrived at has two elements—one referring to the causal relation between self and body, the other referring to the conceptual relation. Under the first head, when a person is said to possess a body, what is implied is that the body is subservient to the self, i.e. its movements are controlled by it. This definition needs some modifications: e.g. a servant should not be regarded as the body of his master, since not all his acts are controlled by the latter. Furthermore, in so far as the material world and selves are interpreted, in Rāmānuja's system, as constituting the body of the holy Power, a teleological account of changes in the world is needed. Thus the subservience of body to self here is taken to imply that the movements of the body are instrumental to the realization of perfections or excellences. Thus Rāmānuja conceives of matter as possessing two forms, its fine or potential form and its gross or actualized form. The Lord, in his creative activity makes potential matter manifest. Again, since selves are in some sense the body of God, the Lord brings about, through successive rebirths, etc., their ultimate perfection—the state of release in which they bask in his glory. It may also be noted that apart from the purpose of bringing about such salvation, the Lord's creative activity is thought of as a kind of sport or play, so that the manifestation of potential matter is something which he likes doing for its own sake (but not out of a sense of boredom or frustration, but because of the positive enjoyment he gains from thus exercising his body). Thus, from the causal point of view, a body is defined as that which is instrumental to a self: it is what the self uses to bring about the realization of certain ends.

From the conceptual point of view, Rāmānuja held that the relation between body and self is one of inseparability. That is, not merely is there a continuous association between body and self, so that they are never in fact separated: but also the two are mutually defined. Thus every body is by definition a body *of* some self, and conversely a self is by definition something having a body. This correlation of a one-many one, in so far as selves or life-monads transmigrate, i.e. a single self is associated with many bodies. But because of the doctrine of inseparability it is held that even in the state of release the liberated self is embodied (only the body is a peculiarly refined and resplendent sort). This complication is by-passed if we say that at any given time there is a one-one correlation between any given self and its body. However, both the definition in terms of causal subservience and that in terms of inseparability fail to show the difference in nature between self and body. For it is in principle possible for two material objects to stand in a relation of inseparability; and for one material object to be causally controlled by another. Of course, the idea that the body is instrumental to the *purposes* of the self implies that the latter has conscious ends: thus the difference between self and body is that the latter does not itself posess experiences, but conditions the experiences of the former. Thus one might say, on the Rāmānujist account, that a self always has experiences from a certain *point of view*, and it is the body which provides this point of view.

It is clear from the foregoing that so far the concept of body *(śarīra)* is in a sense a limited one, That is, the English 'body' is used of all kinds of inanimate and never-animated things (e.g. we talk of a body, such as a stone, having inertia). The limitation of the Rāmānujist notion of a body, which is quite in acord with the usage of the Sanskrit term, is brought out if we exhibit the above notion of inseparability as involving that there is a contradiction both in the idea of a disembodied self and in the idea of a selfless body. That is, body here means 'organic body' or the kind of body which exhibits life and self-movement. We shall have occasion in a later chapter to discuss Rāmānuja's comprehensive critique of the Indian 'proofs' for the existence of God. But clearly he would not be so easily in a position to deny the validity of natural as opposed to revealed theology if he thought that all material bodies are of necessity animated, since the cosmos as a whole could then be argued, without further recourse to revelation, to possess a self, and this would be God. Of course, *in fact* Rāmānuja believed this, but only on the basis of scripture. The point is that he did not consider that it was self-evident that the cosmos is a body of the sort under discussion. However, *given* that the Lord exists, and *given* that the cosmos is his body, it follows that the two are inseparably united, and that there is no possibility of God's having one existed and the cosmos not. The notions of the cyclical creation and dissolution of the cosmos are explained in the transformations of subtle into gross matter, etc.

It will be seen that Rāmānuja is trying to make a sense of the notion that the world is in some sense part of the one holy Power which sustains everything by an *analogia corporis*—or perhaps more properly an *analogia personae*. As a person is indivisible, but yet has two aspects, his consciousness and his bodily states, so the Absolute has its two sides, the Lord as supreme Self and the cosmos as his body. But still something needs to be said to reconcile the supposed changelessness of God with the obvious changes going on in the world. If the world is part of God, then, God is changeable. Once again the analogy with finite selves is brought into play. It is argued that the existence of a self is presupposed by such expressions as 'I know P', 'I remember E', etc. Further, it is not possible to rest the notion of personal identity upon memory-states, since these themselves presuppose a self which remembers and which remains identical through the flow of events remembered, etc. Thus there must be an identical self underlying the various cognitive states. It follows that something changeless underlies psychical changes. Likewise, it is possible to see God as a pure self, in which aspect he is unchanging. On the other hand, changes are ascribed to the person who comprises both self and body; and like-wise changes occur in the Lord's body. Thus God can be both changeless and changing without contradiction.

As well as using the particular analogy between self and body on the one hand and Lord and cosmos on the other, the Qualified Non-Dualists also made use in this context of the concept of a substance and its features or attributes. We can for the sake of analysis distinguish between the thing or substance which we recognize through its features and these latter qualities or relations. But though the distinction can be made, the two aspects are of necessity inseparable. It makes no sense to speak of a featureless substance, nor is it possible to have a set of qualities inhering in no substance. Indeed, the impossibility of a featureless substance is one reason for Rāmānuja's objection to Śaṅkara's doctrines, which implied that the Absolute—the higher Power, as distinguished from the Lord conceived as having personal and other qualities—is featureless. Given then the possibility of distinguishing between substance and quality, and given too the inseparability of the two, there is an analogy with the relation between God and the world—or more precisely, this relation is an instance of the substance-features relation.

So far we have discussed Rāmānuja's attempt to give a proper explanation of the identity-in-difference between the Lord and his creation in terms of his having the cosmos as his body. But Rāmānuja of course wished to maintain—in opposition to Śaṅkara—that there are many finite selves distinguished in some manner from God, and also—in opposition to the Materialists and Buddhists—that such selves are not simply comprised by a series of bodily or bodily-cum-mental states. This insistence on the existence of selves created some complication in applying the *analogia personae*. For Rāmānuja had to affirm not only that the material world is the body of God, but that in some manner life-monads too were part of the one holy Power. Consequently he evolved a (so to say) 'two-decker' self-body relationship. Just as human selves, for example, animate human bodies, so God is the self underlying these selves. In brief, selves are God's body too. They can thus be considered on two levels—as spirits in relation to bodies, as body in relation to the Lord. This notion, clearly, involves stretching analogy far. But it had an important application in Rāmānuja's doctrine of dependence upon God.

The Lord in so far as he underlies the working of selves is the inner controller *(antaryāmin)*. Not only this, but he controls the material world, in that it is his body. But he allows selves a sort of freedom, to realize their desires through the operation of their bodies: but only because God so wills it. That is, Rāmānuja holds to a permissive occasionalism. Further, as inner controller, the divine Being tends to influence certain sorts of people—those who rely upon him and call on him with faith are given his grace *(prasāda)*; those who reject him strongly are led farther astray by the implanting of wrong desire. This doctrine of grace and its opposite was not fully worked out by Rāmānuja, but its elaboration much exercised the Rāmānuja school. By consequence, there was a division into two sects—those who held (taking Rāmānuja's occasionalism to its logical conclusion) that salvation or release comes solely through the grace of God: and those who held that human effort or works is also a necessary condition. The two sects were known respectively as the cat and monkey schools: the cat carries its kitten from A to B by the scruff of its neck, so that the kitten makes no effort (thus is expressed the theological determinism which can be educed from Rāmānuja's hints); on the other hand, the monkey leads its young along from A to B, and so the co- operation of the self with God is necessary.

Rāmānuja's system, so far, is a way of introducing a distinction between the self and the Lord, while retaining a sort of non-dualism or monism. Since Śaṅkara had argued that the world of change is illusory, he resolved the problem of the relation between the unchanging Absolute and the world of change in a different way. It was necessary for Rāmānuja and his followers to show that the notion of a universal illusion (or almost universal—the experience of identity with the holy Power was, according to Śaṅkara, no illusion) was scarcely satisfying. It is not necessary for us here to describe the various arguments employed, since some of the more important are relegated to a later chapter. Suffice it to say that two principal points were adduced as against the Non-Dualists. First, the notion of illusion gains its application by contrast with what is not illusory; by relegating all perceptual knowledge to the sphere of illusion, Śaṅkara makes nonsense of the idea of perception. Second, all illusion in any event is simply the wrong perception of what exists—for example, mistaking a stretch of rope for a snake involves perceiving the rope and ascribing to it the wrong qualities. Rāmānuja and his school therefore argued that knowledge is in general self-authenticated, and that it is absurd to argue from the occurrence of particular mistakes to the possibility of the universal unreliability of perception, etc.

Rāmānuja's cosmology follows that of Distinctionism, with one or two modifications. Nature is identified with the body of the holy Power in its subtle or fine form, and the rest of the evolution of the various states of the cosmos corresponds to the Distinctionist account. Thus the cosmology is Distinctionism given a theistic background and interpretation—so that ultimately God, not nature, is the material cause as well as being the efficient cause of the manifested creation. It needs to be repeated here that there is no question here of creation out of nothing: or of a prior state in which the Lord exists and the cosmos not. It is a necessary fact that the Power qua supreme Self and qua body should externally coexist; nevertheless, the visible world is the consequence of a transformation of the Lord's subtle body. Thus Rāmānuja holds to a form of the identity theory of causation, i.e. that the effect (in this case the manifested cosmos) pre-exists in the cause (the subtle body). It may be noted too that the Rāmānujists rejected atomism as implying the existence of minute and unobservable material entities. In these various respects Qualified Non-Dualism has close affinities to Distinctionism in regard to its doctrines about the material world.

The Rāmānujists did, however, have a kind of atomism, but about the selves or life-monads. These are conceived as atomic and localized in a particular place in the body. One reason for the vacillation in Indian thought between treating selves as (so to speak) spiritual points and treating them as all-pervasive is that spatial attributes do not seem to apply in any ordinary manner to souls. But treating life-monads as points or atoms created a problem of how it is that one has sensations and perceptions which in some sense belong to the self and yet which are associated with various parts and organs of the body. The Rāmānujists introduced an entity to bridge the gap between atomic selves and extended bodies, namely a substance known as attributive intelligence *(dharmabhūtajñāna)*. This was conceived by analogy with light, which serves as a medium for illuminating objects in relation to a percipient. Similarly, attributive intelligence pervades the body and makes the self aware of various sensations, etc. This substance is in principle capable of infinite extension, and indeed in the case of the Lord is all-pervasive, since his body is constituted by the whole of the spatial world. In so far as it is finite, in the case of life-monads implicated in the round of rebirth, this is explained as due to karma and ignorance. However, in the state of release, the self puts off this limitation. It may be noted here that the Qualified Non-Dualist concept of attributive intelligence corresponds in some measure to the Jain idea of the life-monad, which (as we say) is regarded as filling the space of its body, and liable to expansion and contraction.

In the state of release the life-monad, according to the Rāmānujists, realizes its essential God-like properties. It more clearly reflects the nature of the Lord (and this allows Rāmānuja to interpret 'That art thou' and similar sayings in the Upaniṣads as meaning that the self has divine attributes, rather than that it is literally identical with the supreme Power). The self in this state is, for instance, infinitely blissful and omnipotent in the sense that no desire is frustrated. However, the capacities for creation and dissolution and for bringing about salvation remain the Lord's alone. Thus the liberated life-monad leads an eternal life of bliss in which it is aware of its dependence, for that joy, upon the Lord. Opponents of Rāmānuja complained that one could not gain complete happiness unless one were totally self-sufficient, and the notion of happiness through dependence was defective. But Rāmānuja replied that happiness has to be seen in relation to man's true nature: and if the latter is in fact determined by his situation as a creature, the highest happiness will involve, and arise out of, a sense of dependence upon God. Interestingly enough, however, the Rāmānujists did not deny the possibility of another, but lower, form of release in accordance with the underlying assumption of such critics. Both for the Non-Dualist and for the adherent of Yoga, release involves the realization, in contemplative experience, of one's self. From the point of view of the Rāmānujists, the Non-Dualists were of course in error in supposing that there is but one self, identified with the supreme Power, and consequently their attainment of a non-dual experience was interpreted as similar to, or the same as, the Yogin's achievement of the release of the self in a state of isolation. Hence, with a certain magnanimity, the Rāmānujists recognized this release in isolation as a real possibility. But it is a lower kind of salvation, for the isolated self does not share in the joy of basking in the glory of the Lord.

This is especially relevant for understanding the inner motivation and religious concerns lying behind the whole Rāmānujist scheme. It needs to be emphasized again that Rāmānuja, in rejecting natural theology, rests his case primarily on revelation: the arguments employed in his commentary and elsewhere are largely apologetic—to show the inadequacy of conflicting views and to exhibit the accord between his general position and common sense (e.g. in regard to the self-authentication of knowledge). But though he rests his case on revelation, so too do the other Vedāntists appeal to the scriptures. We therefore need to account for the divergences in interpretation of the texts. The doctrine of two levels of release gives us an important clue as to why Rāmānuja elaborated the scheme he did. For the relegation of the contemplative or yogic path to a secondary place in the pattern of salvation is a direct consequence of his elevation of the religion of devotion and grace. As we suggested at the beginning of this chapter, Śaṅkara's Non-Dualism ultimately made worship and adoration pointless. The worshipper sees himself as distinct from the object of his worship, and the stress on the need to love God in Rāmānuja and his predecessors among the religious poets of South India implied a distinction between the lover and the Beloved. But to say, first, that the self is really all the time identical with God, and to affirm, second, that the Lord Himself as creator of the world and object of worship is himself implicated in the grand illusion—such a thesis destroys the heart of devotionalism. Thus Rāmānuja reverses Śaṅkara's priorities. His doctrine of salvation is Śaṅkara's upside down. Instead of elevating the contemplative knowledge of the self to the supreme place in the religious quest, and relegating worship to a subsidiary means he raises the life of devotion, reflected finally in the sense of dependence the soul has in heaven, to the first place and demotes contemplative gnosis to a subordinate position.

It may be noted too that though dualism between self and God expresses a certain form of religion—the devotional—superficially there is not the radical distinction between God and the world (including souls) that one might expect by analogy with the similarly-oriented theism of the West. Indeed the doctrine of the world as God's body looks rather like pantheism. However, Rāmānuja's use of the concept of the holy Power as being among other things the material cause of the world enabled him to stress strongly the continuous dependence of the world upon God. As we shall see in regard to Madhva, there is some conflict in the Indian tradition (which does not recognize creation out of nothing, but rather creation as the periodic reordering of the cosmos out of chaos) between the requirement of a devotional faith to express the distinctness of God and the world and the requirement to express the dependence of the world upon God.

It needs to be borne in mind also that Rāmānuja was being loyal to the monistic import of many scriptural passages, as well as to those which expressed the idea of a personal Lord. Furthermore, it is doubtless true that a form of Absolutism, in which both the divine and visible aspects of reality are seen as constituting a kind of unity has an intellectual attraction which theistic dualism appears to sacrifice.

CHAPTER IX
DUALISM AND ŚAIVITE DOCTRINE

The reaction against Śaṅkara's doctrines expressed by Rāmānuja and his followers was carried farther by Madhva, who abandoned any semblance of a monistic system. The structure of his metaphysics depended on the distinction between three sorts of entity—the Lord, life-monads and non-intelligent *(acit)* substances. A fourth entity, nature, which forms the material cause of the cosmos, is also listed as one of the fundamental entities: its chief function is to avoid the claim that God is in some way the material cause of the world. In short, the introduction of nature—and with it some of the evolutionary paraphernalia of Distinctionist cosmology (Distinctionism, as we have seen, very often formed the starting point for cosmological doctrines, which is one of the reasons why it has become fashionable to treat the different viewpoints as validly treating different aspects of reality, despite their conflicts)—made quite clear the divide between the Lord and the cosmos on which Madhva was keen to insist.

Not only this; Madhva was also concerned to maintain the distinction between selves and non-intelligent substances, and between individual selves and individual material entities. Thus he operates with a fivefold set of distinctions: between the Lord and life-monads; between the Lord and material substances; between life-monad and material substances; between life-monad and life-monad; and between material substance and material substance. Of course, Rāmānuja also held that there are many selves. But Madhva further (and unlike Rāmānuja) held that each has its individual peculiarities. While Rāmānuja regarded selves as having the same essential nature, and thus being indistinguishable in the state of release, Madhva argued that differences remained even in that state, so that each man's salvation has, as it were, a different quality from every other person's. In connection with this, and for various reasons,

Madhva employed a theory of relative particulars. First, of all, Madhva rejected the doctrine of real universals. Hence qualities belonging to substances ought to be regarded as parts or aspects of them, and in so far as we use general words, this is because there is a relation of similarity between the aspects or parts in question. However, the aspects could not be regarded as identical with the substance underlying them—for then the disappearance of a quality should entail the disappearance of the substance. Hence, Madhva argued that a substance contains an indefinite number of relative particulars, i.e. those aspects, etc., of it which we refer to in saying 'This is blue' and so on. However, the aspects referred to themselves do not count as qualities or relations, etc., which further require a point of reference— since this would imply an infinite hierarchy of relative particulars. Thus there are certain basic aspects of a substance to which we refer qualities, etc. In short, we can regard a substance as a conglomeration of particulars, and these are relative to the point of view from which we wish to describe the substance (or rather, since the ascription of predicates is not a matter of convention, from which we *have* to describe the substance, in accordance with the particular facts of the situation). This theory has some connection with the Jain doctrine outlined earlier and does not carry the implication that all judgments are purely relative, in a sense which destroys the notion of truth. But rather, every substance stands in relation to a host of others, and a genuine description of its qualities needs to take account of these complex relations. Madhva was keen to point out that it is a fallacy to suppose that because the qualities, etc., of a substance are determined by its causal and other relations to other substances, therefore these qualities, etc., are not genuinely part of it. It should be noted that in all this discussion 'substances' does not merely refer to inanimate substances mentioned above, but to the life-monads, etc. Since each substance has a different place in the whole system of reality, each has its own peculiar characteristics as determined by its relations to other entities. This is the chief ground for Madhva's doctrine of the essential difference between one life-monad and another—a difference which constitutes its ineluctable individuality.

It may be noted, incidentally, that Madhva was charged with the common retort, in regard to his theory of the use of general words in terms of similarities discovered in individuals, that similarity itself must be a universal. Madhva's reply to this is to argue that since relative particulars are indeed relative to the point of view from which they are examined, there is some difference between the similarity of A to B and the similarity of B to A. That is, similarity is not a properly symmetrical relation. Nevertheless, there is sufficient likeness between a group of individuals described as similar to one another to justify the application of the same name or general word.

All this, then, implies that there are ineluctable, if sometimes subtle, differences between all substances in the universe. Consequently, Madhva felt justified in adopting a pluralistic account of the entities in the cosmos, as well as a radical distinction between the cosmos and the Lord. The complex of material entities forming the world is, however, something which God causes to evolve out of nature. As has been mentioned, this concept of a unitary nature underlying the varied substances of the world is a means of maintaining the transcendence of God. On the other hand, it is under the Lord's control and is, as it were, his instrument of governance. From a mythological point of view, it is personified by the Dualists as God's consort Lakṣmī; this doubtless represents an accommodation of metaphysical ideas to traditional Vaiṣṇnavism.

In an important sense, according to Madhva the material world plus the selves depends upon the Lord. Indeed the most vital distinguishing characteristic which God possesses is his self-dependence. Other entities are dependent upon him. This distinction has various applications. First, at a period of major dissolution (there was also the conception of a less radical form of destruction intercalated between periods of major chaos) the world of inanimate objects is dissolved into primeval nature, thought of as a powdery substance vastly more minute in texture than the atoms of the Distinctionist school. Under such conditions nature becomes virtually undifferentiated chaos, and solely has the function of producing instants of time. Time, it may be remarked, is viewed as a sort of substance generated directly by nature. Thus the material entities of the cosmos are subject to transformation, through the agency of the Lord. On the other hand, the Lord is changeless and is not liable to evolutionary change. Thus dependence here involves being liable to change by God; independence *(svatantra)*, being incapable of change by anything else. It may be noted too that though nature is somehow regarded, as we have seen, as constituting or representing the power of the Lord, it is subject to the transformation into the myriad entities of the cosmos. This somewhat ambiguous position occupied by nature is a consequence of its being an intermediary between God and the things of ordinary experience, and suffers from the troubles intermediaries typically possess.

The relation between life-monads and the Lord is rather different. Considered in themselves, without regard to the ignorance and the material aspects with which they are clothed during their time of transmigration in the world, they are changeless. Thus the distinction between God and the material world, namely that the former does not undergo transformation, while the latter does, does not hold in this case. However, the fate of the life-monads—as to whether they gain release and their status in release, etc.—is determined by God, to whom are due the operations of ignorance which veil life-monads' intelligence and thereby implicate them in the round of rebirth. Thus the circumstances of selves are affected by God's activity—the circumstances, for instance, of whether they enjoy bliss or pain and so forth; but on the other hand the circumstances of the Lord in these respects are unaffected by the activity of other entities in the universe. Consequently, God is independent, but life-monads are dependent *(paratantra).*

As in Rāmānuja's system, the selves are regarded as atomic; but through the possession of consciousness they are enabled to pervade the bodies which they inhabit, rather as light from a source pervades a volume of space. But whereas for Rāmānuja the divergences between selves, in regard to their embodiment and status in the world, are the direct consequence of karma, which in turn is simply the expression of the Lord's will, the Dualists argued that the difference in the fates of different individuals is traceable to their individual characteristics. That is, each life-monad has certain qualities which necessarily determine its whole course of existence. The Lord in controlling the world and thereby arranging the destinies of the life-monads is realizing what is inherent in them.

As in the case of Non-Dualism, the condition which causes souls to be bound down to the beginningless round of rebirth is ignorance.

However, and unlike Śaṅkara, Madhva does not conceive of ignorance as a unitary phenomenon, but each individual's ignorance has its own peculiar characteristics. Thus the 'imposition' by the Lord of ignorance on the life-monad does not involve foisting on it a spiritual darkness which is extrinsic to the individual. We have mentioned above, further, the fact that Madhva differentiates between the release enjoyed by different souls. He also—and uniquely among the great Hindu theologians—holds that some selves are destined for eternal punishment in hell. Some selves also will just go on transmigrating. Thus Madhva not only postulates various grades of release, but different grades of non-release.

The doctrine of predestination to eternal damnation, uncharacteristic of Indian religious thought, has inclined some scholars to see Christian influence on Madhva. The West coast of India round Mangalore certainly is an area where there were early Christian settlements. Moreover, Madhva's mythological teachings make the god Vāyu (literally 'Wind') a central intermediary between the Lord and men. Legendary accounts of Madhva's life, further, describe him as walking on water, and there are other incidents reminiscent of the New Testament. But there are other ways of explaining these facts, and it would be rash to ascribe to Madhva a Christian ancestry. For instance, Vāyu is a Vedic deity, and there is no need to see him as an importation of the doctrine of the Holy Spirit. Again, legendary miracles of all kinds abound in the lives of the Indian saints, and it is not impossible to find parallels nearly everywhere to their Western counterparts. Finally, and most importantly, the predestinationism of Madhva is more easily explained by the internal dynamics of his system. Given the necessary differences in the destinies of individuals, it is not surprising that some should achieve the worst possible fate.

It is easier to detect in Madhva the genuine influence of Jainism, prevalent in the area in question, especially during the mediaeval period. The doctrine of the infinity of life-monads and their being closely-packed throughout the cosmos is reminiscent of the Jain view. It is not unnatural that one who wished to affirm a dualistic thesis should have been favourably disposed towards a tradition which asserted the infinite number of life-monads. For Dualism presupposes that there are many selves, and that they are not all united as it were in the single holy Power underlying the visible world. Also, just as Jainism made a hierarchy of the gods (conceived of course as existing within the cosmos), so too Madhva, with his passion for differentiation, assigns different roles and statues to a whole string of traditional gods, who form, so to say, a hierarchy of officials administering the Lord's commands.

Like Rāmānuja, Madhva was committed to the self-authentication of common-sense knowledge (as opposed to the illusionist doctrine of the Non-Dualists), and there are certain details of his epistemology which are of some interest. These will be discussed later in connection with the arguments used. Also, as has been mentioned, Madhva elaborated his own scheme of cosmology: but as this is based on Distinctionist ideas, its details are of little concern to us here. But there is one aspect of his doctrine about life-monads which needs to be mentioned. Like the Non-Dualists, Madhva made use of the concept of the apperceiver or witness—the self as conscious who, as it were, inspects the data provided by the senses, etc. More important, it is the source of intuitive knowledge which is indubitable—for example, knowledge of one's own existence is of this sort, since doubt presupposes a self which doubts; the apprehension of space and time is also a function of the witness. In Western terms, therefore, it is a faculty of *a priori* cognitions. But, like ignorance, it is not, so to say, common to different persons, as in the Non-Dualist account, but is individual to each person.

Although formally Dualism seems to be nearer to theism as it is usually formulated in the West than is Rāmānuja's system, there is a certain paradoxicality in the situation—to which we referred in the last chapter. For although the separation of God from the world and from the selves is radical in Dualism, and although Qualified Non-Dualism has something of a monistic air and thus superficially resembles pantheism, the concept of grace is much more strongly stressed in the latter system. This is part of the greater emphasis on the dependence of the self on the Lord—a dependence which arises from the fact that the Lord is the inner controller and forms the material cause of the cosmos. Thus Madhva, by affirming the eternal co-existence of selves and the Lord, and by holding that there is a kind of inner determination of the individual souls which provides them with their destiny, blurs the notion of independence. As we have seen, he certainly wishes to attach weight to the distinction between the Lord and life-monads in terms of the self-dependence of the former. But there is not the same sense, in his system, of the dependence of souls on the activity of God as there is in Rāmānuja's, since the careers of souls are only the working out by God of what is already inherent in them. This is where the absence of a doctrine of creation out of nothing alters the dynamics of Indian theology and implies that the superficially pantheistic concept of God as the material cause has a closer resemblance to Western theism than the strictly dualistic account which Madhva attempted to introduce. (In making these remarks, of course, I am not at all intending to pass judgment on these various versions of theism, but merely to show that devotionalism, which requires a form of theism for its expression, may well have a more intense expression in what is superficially pantheistic in the Indian tradition than in what looks at first sight closer to Western orthodoxy. It is of course an open question as to whether a strong emphasis upon devotionalism is a good thing.)

The motive of Madhva in formulating his metaphysics was, like Rāmānuja's, a desire to combat the monistic view of Śankara—a view which, as Madhva's biography explicitly affirms, cut at the root of worship and devotion. Thus, as an intensely pious Vaiṣṇavite, Madhva wanted to elaborate a theology in consonance with that form of worship. Nevertheless, although devotion and individual worship are central parts of the path to salvation, Madhva's prescription on how to lead the true religious life involves the necessary practice of meditation. This is what brings a direct knowledge of the Lord. Now in so far as there is a contrast running through the Indian tradition, especially in the mediaeval period, between yogic practices centred on meditation and devotionalism, it would appear that, paradoxically, Madhva both stresses the distinction between the self and the Lord (a theological reflection of devotionalism) and also the necessity for meditation (which is reflected doctrinally either in self- or soul- or life-monad-pluralism or in the non-dualistic identification of the self with the one holy Power, i.e. release in either case is conceived as a realization of the self). But this appearance of paradox is misleading, when we come to examine what Madhva meant by meditation. For him, it consisted in a contemplation of the Lord. It involved too a reflection upon the eternal fivefold distinction outlined earlier between God, souls and inanimate objects.

Here there is some contrast with much of classical Indian meditation. In Non-Dualism and in Yoga, as well as in Buddhism, methods of contemplation essentially involve the emptying of the mind of images and objects of thought. Through the attainment of a pure state of consciousness, one realizes the self—whether conceived as identical with the Power, as in Non-Dualism, or as individual and in isolation. It is true that such contemplative attainments need to be seen by the practitioner in the light, so to speak, of the path which they are treading—and in this sense they have a sort of conceptual ambience. But essentially it remains true that there are not discursive objects of thought in the higher states of mysticism in the Indian tradition: this helps to account for the Śaṅkarite doctrine of the featurelessness of the holy Power. But for Madhva meditation has as its object the Lord: indeed he should be its sole object. Thus his mysticism has some analogy to theistic mysticism in the West, where the distinction between God and the soul is retained, and where God is the object of loving contemplation. Hence we can say that Madhva provides a sort of bridge between the atheistic mysticism of schools such as Yoga and Jainism and the devotionalism expressed by Rāmānuja. It may be noted too that like these schools, Madhva recognizes the ideal of living-release (of the saint or yogi already liberated in this life) which in one way or another is characteristic of the contemplative schools of the Indian tradition, from Buddhism, Jainism and Yoga through to Non-Dualism. Rāmānuja on the other hand does not so recognize it (in this doubtless as elsewhere he was stressing the dependence of the saint on God's grace: the notion of living-release appears to make him self-sufficient in his latter days). All this may serve to reinforce our earlier interpretation of Madhva as adapting soul-pluralism to the needs of theism.

We have so far observed how both Rāmānuja and Madhva represent a reaction, in the interests of devotional religion, against the contemplative monism of Śaṅkara. It might be thought that this is due simply to the fact that both these theologians were committed to Vaiṣṇavism (while Śaṅkara was a Śaivite). It is therefore of great interest to observe the features of Śaivite Doctrine as elaborated by Meykaṇḍa and others. It does not rank as Vedānta; and arose in a sense outside the orthodox Brāhmanical tradition. But its similarities to Dualistic teachings is a good indication that the same religious impulses as underlie Madhva's metaphysics are at work here also. It is principally for this reason that I have included this school within the purview of this account of the major systems of Indian metaphysics. Since its main concerns—even more than Madhva and Rāmānuja—were theological; and since also it borrowed some of its epistemology, etc., from Logic-Atomism and some of its cosmology from Distinctionism; it does not figure a great deal in the philosophical debates of the various schools. One indication, indeed, of the Śaivite Doctrine's lying outside 'mainstream' Indian metaphysics is its use of its own particular terminology, some of the key items of which are not found elsewhere.

The teachings propounded by Meykaṇḍa can be briefly described. First, the Lord is identified with Śiva; and he is the cause of the world, but not its material cause. The latter is nature or the creative-substance, which is transformed in various ways by the agency of God, through his energy *(śakti)*. The latter is sometimes considered as an intermediary between God and the world, and is therefore hypostatized mythologically as the female creative energy who is the consort of Śiva. There is a parallel here with the Dualist use of the mythological figure of Lakṣmī to represent nature as the Lord's instrument of governance. In the Śaivite case, however, the intermediary is at one farther remove. The creative-substance is acted upon by God and is transformed into bodies, organs, objects of experience and inorganic beings: and the organs, including inner or psychic organs, such as the mind-organ, when associated with a self give rise to consciousness. According to the Doctrine, the selves initially are immersed in an obscuring substance *(āṇava)*, which make them incapable of knowledge either of themselves or of the Lord. By being associated with matter, and further by being tainted by impurities *(mala)*, the selves gradually learn the transiency of existence in the world, self-awareness and ultimately release in the sight of the Lord. All this is due to the operation of God's energy, which not only makes the souls conscious, but leads them on to release. Thus Śaivite Doctrine here assumes the existence of three categories of being—the Lord, who is Master of the world, the souls who are subject to him, and the world itself which constitutes their place of bondage. It is thus in its formal structure similar to Madhva's system.

There are variations among the beliefs of followers of this school, and so not all the following ideas have universal acceptance there; but they serve to illustrate the religious atmosphere underlying the above doctrines. The self as we have seen is subject to God. This entails not only that the adherent should throw himself entirely on the mercy of God, but also he should learn from a teacher or guru (regarded as an incarnation of Śiva). Through initiation into the Śaivite way of life he can ultimately attain to a union with Śiva through contemplative knowledge, and this is sometimes likened to the union of male and female (or in the language of Western mysticism the spiritual marriage). There is thus a living-release possible for the saint, as with Madhva. However, in the liberated state, the soul retains the shadow of its former obscuration and impurities: this is no more than the potentiality for lapsing under the influence of them again. Thus living-release, and indeed final release itself, do not bring with them an inner guarantee, as it were, that salvation is for eternity. In this further way the self is dependent upon God's grace.

We may see in all this strong analogies to the Dualist position. There are many infinite life-monads, immersed in a real world, and ultimately controlled by God. Release comes through treading a path of adoration and self-abasement before God, and a dualism is implicit in the description of the relation between God and souls. Nevertheless, mystical or contemplative gnosis plays a large part in the scheme of salvation, but it is likewise—as with Madhva—contemplation seen from the position of devotion and of belief in a personal Lord. Thus Śaivism has its counterpart to the non-monistic doctrines of Vaiṣṇavism.

With Dualism and the Śaivite Doctrine outlined above we by no means exhaust the variety of theologies and metaphysical systems of the mediaeval and later periods. However, it is fair to say that our survey of the three great forms of Vedānta, together with the Śaivite Doctrine, gives a fair idea of the main types of doctrine elaborated. The other systems represent variations on, or intermediate positions between, these viewpoints. Thus, for instance, later Śaivite teachings, in so far as they take an orthodox form and involve an interpretation of revelation, are not dissimilar to the viewpoints already discussed. It is not necessary for our present purposes to catalogue all the varieties of theology to be met with, and it is sufficient that some important and representative examples have been exhibited. This will enable us not only to analyse them further, in order to see more clearly why these various patterns of metaphysical belief have emerged in the Indian tradition, but it will also, for the second part of the book, be a sufficient indication of the background to the discussion of philosophical topics which have figured prominently in Indian metaphysics.

CHAPTER X
ANALYSIS OF THE RELIGIOUS FACTORS IN INDIAN METAPHYSICS

As has been indicated earlier, it is possible to show roughly why the various viewpoints and schools of Indian metaphysics assumed the shapes that they did. It is often the case that a metaphysical system is a coherent elaboration of a single main thesis, or of some few central theses. From a cluster of insights (or supposed insights) a whole set of doctrines is excogitated. In the case of Indian philosophy, with its powerful connection with religion, it is necessary to look for the determining religious motivation behind the various viewpoints. This, as we shall see, does not quite work in every case—especially Logic-Atomism—but it works in a sufficient number to justify the procedure. It needs to be remembered, too, that Indian philosophy is on the whole markedly *traditional*. That is, the roots of the different viewpoints and schools usually go back a very long way, sometimes to disappear into the recesses of unknown antiquity. Consequently, the shape of a system is often determined, so far as we can see, by factors other than those of speculative inquiry. This is a further reason why there is a need to consider the systems in relation to underlying religious intuitions which, more often than not, they express.

All this is not to say that the arguments which we shall be describing in Part II are valueless because they (so some might think) are mere rationalizations designed to bolster existing prejudices. Such a view would be quite misleading, for at least two reasons. First of all, though an analysis of religious motives will serve to illuminate the underlying reasons for the main shape of the various systems under discussion, it only does that. It cannot hope to be an account which explains all the details, and where the latter are concerned with, for example, epistemological issues, it is wise to consider them as determined, so to say, by reason rather than faith. Second, the validity or otherwise of arguments, and their intrinsic interest, do not depend upon their provenance or upon who utters them. It would be as foolish to ignore the dialectical side of Indian philosophy out of a scepticism about religion as it would be to dismiss Western mediaeval philosophy solely because of its general alliance with theology. It should also be recognized that though the basic insights of a system may be religious in character, the working up of the system which expresses them may be a task exhibiting considerable brilliance. One is inclined to feel this in the case of Śaṅkara. His idealism is perhaps, to eyes unaccustomed to the spiritual intentions of such a form of speculation, bizarre. But there is no mistaking its curious boldness and economy.

In the course of the preceding chapters I have made some brief attempt to characterize some of the religious motivations of the systems, and this will have sufficiently indicated the main features of the present analysis. It will already have become apparent, for example, that the activities of meditation, or yoga as broadly considered, and of worship and devotion to God provide a polarity which helps to account for the shapes of various systems. It is extraordinarily important, if we are to give an account of the matter in terms of religious insights, etc., that attention be paid to empirical religion, and in particular to the religious procedures and activites lying at its centre. It is not sufficient to say about a metaphysician or theologian that, for instance, he wishes to resist a pantheistic doctrine and therefore argues that such-and-such. We want to know further about his distaste for pantheism. We will usually find either that he is resting on some orthodoxy, which puts the problem back a stage, or that (more likely) his feeling for the distinctness of God and man, and therefore his suspicion of its apparent abrogation in a doctrine of pantheism, arises out of his practice of worship and of his consequent religious experience. We can say that there is a correlation between certain forms of religious experience and types of ritual or procedural ambience—the experience of the soul's isolation *(kaivalya)* in contemplative states, for example, correlates with a form of yoga; and the idea of a personal God, met with in prayer, goes with a religion of adoration and worship. Thus it is important to relate doctrines to their earthly manifestation, in the practices and experiences of religion. In this, the Indian tradition constitutes an extraordinarily fascinating spiritual laboratory.

I have referred to meditation and devotionalism as constituting a polarity in religious practice and experience which will help to illuminate the varieties of Indian metaphysics. But devotionalism, in the sense of fervent adoration of, and reliance on, the Lord, is not strictly characteristic of the Upaniṣadic period; but emerges clearly first in the *Gītā* and in the Mahāyāna schools. But it is related to the earlier Brāhmanical religion: for it is the bringing into the formal worship of the holy Power a strong element of love and obedience. In so far as devotionalism occurs in an orthodox context, as in the *Gītā* and the mediaeval theologies, the antique ritualism of the Veda is not repudiated, but reinterpreted as requiring as its inner essence the love of God. This is analogous to the way some of the sacrificial elements in Vedic ritual were reinterpreted from a yogic point of view. But already in the Upaniṣads there is clearly evident a strand of worship, itself going back to the worship expressed in the hymns of the Veda. Thus in an important way the devotional religion of the *Gītā* can be seen as a deepening and personalizing of the formal worship incorporated in Brahmanism. It would therefore be useful to keep in mind that the polarity is not just between meditation and associated yogic practices on the one hand and devotion on the other; but more broadly between yoga and the religion of worship (of which devotionalism is a fervent expression). But since the schools and viewpoints we are considering took their shape for the most part in the later period, I shall simply refer to this polarity as that between meditation and devotionalism.

The presence of these elements needs, as we have seen, to be correlated with doctrines; and for this purpose it is useful to select a few key concepts whose presence and absence in the various systems can be set out. The discrimination of these key ideas will involve comparisons between the schools, and will sometimes necessarily have a certain crudity. But the crudity will not be, I think, of such a degree as to vitiate the results. One cause of the crudity is that metaphysical schemes are organic, or partly so—in the sense that concepts have to be understood in the light of at least a segment of the whole system.

The first of the key ideas I wish to isolate is that of the Absolute. That is, we can ask about a viewpoint: 'Does it affirm the existence of an Absolute?' By Absolute here, as we have seen earlier is meant the inner essence of the observable cosmos, which is conceived in an impersonal manner (i.e. in this way, it differs from the concept of the Lord). As has been argued earlier this idea is affirmed in Mahāyāna schools, but not in the Elder Doctrine: i.e. nirvana as conceived in the latter is not an Absolute in this sense. The use of the notion of an Absolute makes it possible for us to make a direct comparison between the Greater Vehicle schools we discussed in an earlier chapter and Śaṅkara's Non-Dualism. About both Śaṅkara and these Buddhists it is true that they affirmed the existence of an Absolute.

The next key idea I wish to consider is that of the Lord. Here it should be noted that I mean a personal God, but not necessarily a Creator. Thus the celestial Buddha who forms the object of devotionalism in the Greater Vehicle can be counted as equivalent to the Hindu notion of the Lord, even though in Buddhism there is strictly no doctrine of the creation of the world (in line with the Buddha's agnosticism).[1] Then again, in so far as later Yoga developed a doctrine of God, this was simply belief in an ever-liberated soul who was Lord and object of meditation, etc., but not creator of the world. Thus we can ask about the notion of a Lord in a particular system: 'Does the system affirm the existence of such a being?' and also: 'Is the Lord creator of the world?'

A third key idea is that of an eternal soul, self or life-monad (these are essentially equivalent in the Indian tradition). Since this is distinguished from the empirical ego and the psycho-physical organism, we can ask, in regard to each system: 'Does each phycho-physical organism possess an individual self?' Thus we would answer 'No' in regard to Non-Dualism. This viewpoint does, however, make use of the concept of an eternal (but unitary) Self, but in view of its identification with the Absolute, we may neglect framing a separate question to cover this case. As we have seen, there are differences within and between the various viewpoints as the constitution of the selves, but these variations will be neglected for the time being.

A fourth key idea in the Indian tradition is that of rebirth or reincarnation. All systems save Materialism share this belief: but it needs to be distinguished from belief in an eternal or everlasting self, since (as in Buddhism and in Non-Dualism) one can have the concept of a transmigrating person who does not possess an individual eternal self.

Fifth, throughout the tradition, except for Materialism, there is belief in the possibility of release. Again, there are variations in the way in which it is described, and some variety in terminology (for instance, nirvana, one of the words for release in the Indian tradition, has virtually replaced its rivals in the description of Buddhist salvation).

As a preliminary move we can draw up a table to exhibit the pattern of belief in terms of these key ideas in relation to the meditation-devotionalism polarity. But in virtue of the close association between some schools—Distinctionism and Yoga, for example, certain differences of emphasis may be obscured. Thus though both Distinctionism and Yoga, typically of mystical or contemplative thought, lay stress on inner knowledge, the former school is more 'intellectual' in its emphasis. Likewise the Void school in relation to its close relation, Buddhist Idealism. By 'intellectual' is meant here that the part played by reflection on metaphysical truths, so that they acquire an existential impact, is given more prominence than the psycho-physical postures and exercises of yoga. However, this merely represents a further polarity within the conception of meditation in the Indian tradition. As we have seen earlier, the contemplative path is undertaken in terms of a certain conceptual ambience, and a grasp of metaphysical truth is supposed to go alongside the attainment of contemplative states (thus both insight and peace are elements of nirvana). The pursuit of this gnosis thus has two sides to it; and the polarity between metaphysical knowledge and yogic experience sometimes leads to a bifurcation between the two sides.[2] One may compare the bifurcation between faith and works within the sphere of devotional Christianity. Thus in our preliminary table, I shall use the category meditative knowledge to cover both sides of the polarity. We shall then further have to see what difference it will make to our correlations if a distinction within this category is made.

There is a further complication to take account of. Both Śaṅkara and some Mahāyānists affirm both belief in the Absolute and in a Lord. But it is important for our purposes to distinguish between the emphases the two ideas have. This difference metaphysically is represented by the fact that the Lord is conceived as being connected with an illusory world and so shares in its illusoriness or insubstantiality. It is therefore an idea at the 'lower' or ordinary level of truth that is in use when we make empirical statements, etc. It is therefore convenient to insert a further question about the systems, namely 'Is the cosmos a reality?' This will show in a general way whether a system is idealistic or not. Where the answer to the question about the cosmos is 'No', it should be kept in mind that the idea of the Lord has merely secondary importance. We may now consider our questions in relation to the systems, by means of the following table. 'X' means that the idea is affirmed; 'O' that it is either absent or denied. In the lines of the table referring to devotion and meditation, the symbols mean that one and not the other is the dominant spiritual practice: but we shall later have to investigate the relation between the two in a little more detail. For convenience, I have arranged the table so that, where possible, the neighbours of a system show the nearest similarities to it.

Some significant facts emerge from a contemplation of this table. It happens, however, that Logic-Atomism and Yoga are, for idiosyncratic reasons which I shall come to, jokers in my pack. If we neglect them for the moment, our list of correlations is increased, and I shall then explain why my analysis of the situation does not, superficially at least, fit these viewpoints. Our facts, then, are as follows.

(1) Where devotion is important, there is belief in a Lord.
(2) Belief in an Absolute is coupled with belief in a Lord at a lower level of truth.
(3) Stress on meditation as primary implies that the Lord is not regarded as primary.
(4) Belief in the Lord as primary correlates with a belief in many selves.
(5) Where meditation is primary, there is no belief in a genuine creator (column 1 shows a creator; but one that is implicated in the grand illusion).

We may also observe from the table that similarities are cross-religious: Hindu Non-Dualism is close to Buddhist Voidism: Jainism is close to Distinctionism. Vaiṣṇavite Dualism and Śaivite Doctrine are akin. These facts serve to encourage an analysis in terms of religious

	NON-DUALISM	VOIDISM	IDEALISM	QUALIFIED NON-DUALISM	ŚAIVITE DOCTRINE	DUALISM	LOGIC-ATOMISM	YOGA	DISTINCTIONISM	EXEGESIS	JAINISM	ELDER DOCTRINE	MATERIALISM
Absolute	X	X	X	O	O	O	O	O	O	O	O	O	O
Lord	X	X	X	X	X	X	X	X	O	O	O	O	O
Creator	X	O	O	X	X	X	X	O	O	O	O	O	O
world real	O	O	O	X	X	X	X	X	X	X	X	X	X
selves	O	O	O	X	X	X	X	X	X	X	X	O	O
rebirth	X	X	X	X	X	X	X	X	X	X	X	X	O
release	X	X	X	X	X	X	X	X	X	X	X	X	O
devotion	O	O	O	X	X	X	O	O	O	O	O	O	O
meditative knowledge	X	X	X	O	O	O	X	X	X	O	X	X	O

experience, since such an explanation ought not to apply to one tradition alone: that is, the idea that a certain type of religious experience is specific to one tradition alone would explain little.

The above-listed facts clearly indicate the correlation between devotionalism and theism. But they leave obscure the reason why it is that a primary emphasis on meditation should result either in Absolutism or atheism. Nevertheless (2) provides a hint. The hint can be followed up by further considering the relation between meditation and devotion and worship in the principal systems we are considering. Now if we contrast the Elder Doctrine with the Mahāyāna schools we note that in the latter, though devotionalism plays a sub-ordinate part, it certainly exists. That is to say, with the Mahāyāna, as we have seen, there was a considerable growth of popular religion, and with it the development of a fairly fervent a considerable growth of popular religion, and with it the development of a fairly fervent devotionalism. This was, in a sense, tamed by the orthodoxically Buddhist insistence on the contemplative life as the culmination of the Path. But in comparison with the Elder Doctrine, which even in later days does not recognize the worship—in the proper signification of the term—of the Buddha, and which of course does not accept the idea of a transcendent Being who might serve as the object of worship, the Greater Vehicle schools show a remarkable degree of devotionalism. It becomes indeed a secondary means of salvation, for faith in the Buddha helps towards the realization of a more refined spiritual life, whether in this world or in some heaven. It becomes part of the way of the Bodhisattva. A very similar situation obtains in regard to Non-Dualism. For the religion of worship is recognized as part of the preparation for the ultimate realization of non-duality. Even if it be an inferior form of faith, it is *praeparatio mystica.* In both the Greater Vehicle schools and Non-Dualism, therefore, devotionalism is an ancillary to meditative knowledge. (The doctrine of rebirth clearly makes it easier for such a view to be taken: though the lower-level truth may be inferior, it can be of use to people who are at a certain stage of development, and may assist them to higher attainments in one of their lives to come.)

We might signalize this relation between meditation and devotion in the Absolutistic schools by assigning different weights to the two forms of religious life. In revising the bottom two lines of our table, we shall adopt this procedure. But meanwhile a further problem afflicts us—namely what we are to say about, for intance, the religious life of the Dualist school. As we saw earlier, in dealing with this system, Madhva certainly makes a form of meditation central to the spiritual life. However, what he meant by meditation does not quite correspond to its significance in Non-Dualism, Yoga and elsewhere. For meditation involves an awareness of God as its object, according to Madhva. That is, it is the contemplative life suffused with, and seen from the perspective of, devotionalism. It would not be misleading to describe this as devotional meditation, and assign it to a separate category for the purposes of this analysis. For since it is meditation somewhat suffused with a theistic attitude, it would be unclear, if we wish to show the relative weights of devotion and meditation in the various systems (or in the religious life correlated with them), to pigeonhole it simply either with one arm of our polarity or the other. Thus Dualism is correlated with both devotional meditation and the purely devotional religion of worship which Vaiṣṇavism tends to express. Similar remarks can be made about Śaivite Doctrine, as we saw in our discussion of that school. The concept of devotional meditation will also be of use when we deal with one of our 'jokers', namely Yoga. Yoga in essence was almost certainly atheistic until a fairly late period, and the grafting on of belief in a Lord was little more than the recognition that orthodox Yogins by then were already using a form of meditation, in addition to the mainstream practices distilled in Yoga, one which involved meditation upon the splendour of the Lord, as a means helping the adept towards his ultimate goal. In this way, Yoga was affected, but only very moderately and marginally, by the growth of devotional religion in the period from the *Gītā* onwards.

There are some remarks too which need to be made about the other 'joker', namely Logic-Atomism. Here it is indeed hard to account for the shape of the system by reference directly to the religious insights, etc., which it wished to express. Not only was it probably atheistic; but also, it seems to have grafted on to itself elements from orthodox religion in a very formal way. In view of its origins, it was not primarily interested in presenting any sort of way of salvation. In theory, however, it was intellectualist in its prescription for release. Knowledge of the true system was adequate for salvation. Superficially therefore it looked like Distinctionism. But it would be spurious to explain its features directly by reference to the forms of the religious life we are now considering; and so I shall continue to neglect it, for the time being, in this analysis.

Logic-Atomism is, in a sense, doubly the converse of Exegesis. The latter is a very curious phenomenon. It arose, of course, from the need to give a reasoned account of ritual. But ritual itself was in origin merely a highly formalized means of expressing men's relations to the gods of Vedic religion. It thus springs from the activities of worship and sacrifice, which themselves foreshadow the more intensely personal devotionalism of later Indian religion. But the growth of ritualism detached the ritual from the gods, and the holy Power came to be conceived—not as a single being underlying the many gods, its variegated manifestation—but as something implicit in ritual activities: a force to be manipulated. In some respects, this was not surprising—since the concept of an impersonal power implicit in ritual or other objects is not uncommon in early religion. But in effect Exegesis represents a stage where the outer manifestations of religion which had a direct connection with worship have become quite detached from that ambience. This is why, in our table, neither side of the polarity is represented in the column devoted to Exegesis. I have said that Logic-Atomism is its double converse. First, it makes formal recognition of God and thus includes what is so oddly omitted from Exegesis. And second, the detachment of Logic-Atomism from the springs of religion occurred in a way opposite to the manner in which it happened to Exegesis. Exegesis has moved away, as it were, from the religious origins from which it sprang. Logic-Atomism was without such religious origins, but moved towards a more orthodox religious form by engrafting a doctrine of God (as well as recognition of revelation).

There is one further point about the revision of the bottom two lines of our table. Rāmānuja, as we noted, recognized (perhaps grudgingly) the possibility of a form of release through identification with the self in yogic experience. It was an inferior form: but it should be registered on our table (it is interesting that in the *Gītā* there is a rather similar doctrine of priorities in release as between those who follow the path of devotion and those who isolate the self in inner experience).

The lower part of the table can now be revised as follows (where the numbers register in an unavoidably crude way the priority-relations between the different forms of spiritual activity, etc.):

	ND	VO	ID	QN	DU	SD	YO	DI	EX	JA	ED	MA
devotion	1	1	1	3	2	2	0	0	0	0	0	0
devotional	–	–	–	–	2	2	1	–	–	–	–	–
meditation–knowledge	3	3	3	1	0	0	3	4	0	4	4	0

This revision clarifies a number of things not quite obvious in our previous correlation of doctrines and religious attitudes.

(1) An element of (pure, i.e. neglecting devotional meditation) devotionalism implies a doctrine of a personal Lord.

(2) Where meditation outweighs devotionalism, but where the latter exists, there is a doctrine of an Absolute.

(3) Exclusive concentration of meditational means of salvation is correlated with a belief in a plurality of selves or (in the Elder Doctrine) with a virtual pluralism, and certainly not with a monistic doctrine.

(4) Where devotionalism outweighs the meditative side of the polarity, there is a doctrine of the Lord as the supreme reality.

We can also note certain points about one or more of the systems. Thus Rāmānuja represents Non-Dualism upside down, so to speak. It contains an exact reversal of priorities. Again, Qualified Non-Dualism, Dualism and the Śaivite Doctrine involve roughly equal elements of devotionalism, though it is more intensely expressed in the first of the three. It is perchance no accident that these three come closest to theism as it is conceived in the faiths of Semitic origin. Again, Yoga among all the systems which include a Lord, has the weakest devotional element: it should thus occasion no surprise that the position of the Lord is rather marginal in the history of the viewpoint and that he is not conceived as having the creative powers usually ascribed to the Lord elsewhere in Hinduism.

A reflection on all this serves to show an important point about the Absolutistic schools. They succeed in integrating the doctrine of God into an essentially meditative ambience in such a way that it is quite clear that worship and devotion are quite secondary. This contrasts with the status of the Lord in Yoga (which might up to a point be thought to be expressing a similar priority), which is both semi-detached and something of an afterthought. In any event for Yoga there was not the same compelling need as in the Greater Vehicle to integrate popular religion with the quest for nirvana. The forces of devotion were more powerful there, and had important associations with a strong ethic of compassion and self-sacrifice. Thus we might claim that the notion of an Absolute (which is sometimes thought to be typical of mysticism—the seeing the One in All) only emerges in the fully-fledged form which we find in later Buddhist and mediaeval Indian religion as a concept which paradoxically owes its application to devotionalism rather than to mysticism pure and simple. To put the matter in another way: the typical expression of contemplative religion in India is pluralistic, not monistic.

One main reason for this paradox is as follows. The more advanced or developed forms of devotionalism move unmistakably in the direction of a single object of worship—or at least a unified complex of such lords. The many gods are seen as subordinate manifestations of the supreme Lord: the many Buddhas and Bodhisattvas are the one Being, essentially. Thus devotionalism increasingly requires an underlying unity in the objects of its expression. By conceiving of the Buddhas as united mysteriously in their Truth-Body, and by the identification of this with ultimate reality, the Greater Vehicle schools provided such a unified focus to popular religion. It is interesting by contrast to notice the situation in the Elder School. For the Elders, there was no question of worshipping the Buddha, for doctrinal reasons. There could thus be no outlet for devotionalism in accordance with Buddhist orthodoxy, save in relation to existing, non-Buddhistic cults. Thus polytheism was retained, on condition that it was to be seen by the faithful as in the last analysis quite irrelevant to spiritual welfare. The gods were overcome by being ignored. Polytheism was transcended not in the direction of theism, but by nirvana, which had nothing to do with worship, etc. But, as we have said, the situation in the Greater Vehicle was very different. Devotionalism was incorporated into the faith, and was recognized through doctrines which approached theism but at the same time were themselves subordinate to the concept of an Absolute with which the contemplative could identify himself through inner experience.

The Absolute, therefore, in Buddhism served two functions. First, in its emptiness, its Voidness, its impersonality, it retained the qualities of nirvana: that is, it was recognizable that the contemplative goal of the Greater Vehicle had strong analogies to the nirvana conceived in the Lesser. Second, and relevantly to our remarks about the paradox of the Absolute, the Absolute served as a substratum in which the Buddhas manifested to the religious imagination of devotees could inhere. It was not surprising, then, that in later developments of the Greater Vehicle there should emerge a tendency to treat the Absolute itself as a personal Being, and for a form of theism (or something close in spirit to theism) to usurp the quest for nirvana as originally understood. It was not surprising, for it meant that devotionalism had broken through the barrier which the classical Mahāyāna concept of the Absolute presented. This barrier lay in idealism of one kind or another: the notion that the ordinary world of experience is self-contradictory if taken as independently real. Such an idealism was co-ordinated to a two-level theory of truth, as we saw. Thus the Absolute was the higher truth—the goal to which, like fingers pointing at the moon, the doctrines ultimately refer. But the Lord belongs to the lower realm—the ambit of men's imagination. Thus in the Greater Vehicle schools, devotionalism, together with something approaching theism, is incorporated, but made subordinate to the contemplative knowledge of the Absolute.

This transition from a virtually pluralistic system (as carried on by the Elder School) was made the easier by the form of that virtual pluralism. The repudiation of the doctrine of selves meant that the Buddha, while retaining the rough form in which early Indian mystical religion was expressed—in Jainism and the precursors of Yoga, for example—had strictly speaking gone beyond soul-pluralism. It was thus a possibility that sooner or later nirvana might be conceived as a monistic reality, rather than as a state attained separately by diverse individuals. Thus the way was open to the Greater Vehicle reinterpretation of the transcendent.

The Absolutism of the Greater Vehicle of course had a considerable influence upon Śaṅkara; and we can see similar factors at work in his metaphysics. Again, the two levels of truth mean that he can incorporate devotionalism without allowing it to capture the castle.

We may note too that though idealism or illusionism is a means of expressing the lower status of devotion and of ordinary life, when compared with the resplendent attainment of contemplative insight, it also directly expresses something of mysticism itself. In the pluralistic systems which concentrate upon yoga and meditation, release means that the soul vanishes from the world. The world is conceived as real, and the soul simply vanishes from it. This concept of liberation reflects the 'voidness' of the contemplative's consciousness—voidness, that is, in terms of the perceptions, images and thoughts arising out of, and referring to, empirical existence. But in Śaṅkara the situation is, so to speak, reversed: the world, looked at from the standpoint of the illuminated self, vanishes. And though for ordinary purposes one still has to go on living in the world and uttering statements about empirical matters, the world no longer looks as it once did: it is an insubstantial wraith, a dream, a grand illusion, God's conjuring trick.

It may be objected to the above analysis of how injection of devotionalism turns contemplative pluralism into a doctrine of the Absolute, that it is not sufficiently historical. For if Śaṅkara be a case in point, surely it should be recognized that he derives his monism from the Upaniṣads. There are several remarks to be made about this. First, though there are Non-Dualistic elements in the Veda, we still need to explain why Indian theologians and metaphysicians came to interpret revelation in such differing ways. Our analysis is clearly relevant to the various emphases placed upon different statements in revelation, which justify the various interpretations. Second, the analysis fits the Greater Vehicle schools, and these in turn influenced Śaṅkara, as we saw. Third, a similar analysis has to be given about Upaniṣadic non-dualism itself. That is, the Upaniṣads unmistakably manifest the importation into Aryan religion of yogic elements, including belief in rebirth, which were not characteristic at all of the early parts of revelation. In short, the sacrificial religion of the earlier period, and the worship of gods and God, is seen here for the first time in relation to the yogi's inner quest. The identification of the holy Power with the self within represents the supreme expression, in the Upaniṣads, of the synthesis between these two forms of religion. That an impersonalistic interpretation of the Upaniṣads was possible for Śaṅkara and others, through the doctrine of the Absolute, was facilitated by the fact to which we have already referred—that the Power was conceived not merely as a holy Being sustaining the cosmos in a personal way, as Creator, but also as the force implicit in the sacrifice: an impersonal force. A generalization of this sacrificial idea meant that the whole cosmos was one great ritual in which and through which the Power worked. It followed that in the Upaniṣads there is a considerable ambivalence between the personal and impersonal aspects of the holy Power. Thus again, it is as well to see Upaniṣadic religion as a synthesis between the cult of the numinous, whether personally or impersonally conceived, and the interior yogic quest. Here too there was a tendency for soul-pluralism to be swallowed up into a monistic doctrine. Nevertheless, it would be wrong to see any one teaching as running consistently through all the classical Upaniṣads, and this is one reason for the divergence of interpretations. But in this connection our first remark in reply to the objection must be repeated with emphasis: we want to know why one interpretation rather than another was put upon revelation, and here the analysis in terms of different strands of religious practice and experience is extremely relevant.

The thesis that Distinctionism, Yoga, Jainism and Buddhism represent a common stream of non-Aryan religion (a thesis which lies behind the remarks above about the importation of yogic elements in the Upaniṣads) is seen to have some force when we contemplate the first table. If we remove the notion of a Lord from Yoga (in accordance with its most probable state early on in its development), we note that Distinctionism, Yoga and Jainism have an exactly similar pattern, and Elder Buddhism diverges in only one main particular. However, it is not merely doctrinal likeness that the thesis is based on, but mythological similarity also (especially as between Jainism and Buddhism).

We may sum up our results so far by enunciating the following principles which appear to determine the shape of the main systems in the Indian tradition:

(1) Contemplative religion, in its 'pure' form, i.e. where devotionalism and worship are neglected as irrelevant to release, etc., is either pluralistic or (in the case of early Buddhism) starts from, but transcends, pluralism.

(2) Devotional religion is correlated with a doctrine of a Lord, regarded as distinct from souls and the world.

(3) Contemplative religion is formulated as the quest for identification with the Absolute when it receives a strong injection of devotionalism and worship.

In brief, the various patterns of Indian metaphysics reflect a varied emphasis upon meditation and devotionalism.

That Indian mysticism should, in a sense, be typically pluralistic, and, in Buddhism of an early period, non-monistic; and that it should be typically atheistic or agnostic;—these ideas may strike some people, brought up in the tradition of the West, as strange. We are accustomed to think of mysticism and the contemplative life as directed towards God or a transcendent Ultimate Reality. It is also usual to think of monism as expressing an important aspect of mystical experience, the seeing of all things in One. This is 'panenhenic' mysticism, of which Professors Zaehner and Stace have written. Nevertheless, though I would be far from denying that the experiences of seeing all things in one, and of gaining an ineffable *rapport* with nature, are not absent from Indian religion (it may be that some passages in the Upaniṣads reflect such an experience), the inner quest for a luminous state of pure consciousness, however this may be theologically interpreted, is much more central to the mystical tradition, both in East and West. It is an experience in the depths of the soul, not directed to outer reality as the panenhenic feeling is. Now in regard to interior contemplation it is certainly necessary to distinguish between experience and interpretation (as we remarked earlier). Those who tread the contemplative path do so in a certain conceptual ambience, and a certain religious milieu. The way they interpret their experience is obviously much affected by that ambience and milieu. Moreover, the differing conceptions of the nature of the path may directly affect the experience itself—injecting into it, as it were, an unconscious interpretation. It is for this reason extremely hard to tell about a given description of mystical experience how much is due to interpretive elements and how much to the experience itself. It is thus a dangerous procedure to say that, in regard to diversely described interior visions, there are in evidence different *types* of experience. For this reason I would be somewhat disinclined to assert that the soul-pluralistic mysticism which typifies yoga is a different variety in essence from the theistic mysticism of, say, the Theravāda. It may perchance be so: but there is little advance in explanation where we account for the idiosyncrasies of different theologies and metaphysical schemes merely by postulating a different kind of experience to go with each. It is true that we need to distinguish more than one kind of religious experience if any explanation in these terms is possible: but our division between the religion of worship on the one hand and mysticism on the other seems to supply sufficient material with which to explain the varied patterns of Indian theology—the diversity of pattern arising from the varied strengths of the two ingredients.

Moreover, it is not unnatural at all that mysticism should in its 'pure' state be interpreted in a soul-pluralistic way. Only if you already possess the concept of God, for instance, does it make sense to interpret the inner vision as a vision of such a transcendent Being. If one's religious quest is simply concentrated upon inner contemplation, and if God and worship are irrelevant, and the gods peripheral, it is very natural to see the yogic experience as a realization of the eternal element lying 'within' the individual. It is at first sight, moreover, natural enough to think of there being many such souls. This of course is especially likely if there is already the belief in rebirth with its attendant assumption that there is an everlasting something which transmigrates from body to body. It is therefore most understandable that pluralism should be the typical form of non-theistic mysticism in the Indian tradition—only to be modified when it comes into synthesis with other religious elements.

But it is also intelligible, as we have seen in discussing the Elder Doctrine, that a transcendence of such soul-pluralism should be taught as a further, and in many respects more subtle, interpretation. For since the experience of the yogi involves going beyond the ordinary discriminations of perceptual, imaginative and ratiocinative experience, thus attaining a certain 'voidness', looked at from the point of view of the world, it is rather hard to distinguish one mystic's content of experience from another's. The undifferentiated nature of the experience thus opens the way to the abandonment of the notion of individual souls or selves, though without the implication that therefore there is just one Self. (Where discriminations do not apply, neither do numbers, including the number *one!*) Thus the Buddhist position of, so to say, starting from a pluralistic base but going beyond it is an intelligible development from soul-pluralism. Of course, other motives and reasons entered into the Buddhist denial of the selves, as we saw: it is, for one thing, part of the attack upon the notion of the substantial permanence of things. It is worth remarking too that of all the systems, the Elder Doctrine has the least element of interpretation in its account of the contemplative attainment. Neither Lord nor self is invoked in the description of nirvana. It is thus 'pure' mysticism, not only in the sense of not including worship and devotionalism as central to its concerns—indeed these, especially at an early stage, were quite neglected, and even later given no doctrinal sanction or justification—but also in the sense of having a minimal amount of doctrinal ramifications built into its descriptions.

It is worth commenting too on the way in which the religion of worship is expressed by the notion of a distinction between the Lord and selves. For the attitude of worship, and a sense of the holy or numinous other, as object of worship, implies a distinction between the worshipper and the Object of worship. This has, for instance, a very vivid expression in the prophetic faiths of Semitic origin. But also too in the Indian tradition, the proponents of devotionalism as being the centre of the religious life stress the difference between God and the soul. Thus it is that Madhva and Rāmānuja felt clearly the need to repudiate Śaṅkara's monism, since it ultimately made nonsense of the worship of Viṣṇu as supreme Being. Nevertheless, the strong emphasis on mystical experience in the Indian tradition, with its accompanying tendency to be expressed, where the concept of a Lord was present, as union with that Being, makes intelligible both the Upaniṣadic and the later Absolutistic identifications between the object of worship and the object of mystical experience. The non-duality of the experience, the absence from it of empirical discriminations, etc., lead very naturally to this idea of union. But where the union is interpreted as identity, clearly the notion of a Lord as a distinct being and object of worship is seen to be illusory. What the worshipper sees as an Other is, in the last resort, identical with him. So that in Mahāyāna Absolutism, the devotee in worshipping the Buddha is in effect worshipping his own future state, when he has attained non-dual enlightenment *(bodhi)*. Hence it is of interest to note that many theistic interpretations of the mystical experience attempted to express the union, not as identity, but as a kind of spiritual marriage: here there is intimate union—the most intimate possible—and yet a distinction (expressed in another tradition through the phrase 'one flesh'). Thus, for example, in Śaivite Doctrine, there is the image of Śiva as Lord, who moves the selves through his energy, so that they gain a union with him; and both the energy and the selves are feminine: so there is a marriage, so to say, between the selves and God's energy or grace working in them, and the Lord. It is, of course, clear that a distinction between the Lord and the devotee implies that if there are any eternal selves, there are more than one. That is, dualism goes with self-pluralism. (In principle one supposes that it might be possible to have a doctrine that all selves are united in one Self and that this Self is distinct from the Lord whom it worships; but as far as I know such a doctrine is not propounded in the Indian tradition, and has a certain intuitive bizarreness.) The alliance between dualism and soul-pluralism may indeed help to account for possible Jain influences on Madhva. But at all events, it meant that typical yogic mysticism could be incorporated into, but subordinated to, a devotional theism. Thus we might express the relation between yoga and theism in the orthodox Indian tradition by the following principle: where devotion and meditation are combined, a preponderance of the latter leads to soul-monism, where the Self is identified with ultimate reality; where on the other hand, there is a preponderance of devotion, yoga retains its typical shape as involving a doctrine of soul-pluralism. It is perhaps a paradox (but we have seen already why it is so) that yoga, when it takes on the ambience of a devotionalism it ultimately seeks to swallow, loses its typically pluralistic expression; but when it is tamed by devotionalism it is allowed its doctrine of many selves. These remarks, however, have to be somewhat adapted when dealing with the Buddhist situation. For, as we have seen, it is only a virtual pluralism which is discoverable in the Elder Doctrine. Thus in those later Mahāyāna schools which emphasized the personal nature of ultimate reality, and a religion of devotion, rather at the expence of the contemplative goal which hitherto had formed the centre of Buddhist aspirations, one meets a situation analogous in some ways to that of pre-Christian Judaism: a belief in the Supreme Lord, but no doctrine of the eternity of the self.

There is one further feature of the pattern of Indian religion and metaphysics which needs to be kept in view. Already we have noted, in the case of Exegesis, the phenomenon of 'detachment', whereby an integral element in a form of religion has become detached and made central to the scheme. For 'Exegesis, this element in ritual. There is something similar to be observed in the case of Distinctionism. We have already noted the polarity within one arm of our main polarity between meditation and worship, namely that between reflection upon metaphysical truths as means of salvation and yogic self-training. But the two in fact are integral to one another in a way in which devotionalism and meditation are not. For, as we have repeated frequently enough, the contemplative quest has a conceptual ambience whereby it is interpreted. The doctrines enshrined in that ambience are not merely objects of speculation, but have to be realized existentially through contemplative experience. Thus doctrine and yoga go side by side. Consequently, when knowledge or insight is spoken of in the Indian religious tradition, it does not just mean the kind of theoretical understanding which might accrue from, say, the study of physics. Knowledge is spiritual: and it involves 'seeing' in inner experience the truth of what is taught. Nevertheless, the phenomenon of detachment does occur, so that some distinctionist writers can appear to say that one can gain release from doing metaphysics.

The respective emphasis upon knowledge and yoga accounts for the contrast between the Void and the Idealist schools of the Greater Vehicle. Nāgārjuna's elaborate critique of common-sense concepts and of views about ultimate reality were, of course, intended as part of a process whereby the aspirant could come to the non-dual experience of the Void: it formed an intellectual yoga to be conjoined with the classical methods of Buddhist meditation. But the intellectualist emphasis (a paradoxical one, since the philosophizing was designed ultimately to break down intellectual constructions put upon reality—a kind of metaphysical judo) could easily lead to some neglect of the heart of the Buddhist life. The Idealists, therefore, while holding a general metaphysical position which was pretty close to that of the Void school, preferred to stress the concept of consciousness in their scheme. This reflected the practical training of the Buddhist yogin in purifying his mind of the ordinary discriminations of empirical experience. Thus the relation between the Void school and that of the Yoga-practitioners corresponds somewhat to that between Distinctionism and Yoga *(Yoga)*. But in so far as the Voidist doctrines have remained a living force within the religious life of Buddhism, while Distinctionism tends to serve only as a theoretical background to Yoga and a supplier of cosmological ideas to other schools, one can observe that Distinctionism exhibits the phenomenon of detachment—it is a metaphysical system which has become somewhat removed from its sources in religious experience.

We may note another appearance of detachment. Jainism has the same yogic roots as Distinctionism and Buddhism, though it retained the ideal of inner mystical knowledge, it was also very considerably preoccupied with one aspect of the path of self-discipline. Its rather materialistic notion of karma lent added weight to this tendency to stress asceticism. It was not only in Jainism, of course, that such fierce austerity was practised. Some degree of asceticism is indeed, it appears from the history of religions, integral to contemplative mysticism. But in Jainism there was a trend towards making fierce austerity itself a means of release. The Buddha, who wished to gain enlightenment in experience, and not simply escape from a sorrowful world, evidently found that such an exclusive emphasis on self-mortification was scarcely helpful in this aim. Thus we might say this: while Distinctionism leans towards intellectualism,

Jainism leans in the opposite direction, and again away from the central concern of yoga, towards austerity.

We may sum up our analysis of the systems with a series of thumb-nail sketches, beginning from the right of our table.

Materialism: a repudiation of all religion, but crippled because its scepticism cut at the roots of protoscience.

Elder Doctrine: a scholastic elaboration of early Buddhism, wherein pure mysticism is given a minimal interpretation, but with a pluralistic flavour—it lies genuinely between Jainism and Materialism.

Jainism: contemplative soul-pluralism with archaic roots, but leaning heavily towards the cultivation of austerity.

Exegesis: here ritual has become detached from worship, and neither meditation nor devotion are relevant—so there is heaven without God and without isolation.

Distinctionism: soul-pluralism which has an intellectualist slant, but arises out of yogic mysticism—it is the supplier of cosmology to many systems.

Yoga: atheistic soul-pluralism which has grafted on a Lord, despite its almost exclusive concern with meditation and neglect of genuine devotionalism.

Logic-Atomism: an elaboration of protoscience and of patterns of dialectic, which has conformed to orthodoxy by importing theism.

Śaivite Doctrine: the Śaivite theist's contrast to the Śaivite Śaṅkara, wherein devotionalism infuses the meditative life.

Dualism: the Vaiṣṇavite counterpart to the foregoing: but though formally more theistic (by Western standards) than Rāmānuja, there is a less intense expression of the soul's dependence on God, since devotionalism, though it infuses meditation, is less strongly expressed.

Qualified Non-Dualism: while preserving the appearance of monism, it emphasizes God's grace and the soul's dependence—it shows most strongly the logic of devotion at work in the Indian tradition.

Idealism: here the Buddhist yogi stresses a side that could be neglected in Voidist Absolutism.

Voidism: the Absolutism par excellence of Buddhism, wherein mysticism is expressed monistically, because of a strong injection into the Buddhist tradition of devotionalism.

Non-Dualism: like the foregoing, it is an expression of contemplative religion which incorporates, rather than ignores, the religion of worship.

So much for our general analysis. The account involves reference to one main polarity—between worship and yoga. Within each arm there are others: between the devotional side and the ritual, in the case of worship; between knowledge and meditation on the yogic side. The detachment of ritual from its proper objects (God or the gods) led to the Exegete position; the detachment of metaphysical knowledge from its roots in mysticism led to the Distinctionist position. Likewise the powerful emphasis on austerity (some degree of which is an element in all yoga) was expressed by the Jains. Our whole account is, quite obviously, a tremendous simplification of the complex facts. But it is to be hoped that thus the wood can be distinguished, and not, as so often, only the trees. It involves too the assumption that the determination of metaphysics by forms of religious experience and practice occurs that way round and not conversely. Now it is of course perfectly true that individuals are much influenced by the doctrines which they are taught and in this sense it is certainly true that theology and metaphysics are in some degree determinative of religious experience. Nevertheless, the assumption, as a general thesis, requires little justification—it would be indeed odd if metaphysics, considered as sets of propositions to be entertained and believed by people, should have the enormous effect of creating out of nothing the powerful religious experiences of both great teachers and ordinary folk. It is easier to explain a dualism between God and the soul by reference to the experience of prophets and worshippers than to explain the latter by reference to a current doctrine of dualism. It is easier to see that the Lord who is worshipped is also the God of metaphysics than to see why the God of metaphysics should be worshipped at all. In any event, if the correlations between doctrines and forms of religious life in the Indian tradition which I have been outlining is a valid one, some light will have been thrown on the situation.

I have, of course, not attempted to argue that one shape of metaphysics is better than any other. Nor have I attempted to argue for or against the veridical nature of devotional or meditative experience. These issues lie quite outside the tasks of description and analysis, though of course these tasks are relevant to the questions of truth. One has to understand in order to believe—or not believe.

Part II

CHAPTER XI

ARGUMENTS FOR AND AGAINST THE EXISTENCE OF GOD

Although religious concerns are, as we have seen, prominent throughout nearly all Indian metaphysics, the atheistic character of much Indian religion has meant that there has been a lot of discussion about the existence of a Creator or Lord, and about the validity of arguments adduced for his existence. These are varied in character. First, arguments for the truth of revelation are often by implication reasons for belief in God (though, of course, revelation was often interpreted in a non-theistic sense). Second, some supposed proofs of the Lord's existence depend on particular features of a viewpoint. Third, some depend on concepts, such as karma, peculiar to the Indian tradition. Then there are arguments, such as the Teleological, which do not so depend. We shall also note some considerations of a theological or doctrinal nature which are introduced into the discussion. Ranged against all these 'proofs' there are some powerful counter-arguments.

The doubtfulness of such proofs has not, however, always been taken in an anti-theistic sense. For the truth of revelation may still be affirmed, and any emphasis upon divine grace can be taken to imply that it is through God's revealing activity, rather than the intellectual efforts of men, that the truth about him is known. In this connection, a variety of positions is adopted. First, there is the rationalistic approach of the Logic-Atomist school: revelation is valid, because it is the work of an omniscient author, and the existence of the latter can be established by inference. Thus the trustworthiness of scripture is not intrinsic, but is based upon the theistic proofs. Second, at the other extreme, Rāmānuja argues that the proofs are doubtful, because of the powerful objections which can be raised against them. Belief in God therefore rests solely upon revelation. Madhva, thirdly, represents an intermediate position—namely, that though the proofs themselves are doubtful if the truth of revelation is in question, they may become convincing if that truth is already conceded.

But even acceptance of revelation does not settle matters, since, as has been said above, atheistic interpretations of the scriptures were common, as in Distinctionism and Exegesis. Thus the appeal to revelation, in connection with God's existence, needs to be backed by showing that a theistic interpretation of the words of revelation is correct. Nevertheless, it is useful to note here some of the grounds which were advanced for the validity of the scriptures.

One position is simply to say that revelation is simply self-authenticated—a basis of knowledge in itself, comparable to perception *(pratyakṣa)* and inference. Nevertheless, not only is there a wide range of analyses of the character of revelation itself, but also subsidiary grounds for the validity of the texts have in fact been adduced. Under the first head, though Indian religious thought has often considered revelation in a quite straightforward way, as consisting in certain words, viz. the Vedic writings, etc., there are other interpretations which radically affect their status, and thereby shift the locus of arguments about revelation. Thus, for instance, Śaṅkara's division between higher and ordinary knowledge is taken to imply that revelation belongs to the latter—save only the identity-texts, i.e. those passages which affirm the identity of the Self with the Absolute. Yet even these disappear, so to say, in the state of realization and release. In other words, the scriptures are valid at the higher level in so far as they point towards a certain supreme experience. In the last resort, therefore, their truth is pragmatic and provisional. What confirms them is direct experience, and by then they are useless. This clearly modifies considerably the concept of their being self-authenticated. Here Śaṅkara's view is not far from that of Yoga, namely that the scriptures originate from the supreme perception or intuition of yogis. Hence the issue about the validity of revelation is shifted to that of the trustworthiness of mystical—in particular, yogic—experience. On this, the Exegete Kumārila raised a central problem: the experience of the individual may be delusory and so has to be checked by other evidence. Likewise the Jains argued that in so far as spiritual intuition is appealed to in establishing the existence of a Lord, it is as well to ask whether the belief in a Lord derives from the experience or conversely. Kumārila went on to affirm that the other evidence needed to check the intuition was provided by scripture, which is itself accepted by the general consensus.

The Yoga and Non-Dualist positions, as might on other grounds have been expected, have analogies to the scriptural attitude of Buddhism. Thus the authority of the Buddhist writings derives from that of the great Teacher; and the content of their teachings in turn originates from his supreme knowledge or enlightenment. Hence, with the growth of Greater Vehicle ideals, and the notion that the adept himself can achieve Buddhahood, it was not surprising that the ultimate significance or reference of the scriptures should be thought of as the non-dual experience, i.e. the mystical experience of identification with the Absolute, which is also the Truth-Body of all the Buddhas. But in so far as both the Jain and Elder schools held that the authority of scripture derives from the omniscience (differently conceived) of the respective Teachers, there is an analogy with the Logic viewpoint. This generated a wry problem for Vaiṣṇavite theology when the Buddha came to be conceived as an incarnation *(avatāra)* of Viṣṇu: one writer used the situation to argue for the inherent validity of revelation (as opposed to its deriving its trustworthiness from someone's—even God's—omniscience), by pointing out that the Buddha is divine and yet deceived people with false teachings.

Regarding subsidiary grounds for holding that revelation is genuine, it was often argued that its self-authentication implies its eternity (as we saw in Chapter IV, regarding the school of Exegesis)—on the ground that if it ever comes into existence this must be through some agent and then the authentication would belong to the agent. Hence, it was held that it was without personal authorship *(apauruṣeya)*. This was peculiarly important for Exegesis, since this viewpoint denied a Lord and was distrustful of yogic intuition, and mysticism in general. Hence, arguments were adduced against the human authorship of the Veda: for example, that tradition asserts this, that revelation teaches the everlasting law *(dharma)* which necessarily precedes human beings, that revelation introduces extra, supernatural knowledge not given in human experience, etc. These arguments were apologetically important, since they tended to assign to the Veda a superiority over Buddhist and Jain writings, which admittedly owed their origin and authority to persons.

It will be seen from the foregoing that appeal to scriptures was by itself scarcely persuasive in connection with the Lord's existence. Let us now turn to more direct arguments. First, there are one or two depending fairly closely on certain features in particular viewpoints. For instance, there is the interesting Logic-Atomist argument relating to atoms. As we saw, macroscopic entities in the cosmos are built up out of infinitesimally small atoms, and the Atomists postulated two quantum jumps whereby atoms were built up into a dyad, then a triad—the latter having a finite magnitude, by the addition of which the magnitudes of macroscopic entities are generated. We also saw that only unity, but not duality or plurality, inheres in substances: the number of a combination of atoms is thus due to connective understanding—i.e. it is mind-dependent. It follows therefore that at the end of a period of cosmic dissolution—when atoms begin to combine again in a new era of creation, and when there are so far no rational beings within the cosmos (they require bodies, which are built up from atoms)—there must be an extra-cosmic mind. And this is the Lord.

It may be noted that the non-theistic Atomism discussed by Rāmānuja is criticized for the inexplicability of the quantum jump. The introduction of number as the cause, to patch up the theory, raised the epistemological problem solved by the postulation of the Lord as the perceiver of number. But it can always be replied that here, as elsewhere in the theistic arguments, the introduction of God is a sign of theoretical inadequacy.

Another argument which closely depends on idoiosyncratic features of a particular viewpoint is one which stems from the Non-Dualistic thesis that there is only one eternal Self, identified with the Absolute. It follows from this that any proof of the existence of the Self is thereby a kind of theistic argument. In so far, however, as this identification depends upon revelation, or upon a particular interpretation thereof, an essential link in the argument is theological rather than metaphysical. Further, the Power, though it is the supreme reality (according to Non-dualism), is different in concept from creative Lord. In the last resort, the latter, like the empirical world, is part of the grand illusion. Thus the proof of the Lord's existence via the proofs of an eternal self, whether single or plural, represents too extensive a topic to enter into now—and is indeed dealt with in part elsewhere, in Chapter XII.

As well as arguments which depend closely on features of given viewpoints, there is one which presupposes a characteristic Indian religious concept—that of karma. Thus in Śaivite Doctrine, two connected considerations are advanced. First, the doctrine of karma implies that there is an apportionment of good and evil in accordance with a person's deeds. But this apportionment presupposes a perfect knowledge of the moral law, and therefore only the Lord can regulate karma. Second, karma is non-intelligent, and so cannot operate on its own. Nor can disembodied selves, who are without causal power, appropriate to themselves their karma. So some further regulator of karma is required, and this must be God. A similar point is made by Yoga, in rejecting the completely adequate teleology of nature in atheistic Distinctionism.

But the notion that karma is self-operative is too deeply entrenched in Indian religious thought for such arguments to meet with much agreement: and it is commonly urged that karma as an unseen force suffices to explain what would otherwise require an intelligent creator or governor of the world. Moreover, theism and analogous beliefs (such as belief in celestial Buddhas in the Great Vehicle), by making release depend, in some degree at least, upon God, and by therefore considerably modifying the operation of karma, were often held to weaken the sense of individual effort. This is a main reason for the rejection of theism in Jainism and Elder Buddhism. Likewise such beliefs cut at the roots of ritualism as defended by Exegesis. Nevertheless, the fact that, in Logic-Atomism and elsewhere, the operation of karma has been subsumed under the head of an unseen force indicates some of the difficulty there has been in conceiving its mechanism. But given the truth of the doctrine of rebirth, for which independent arguments were advanced (see Chapter XII), it has not been felt implausible in the Indian tradition to consider karma as a law of nature happily or unhappily geared into the moral law.

We now come to arguments which are more general, i.e. they do not closely depend upon features of particular viewpoints or upon any specific religious assumption. The most important of these can roughly be described as a version of the Teleological Argument. It occasioned a comprehensive critique by Rāmānuja. The argument is stated in the *Kusumāñjali* of Udayana (a Logic-Atomist) and else-where. The bare bones are these: that the cosmos is of the nature of an effect, since it is made up of parts. Thus, having an analogy to artifacts, it requires an intelligent author. A secondary argument is that the cosmos has an analogy to a complex organic body, and therefore depends for its functioning on an intelligent principle.

The notion that the cosmos is an effect was criticized by the Jains. If the criterion of being an effect is that something is made up of parts, then space ought to be regarded as such—and yet the Logic-Atomists recognized space as being eternal and thus uncreated. On the other hand, if we adopt another plausible criterion, that of changeability, there is trouble: for if the Lord is supposed to create at a particular time or period, then this represents a change in him; and by parity of reasoning, he is an effect and needs a further Creator—and so on. On the first point, the Logic-Atomists replied that a part is what enters into combination, and so is capable of change in location; this is not true of 'parts' of space. We only speak of such 'parts' of space because they become enclosed by physical entities, and it is only *as if* space were divided into segments. Nevertheless, difficulties occasioned by such arguments as the second Jain point described above led the Logic-Atomists to formulate the argument in a more explicitly teleological form: it is because mountains, etc., have an analogy to artifacts in being wholes made of parts, that one can infer an intelligent agent. To the point that we do not perceive intelligent agents producing wild rice, etc., and have no right to infer to such unseen agencies, it was replied that critics believed that change of place was associated with motion: and yet, though the sun's change of place is perceptible, its motion is not.

Rāmānuja criticizes the above Logic-Atomist arguments on a number of grounds, the chief of which are as follows. First, experience shows that pots, etc., are produced by intelligent agents. But as the material causes of the earth, oceans, etc., are unknown, and as we have not observed their being produced, we have no right to infer an intelligent agent. Second, the existence of an organic body made up of a complex of parts only requires the combination of those parts in a specially intimate relation: there is hence no need to postulate a soul or self as keeping the body together. Third, in any event, intelligence is not the only condition of the continued existence of an organic body. Fourth, there is no strong analogy between organic bodies and nature: e.g. animated bodies characteristically have the property of breathing, but this is not true of the earth, sea, mountains, etc. Fifth, even if the argument were valid, there is no reason to hold that the world has been produced by a single agent: it might have been produced by many finite selves acting in concert. It may be objected that such selves would, in being finite, be ignorant of the material causes, etc., required for the production of the world. But craftsmen can make pots, etc., perfectly well without a full insight into the nature of their materials. Sixth, is the cosmos supposed to have been produced all at one time, or in successive phases? The former supposition is unwarranted, since we have no evidence that the cosmos was created at one time. The second supposition would support the wrong conclusion—for experience shows that effects produced at different times are produced by different agents. Thus we would have to infer creation by many selves rather than by a single Lord. Seventh, we only have experience of inferring a finite agent from certain kinds of things, i.e. artifacts. But we have no experience upon which to base an inference to an omnipotent,omniscient Spirit. Thus we could only legitimately infer a finite self, and this conflicts with the definition of God. Eighth, finite agents operate through their bodies. But if we ascribe a body to the Lord we are allowing that something made of parts can be eternal. But in this case the cosmos can be so regarded and there is no need to infer a creator. If on the other hand the Lord is bodiless this destroys the basis of the inference: for we only have experience of effects produced by embodied agents. Ninth, the stronger the proof, the greater the supposed similarity between finite beings and the Lord. But the Lord is infinitely good, possessing all excellences, and it is therefore repugnant to religious feeling that God should be closely compared with the imperfect beings of this world.

To some at least of the above arguments the Logic-Atomists were able to produce apparently reasonable replies. For example, there is nothing intrinsically impossible in the production of an effect by pure volition. Thus the Lord could bodilessly create the cosmos. The notion that every agent requires a body bristles with difficulties in regard to the self. If the self can, through volitions, move its body, then it is nonsense to suppose it requires a body to do it: for then there would be a viciously infinite hierarchy of intermediate bodies between the body and the self. But it should be noted that some of the disputation here reflected different views of the self: for practically all Indian schools the self or soul is quite distinct from the psycho-physical organism, and is thus only *associated* with the faculties of volition, cognition, etc.; but the Logic- Atomists, by using the category of inherence, were able to hold that volition, etc., could inhere in the self—this in turn made possible the thesis that eternal volition inheres in the Lord. In effect, the notion of inherence bridges the self-body gap. Nevertheless, the Logic-Atomists held that there was no intrinsic or necessary connection between a soul and its body, whereas, as we shall see, the notion of a bodiless self was regarded as nonsensical by the Qualified Non-Dualists. But the Logic-Atomist doctrine allowed them to conceive of a bodiless being in whom volition, etc., inhere. Moreover, as an *ad hominem* argument, they urged that if an opponent insisted that a physical body must invest the Lord, atoms would fulfil this function: but this was, of course, merely an *ad hominem* point, not a doctrine.

Again, in relation to Rāmānuja's and similar criticisms, it was argued that though the cosmos is greater in scale than pots, etc., objection to teleological inferences on this ground would rule out the inference of a person who on first seeing an enormous palace infers that it is the work of an intelligent agent or agents. This raises the question of whether the cosmos could have been produced by a committee of gods. It was argued that either there is a great God who co-ordinates the work of the others, in which case the postulation of the latter is unnecessary, or there is the likelihood of chaos, and this is not borne out by experience.

The Teleological Argument is also found in Śaivite Doctrine: the world as a single complex whole requires one mind to focus the work towards a unified product. Finite souls and matter are inadequate for this task (we may note that, as with the karma argument disembodied selves are here regarded as causally inert). Madhva provided another variant to the argument, namely that the orderly interrelation of selves in the world requires a Lord as co-ordinator. For if any one self had control over the others, the others would have this power also, and the result would be chaos. This is in line with his view of the Lord as guiding the inner determination of the selves.

We have already discussed the atomic argument of Logic- Atomism, which depends upon a particular view about number and quanta. But there is a more general argument from movement, namely that the paradigm case of movement is volitional—e.g. when I raise my arm. Therefore, movement in general needs to be interpreted in the light of this paradigm. Thus atoms, being material entities, are in themselves inert, and their combination, after a period of cosmic dissolution, can only be explained by reference to an intelligent being capable of volitions, or to many intelligent beings. But such finite selves require bodies for their agency, and bodies are complexes of atoms. However, Atomism of the early period was not theistic, and such concepts as gravity (to explain the falling of bodies), unseen force (to explain the circulation of fluids in plants and so on), etc., indicated that no intrinsic difficulty was felt in assigning motion to inanimate objects quite independently of volitional activity. This indeed forms the substance of the Exegete reply to the argument.

The sharp antithesis between soul and body—or more accurately between the self and the psycho-physical organism—in so much of traditional Indian thought provided an argument which might seem paradoxically opposed to the above one. The Śaivite Doctrine argued that the Lord is required to explain the bringing together of selves and bodies. The self is incapable of action without a body, and so cannot (so to speak) clothe itself in a body on its own initiative. But it must be remembered that the real distinction comes between self and organism, as has been indicated above, and not between mind and body. That is, volitional activity was normally conceived as a phenomenon of the material world. It can therefore the more easily serve as a paradigm of other kinds of change within that world. But this, of course, places the difficulty in another locus, and it is therefore a stock argument against such supposed proofs of the Lord's existence that he cannot be effective unless he is embodied in a psycho-physical organism, and then the inference ought to be repeated to account for his body, and so on *ad infinitum*. Again, the dispute has its roots in divergent views of the self.

We have already referred briefly to a Yoga argument. Two others are of interest. A passage in the *Yogabhāṣya* (i.24) (i.e. the commentary on the Yoga aphorisms or *Yogasūtra*) has sometimes been seen as reminiscent of the Ontological Argument of Anselm and others. It is this. 'The Lord's pre-eminence is altogether without anything equal to it or excelling it. For... it cannot be excelled by any other pre-eminence, since whatever might seem to excel it would itself turn out to be that very pre-eminence. Therefore that is the Lord wherein we reach this uppermost limit of pre-eminence.' Further, two equals are impossible, for when they simultaneously desire the same thing, one will necessarily be frustrated and thus will be inferior to the other. But all this differs from the classical Ontological Argument in a number of ways: chiefly because it is an argument to show that the most perfect being is God, and is unique; and because existence as such is not treated as a perfection.

The other interesting argument is more conclusive, since it does not merely try to show that the most perfect being that there is the Lord, but that this being must be omniscient. It is argued that there are grades of knowledge and that there must be a perfect limit to this series, viz. omniscience. But such a property must belong to a distinct soul, namely to the most perfect being, the Lord. But Exegesis found difficulty in this concept. Ordinary perception could not give the Lord knowledge of all things past and present and future. Hence some suprasensible mode of knowledge must be employed. But if this is possible for a self, what is the use of the senses? Another objection, against the general notion of such an inference, is noted below, on p. 201.

There are a few further counter-arguments to theistic belief used in Indian traditional thought. Notably the problem of evil weighed heavily with the Buddha and others. Again, there was difficulty in conceiving God's motive in creating, as he is supposed to be totally self-sufficient and perfect. Again, if the existence of the world pre-supposes a God, the existence of such a Creator presuppoes a meta-Creator and so on. (It is entertaining that in the Upaniṣads, a Brahmin's wife who raises a similar question, namely what sustains the Power sustaining the world, is told that she asks too many questions.) If you can stop at any stage, to evade an infinity of Gods beyond God, why not stop at the first stage and affirm that the cosmos is uncreated?

The theistic arguments also raised questions about the nature of inference. Early Indian Materialism rejected inference, and in particular inductive inference, on the ground that a generalization would always be liable to perceptual falsification. Even if one could observe all positive instances of a concomitance, furthermore, it would be impossible to observe all negative instances, i.e. the invariable concomitance of non-A with non-B. However, as noted, Purandara (seventh century C. E.) allowed inference from what is perceptible to what is perceptible, but not—and here we can see one of the main Materialist motives for questioning the validity of inference—inferences to the imperceptible. Orthodox theologians used these to establish truths about the transcendent realm. Logic-Atomism gave such analogical inference a special name (see p. 80): it was of course a necessary form of reasoning if the existence of theoretically-unobservable atoms were to be supported by argument. Likewise Distinctionism had to use this sort of inference to establish the existence of an underlying nature and eternal souls. But the ban on analogical inference to the unseen imposed too drastic a limit on physical speculations, and so the Materialists were in the position of undermining both protoscience and theology.

Such then were the main issues clustering round Indian theism. Certain other arguments, such as that arts and crafts are handed down traditionally, but are not known to have human authorship—so that it is reasonable to ascribe their origin to the Lord—need not detain us. The fact that different viewpoints and systems of religious belief lived together from a very early period meant that there was plenty of opportunity for debate about disagreements—and the issue of the existence of a Creator was one of these. But it became fairly clear that arguments for God's existence could at best be a subsidiary means of persuasion, as Madhva held. Of more importance, perhaps, was the assumption that religious experience gives an insight into the nature of ultimate reality. This remains central to modern Hindu and Buddhist arguments and apologetics.

CHAPTER XII
ARGUMENTS ABOUT REBIRTH AND THE SOUL

While there was considerable debate, in the Indian tradition, about the existence of God, since atheistic viewpoints were well represented, there is surprisingly little argument which seeks to establish the truth of the doctrine of rebirth. The main reason for this is that only the Materialists denied the belief. Otherwise both orthodox and unorthodox schools were in agreement about it. With the virtual demise of Materialism in mediaeval India, rebirth no longer was a live issue. However, arguments on the topic are not entirely lacking; and some of the points raised have a wider interest, because they bear on the mind-body problem. It is not, moreover, easy to disentangle discussions of rebirth from those about the eternity of the soul or self. Clearly, objections to rebirth tended also to be objections to eternalism *(sassatavāda)* or immortality. Also entangled with discussions about rebirth were those about the manner in which karma operates: since karma and rebirth in effect constitute a single complex of doctrine. It is true that one early Indian teacher held that release is simply the consequence of a person's unalterable destiny, and not connected with human works, and at a much later time the doctrine of grace had a like effect. But otherwise, the idea of rebirth was associated with the belief that one's status in future lives, and the chance of release, depend upon human action.

The principal considerations urged against rebirth by the Materialists were three. First every macroscopic object can be explained as due to a particular blend of material elements. It is therefore necessary to explain consciousness as a product of matter. Admittedly, consciousness possesses some peculiar properties; but similarly the intoxicating quality of certain substances differs from the qualities of the elements which go to make up those substances. Just as intoxicating power supervenes upon certain material processes, so consciousness supervenes when matter is arranged as a certain kind of organism. Second, different types of consciousness are produced in different kinds of animal body: it is an absurdity that the same individual consciousness could successively inhabit the body of an elephant and a man. Third, there is no memory of previous lives, and it is simpler to suppose that the self arises with the body and ceases with it. Of these three arguments the second depends upon the first, since the main ground for holding that types of consciousness differ is the difference in the bodily constitution and behaviour of the different organisms.

One of the difficulties which was felt in the Materialist intoxicant analogy was that the self was known introspectively as a unity, which, so to say, underlies the various states of consciousness. The Materialist thesis seems to give no explanation of this introspective awareness. Furthermore, it is obvious that conscious states do possess qualities not shared by physical states, and the question of whether consciousness is an emergent characteristic from combinations of material elements can only be settled by showing that conscious states do not exist independently of the particular body with which they may for some time be associated. Certainly, it was argued, some mental states can be described without reference to bodily states; and so it must remain an open question as to whether they can actually exist independently of a given body. This is where we are liable to get into inductive difficulties, in trying to apply the method of agreement and difference to the co-existence of minds and bodies.

Thus an ingenious Buddhist Idealist argument went as follows. The concomitance of mental and bodily states can only be perceived directly by oneself; but the causal dependence of the mind on bodily states in the early stage of an individual's life cannot be observed, since there is as yet no consciousness and therefore no perception. But in regard to other people, one cannot observe their minds, and so cannot observe the dependence of their mental states upon their physical states. Conversely, we cannot now on the basis of observation tell whether at death mental states cease. And for the same reason as that given above, a negative observation is impossible on the death of other people. It follows that there cannot be the normal inductive grounds either for believing in or for disbelieving in survival and pre-existence.

Nevertheless (the Buddhists argued), there could be a general argument in favour of the belief, if once it is admitted that some mental states are not totally caused by physical states. Since every event has a cause, such a mental state must have some prior mental state as part-cause at least. Now consider the first non-physically caused (i.e. not totally caused by physical states) mental state in the life of an individual. It must necessarily have as its part-cause a mental state occurring before the conception of the individual. Thus pre-existence is established, and by analogy, post-existence. It is interesting to note that Western philosophers, because of a different religious background, have rarely inferred reincarnation from dualistic premisses.

The above Buddhist argument incorporates the thesis that every event has a cause. Emphasis should here be placed on the expression *event*. Nirvana, for instance, is causeless, on Buddhist theory, but it is not strictly an event, and it is permanent. That is, all impermanent states have causes; and if something were causeless it would be permanent. Thus they argued that if the first conscious state of an individual were causeless, it would be permanent: there would be no reason for it to cease. But this is not borne out in experience.

The Buddhist argument, of course, does not depend upon establishing the existence of a soul or self. Indeed the Buddhists were heavily committed to denying any such doctrine. However, the argument does (we may allow) at least show the possibility of rebirth, even if inductive evidence of the best sort can never be forthcoming. It would obviously be strengthened if empirical support for the hypothesis could be provided. In particular, it was important to say something about the third point made by the Materialists, viz. that there is no memory of prior lives. To these empirical arguments, both of the Buddhists and others, we shall turn in a moment. Meanwhile, briefly, an account of Buddhist reasons for the premiss that some mental states are not totally caused by physical ones can be outlined: first, that the non-perceptibility of the mind indicates that it is not of the same stuff as the body, but *sui generis*, and like effects require like causes. Second, personal identity is a product of memory; but this sense of the individual's unity could not be caused by the body, as being some sort of unitary object, for the body is continually changing and its unity is imposed upon it by the mind, through the mind's *regarding* it as a unity.

The empirical arguments recur in various places in the Indian tradition. First, the Materialist argument about memory was dealt with both positively and negatively: positively, by pointing to instances, or alleged instances, of the memory of former births, both conscious and unconscious. Thus it was claimed of the Buddha and Buddhist saints that they could remember the details of countless previous lives; again, examples of people recognizing places and persons, etc., and being able to supply information about them not based on observation, are used to indicate that they have had experience of them in previous existences. Thus it was believed to be by no means infrequent for yogins and the like to recall earlier lives. Negatively (as against the Materialists) it was urged that the processes of death and then birth were sufficiently traumatic to erase all or nearly all memories. Thus the fact that lots of people have no conscious remembrance of pre-existence should not be accounted a very grave objection.

Two or three other straightforwardly empirical arguments were employed. The instinctive behaviour of children (their capacity to suck milk, for instance) was traced to learning in a previous life; likewise their apparently unaccountable joys and sorrows. Also, the inequalities in character as between various children of the same parents was held to indicate the operation of karma, as indeed was the fact that children differ in their characteristics from their parents. Caraka, the medical writer, also adduced the supposed spontaneous generation of certain insects as evidence: for if characteristics are handed on solely by heredity from the parents, such a phenomenon ought to be impossible. It was thus generally assumed in India that some undetectable mental or karmic causes co-operated with the sperm and ovum, etc., in the determination of the make-up of offspring.

The facts of parentage also provided a further difficulty for those who believed in a self. The self is deemed to be partless and indivisible.

It follows that the foetus cannot get its soul from its parents, as it would then have to transmigrate in bits. Moreover, if the self or soul comes from the parents, and if each person has only one soul, the migration (*per impossible*) of the souls, or bits of the souls, of the parents to the child would involve the death of the parents.

As well as these empirical and partly empirical arguments, religious grounds for the doctrine were employed. The great merit, of course, of the twin ideas of rebirth and karma is, from the religious point of view, their mitigation of the problem of evil. Thus theists could hold that the miseries of existence can all be traced to the actions of living beings, and so physical evil is swallowed up in moral evil. The world, for all its troubles, looks a thoroughly just place, once rebirth is accepted (and provided a retributory theory of punishment is accepted too). The Materialists on the other hand objected that the distribution of happiness and unhappiness in accordance with merit and demerit, as supposed by the theory of karma, runs flatly contrary to much of our experience—for we observe the wicked prospering and the virtuous suffering.

A second theological consideration in favour of rebirth (which, however, is not as far as I know explicitly argued in the Indian tradition, but lies behind much of the religious reasoning and attitudes expressed therein) is the fact that belief in the doctrine chimes in with the idea that there are different grades of spiritual attainment: thus the person of lowly stature now may gain a higher position in the next life...and so on. It is no doubt because of belief in rebirth that Indian views on conversion and in general on religious education are much more permissive than those which derive from the Semitic faiths. Thirdly, at the theological level, it is argued by Caraka, among others, that the scriptures teach the doctrine of rebirth (he is here referring to certain portions of the Upaniṣads, for in the early part of revelation the doctrine was unknown); and since revelation and theologians teach other things for human welfare, for instance moral duties, it is reasonable to suppose that this testimony too is reliable.

The theory of rebirth, together with its twin, the concept of karma, presents certain difficulties to the various viewpoints about the mechanism whereby rebirth, etc., occurs. Thus, as we have seen (p. 85), the Logic-Atomists, because of their belief in rebirth, were obliged to suppose that causality at a distance could occur, at least in the spatial sense. Moreover, their concept of the unseen force as determining the destiny of living beings in effect constituted an evasion of the problem of how karma actually operated. On the other hand, the common doctrine in the Indian tradition that the self or soul is all-pervasive helped to make the concept of causation at a distance acceptable: since it was a determination via the all-pervasive soul of the moral forces left over from a prior embodiment. However, although the early Indian view of karma (doubtless of non-Aryan provenance) was that it operates as a kind of natural law, and that really there was no further problem once one had stated that this was how the world was, later metaphysicians tended to ask how karma operated; and, as we have seen (p. 146), the theists argued that since the operation of karma implies an understanding of the moral law it presupposes the existence of an intelligent being (namely the Lord) to apply it. In short the unquestioned (save among the Materialists) acceptance of karma was used as a theistic proof. But, as we have also seen, the concept of a self-regulating 'moral law' was so deeply ingrained in the Indian imagination that such a proof was hardly likely to be persuasive of the unpersuaded.

The notion that karma was the will of the Lord was not the only way in which the concept of karma as a self-regulating natural law was modified.The doctrine of the transfer of merit in the Great Vehicle implied that through faith rather than the works of self-discipline, etc., the devotee could gain paradise, and thereby propitious circumstances for the attainment of nirvana. Yet early Buddhism (most probably), Elder Buddhism and Jainism were much concerned to defend the self-regulative character of karma: salvation was essentially through self-reliance: and there was fear of the antinomian tendencies of the notion of reliance on others (e.g. the Lord). Likewise the Buddha was concerned to attack early Indian fatalism, which contemporaneously had some currency. He was impressed by the fact that knowledge of causes gives one the opportunity to influence what will happen, so that a proper understanding of the mode of operation of karma should in no way involve fatalistic conclusions.

It is interesting to observe that in so far as Indian philosophers discussed freedom of the will (and this was but slightly), the topic arose in connection either with karma or with God's control of us. For the thesis that all human acts are the result of prior causes was almost inevitably interpreted by reference to the self-regulating law of karma. Thus the problem of free will takes on the form of the question: 'Is it possible by present or future acts to alter the causal sequence already set in train by our previous deeds?' The answer was generally agreed to be 'Yes', on account of the fact that we can perform good deeds which make our future more favourable and, more importantly, in various ways annihilate existing karma or neutralize its effects. The problem in relation to God's control was, of course, a different one. Here the Qualified Non-Dualist answer (it was especially a difficulty for them because of their stress on the dependence of the self on the Lord) was that God gives persons freedom to perform what they desire, and arranges the results in accordance with their desires, by a sort of occasionalism (see above, p. 102). Thus souls are not under compulsion from the Lord. Madhva, on the other hand, though he taught a kind of predestination (e.g. that some selves are destined for eternal punishment in hell, etc.), held that in any event the career of the self was the consequence of an inner determination by its specific nature, different from that of every other self. This was one reason for his doctrine of relative particulars (see above, p. 108).

We have already noted one sort of difficulty, regarding rebirth, which is provided by the facts of reproduction. Still, the need to postulate some bridge, so to say, between one life and another, given the truth of rebirth doctrine, was one consideration in favour of the doctrine of a soul. Yet the concept of the bridge was one of the features of self theory criticized by the Buddhists, in their general onslaught on the belief in a permanent self. We have noted above that, according to their concept of causation, momentary events have momentary causes. In principle, an eternal cause should have eternal effects. But since the events of a person's life are momentary, or at least non-eternal, it follows that the postulation of a self would not help to explain anything about actual events. It would therefore be equally useless as serving as a bridge between one life and the next. If causation boils down to 'first this event occurs, then that,' then it is sufficient to describe the conditions which precede the start of a new life. According to Buddhism, these consist in the conditions of a dying person still in the grip of craving.

The argument from causation was by no means the only, or the most important, Buddhist anti-self argument. There was also, and secondly, the argument from introspection: namely that when one examines the contents of one's experience all one is aware of is the groups (i.e. classes of mental and physical states—see above, pp. 29-30). This raised the question of what, in that case, the word 'I' refers to (and for that matter, proper names, such as 'Nāgasena'). It was argued that these are merely conventional designations, which do not reflect any separate entities in the world. It was not to be thought that because words like 'blue' stand for states of blueness, that therefore there is a state of 'I-ness' reflected by the word. An analysis of supposed substances shows that they are merely congeries of evanescent states. Thus, in general, words for substances are merely conventional labels which we find useful in ordinary intercourse. Further, the sense of personal identity, to which soul theorists appeal, can be explained through the functioning of memory.

However, the Personalist school of Buddhism was uneasy about the destruction of the individual in this manner; and held that there must be something which supports the groups (they appealed to a well-known scriptural passage in which the Buddha is described as referring to the 'carrier of the burden', which seems to bear the implication that there is some sort of ego which carries the burden of the groups: but probably this passage, taken in the context of the whole of the Buddha's non-self teaching, was given undue weight by the Personalists. But the person was necessarily manifested through the states of consciousness and so on comprehended under the classification of groups. Thus the admission of a person, it was held, did not entail the dread heresy of eternalism. This view was suggestive for other Buddhists (not sharing this doctrine) who wished to combat the argument that memory of previous experience implies the existence of an underlying self existing from the time of the previous experience until the present memory, and so by analogy throughout the individual's past and future. Even if, it was argued by the Buddhists, memory requires a subject, it does not follow that the self remembering something now is identical with the subject of the experience remembered, occurring some time back.

We remarked earlier (pp. 89-90) that Śaṅkara's Non-Dualism comes close to the Buddhist non-self doctrine, in its denial of individual selves (whereas all other orthodox schools affirmed a soul-pluralism of one kind or another). The Non-Dualist transmigrating self corresponds very closely to the Buddhist transmigrating individual. Nevertheless, it would be unwise to exaggerate the similarity. It still remains true that the Non-Dualists wished to argue for an eternal something which underlies individual experiences. Thus they found themselves in argument against the Buddhists on the issue of the Self. Thus, for instance, they objected, as against the preceding Buddhist argument, that the memory of a prior event does involve the identity of the two subjects (the subject of the memory and that of the prior experience), for otherwise it would be proper to conclude 'I am identical with that other person who had that experience' rather than 'I am the same person as I was then'.

We have seen, in the chapter on Non-Dualism, that Śaṅkara made use of an argument reminiscent of Descartes': that doubt itself certifies a self, for there must be a self to doubt. But the Non-Dualists objected to the Logic-Atomist thesis that the self is known through *inference*: i.e. on the basis of certain experiences one infers that there must be a subject of such experiences. If the inference is supposed to take the form: 'Here are some experiences, etc.: they must belong to some self', one runs into the difficulty that I have no guarantee that these experiences are mine rather than someone else's. Thus in order to distinguish my experiences from someone else's I must already know them as *mine*. So in order to make the inference work its conclusion must already be known. Consequently, the Non-Dualists held that the self is intuited immediately, or (to use their more colourful expression) the self is self-luminous *(svaprakāśa)*.

The Qualified Non-Dualist arguments on this topic partly overlapped with those of the Non-Dualists. It was urged, first, that in locutions such as 'I know' it is implied that there is a self which is the subject of knowledge, etc., and that such locutions are different in character from 'This is my body' and the like, because their reference is clearly different. Second, in certain states, notably that of rapt concentration, there is no association of experience with the body: i.e. in describing the state, there is no reference to bodily states. Third, the locution 'This is my body' implies that I possess the body and am therefore something other than the body. Unfortunately, the phrase 'my self' also occurs in Sanskrit and might seem, by a like argument, to show that there is a self beyond the self; or alternatively that the self is not to be distinguished from the body (for if there is no self beyond the self, but only the one self, the linguistic fact that we speak of 'my self' does not indicate that there is something separate referred to by 'my'; and hence in regard to 'my body' one could equally well hold that 'my' merely refers to the body). However, it was maintained that the expression 'my self' is merely a convention; it involved redundancy. On the other hand, 'my body' introduced a new concept, viz. that of the self, and could not thus be explained away as pleonastic.

But the Rāmānujists, though agreeing with the Non-Dualists about the existence of a self, were in opposition to them over the number involved. They therefore had to establish the existence of many selves. In one respect, they were in a fortunate position, since the Śaṅkarite argument against the Logic-Atomists, as described above, made use of the notion of *my* experiences, and thus there was a presumption that each individual had a distinctive self. More importantly, the Rāmānujists held that cognitive experience is necessarily dualistic—thus in having acquaintance with something I must be distinguished from the object of my knowledge. Now the Non-Dualists, in order to maintain the unity of the Self, held that the individual intuitions *(anubhūti)* of the Self arose from its self-luminous or self-revealing character as pure consciousness. But this involves, argued Rāmānuja, an incoherence. If by self-revelation is meant that one cannot distinguish between the entity and its mode of manifestation, pains and pleasures are self-revealing. But the Non-Dualists held that a subject of such experiences had to be acknowledged. But a similar argument could then be applied in the case of knowledge itself, or of revelation. If the Self reveals itself, it must reveal itself *to* somebody. Thus, even granting the existence of a unitary Self, it is necessary to postulate the existence of individual selves who will become aware of the Self. In brief, if consciousness always involves the subject-object relation, the concept of self-luminosity is unacceptable.

Madhva, further, argued that individual differences must be due to the differences of the selves which they embodied. Moreover, of course, Rāmānujists, Dualists and others attacked the analogies whereby Śaṅkara and his followers attempted to establish the coherence of the notion that one Being appears in various individuals (see above, p. 92).

A further point at issue as between the various viewpoints was that of the nature of the soul or self. Thus for Śaṅkara the Self was pure consciousness, while for the Logic-Atomist school the self was essentially unconscious until it came into relation with a psycho-physical organism. (Consequently it was hard to distinguish release, in the doctrine of this school, from annihilation.) As we have seen, this viewpoint held that the self had to be established by inference (it was argued that without the existence of a self, the unified understanding and recognition of objects given in sense-experience would be impossible, that it would not be wrong to harm others if we did not believe in selves, and that there was evidence of rebirth). Of more interest, perhaps, are the varying accounts of whether the soul is spatially extended or not. While some (e.g. the Atomists) held it is all all-pervasive and others (e.g. Rāmānuja) that it is atomic, there was the Jain position that the life-monad fills the body, and is capable of expansion and contraction. Both the all-pervasive view and the atomic one are understandable in virtue of the difficulties in holding that the soul is extended. The body-filling view is understandable in virtue of the way in which sensations are localized in various parts of the body.

A determining factor in the discussion was that, in the orthodox tradition, finite (though not infinitesimally small) entities were regarded as subject to change, and so destructible. Consequently there was objection to the Jain naively common-sensical view of the life-monad as occupying the body, and filling it. The dominant view, therefore, was that the selves or souls are all-pervasive. Not only did this account for the non-spatial character of inner experiences, but also it performed two further functions. It covered the facts which supported the Jain thesis—since if the soul were all-pervasive there was no difficulty in supposing that it pervaded the body. Second, it accounted for the way in which karmic effects worked at a distance (e.g. when one person dies and another in the same sequence is born, but in another town). On the other hand, the Qualified Non-Dualists, whose interpretation of karma was that it was the expression of God's will for the individual, had no need of this hypothesis. The Lord was all-pervasive and thus could operate karma at any point he wished. But the Rāmānujist doctrine of the atomicity of the self was criticized for not making sense of the fact that sensations occur at different parts of the body, save through the analogy (used by the Jains also, but more consistently—in that theirs was a materialistic account of both life-monad and karma) of the lamp lighting up an area: likewise the atomic soul illuminates the body with experience. But it is interesting to note that schools advancing the all-pervasive view at the same time made use of the concept of an atomic mind-organ as one of the intermediaries between body and soul.

We have here described the metaphysical and empirical arguments for rebirth and for the existence of an eternal self. Needless to say, appeals to particular texts of revelation were also employed—for example, that since the scriptures speak of the soul leaving the body it cannot be all-pervasive, but must have finite or atomic size. But it is not necessary for us to investigate such discussions here.

CHAPTER XIII
EPISTEMOLOGICAL QUESTIONS

The epistemological issues debated in the Indian tradition took two main forms. First there was disagreement over the so-called bases of knowledge, i.e. over what should be counted as genuine and necessary sources of knowledge. For instance, perception and inference were generally accepted as such bases. Part of the problem in regard to epistemology was to find out what were the minimum bases on which one could build up knowledge of the world, etc. Given that certain things were true about reality, what followed about the grounds upon which these truths were affirmed? Secondly, Indian epistemology had a direct relationship to metaphysical issues, in that some viewpoints and schools, such as Non-Dualism and Buddhist Idealism, denied the reality of the 'external world', save in a heavily qualified and eccentric sense. By consequence, some prominence came to be attached to discussions about perception and illusion.

Among the orthodox viewpoints, three bases of knowledge were generally recognized (in Exegesis, Logic and Non-Dualism some additions to the list were made, of which more anon; and in Atomism a virtual subtraction): namely, perception, inference and verbal testimony. The last of these figures in Indian metaphysics more largely than might have been expected for a special reason. Although *a priori* one might consider that philosophical viewpoints would see their way to dispensing with testimony as an independent basis of knowledge (on the ground that the information conveyed by testimony must have been gathered by perception, inference, etc.), it happened that testimony was normally considered to include revelation (since literally revelation should be translated as 'what is heard', i.e. by the seers *(ṛṣi)* of old and from a transcendent source). Consequently, discussions about testimony tended to be discussions about the necessity of admitting revelation as a source of knowledge about reality. It is hardly surprising that all the orthodox schools admitted testimony as a basis of knowledge, with the virtual exception of Atomism. The latter viewpoint argued that revelation is valid, but not intrinsically. It derives its validity from the fact that it is produced by the Lord, a good and omniscient being: in turn, the Lord's existence is established by inference from the perceptible world. Thus perception and inference are the only independent bases of knowledge which need to be invoked. The recognition of testimony, in the sense of the words of revelation, as an independent basis led to some curious speculations about the nature of language—e.g. that words have eternally fixed and natural meanings. By contrast, the Buddhists argued powerfully for the conventionality of meanings—for two reasons, first because they did not recognize the orthodox scriptures, and second, more importantly, they considered that their analysis of reality, involving a denial of the existence of permanent substances, etc., showed that language, far from having a natural correspondence with reality, tended to bewitch the intellect. Atomism in all this held an intermediate position: meanings are conventional, but the conventions are made by God.

By inference was generally (though not exclusively) meant inductive inference, and we shall later have occasion to examine in more detail Indian logical teachings on this and related matters. However, it is of some interest to consider the predicament of the Materialists, who, as we have seen, attempted to do away with inference as a basis of knowledge. Their motives may have been partly those of philosophical scepticism; but they were also worried because orthodox religion made use of inference to try to prove truths about the transcendent realm. By scepticism about inference, therefore, Materialism hoped to exclude the possibility of religious belief.

A number of arguments were used by the Materialists in order to cast doubt on the validity of induction. First, induction involves establishing an invariant concomitance between two types of events, etc. Cases of concomitance can only be known by perception. But we cannot now perceive all the events of the given classes which occurred in the past, occur at present and will occur in the future. Thus induction is always liable to falsification. Secondly, it is not enough to show that A-events are always accompained by B-events. One must also show that non-B-events are also non-A-events. For example, one must not only show that all swans are white, in one's experience. One must also show that all non-white things are non-swans for if a black thing should turn out to be a swan, the thesis that all swans are white is falsified. But the task of examining all things in the universe other than swans is even more formidable than that of examining all swans.

However, it is not certain what precisely the early Materialist conclusions were from their scepticism about inference. Most likely they accepted that predictions about the future and so on, on the basis of inductive experience, are probable, even if uncertain. This was doubtless sufficient scepticism for them to dismiss the dogmatisms of various religious groups, especially as the reasoning on which transcendental conclusions depend does not always start from perception. But in the early medieval period, it was allowed by at least one prominent Materialist that induction from the perceptible to the perceptible could be valid; but strong objection was still taken to inferences to conclusions about an other realm of existence. It was argued that in inductive inference we observe a sign *(liṅgaṃ)*, e.g. smoke on a hill-side, and infer the presence of fire, the inferendum *(sādhya)*. This is on the basis of the concomitance of the sign with the inferendum in past experience, etc. But there could in the nature of the case be no observed concomitance between the sign and the inferendum where the latter was a transcendent or imperceptible entity.

The problems presented by induction were solved by the schools in differing ways. The Logic-Atomists here made use of their category of universals. Given a sufficient sampling by the method of agreement and difference, one could establish with certainty the concomitance of a pair of universals. On the other hand, the Non-Dualists tended to hold that the criterion of validity is unfalsifiedness. The concomitance between two classes of events, etc., can therefore be affirmed on the basis of a single instance, and the method of agreement and difference is unnecessary. It is interesting that the concept of non-falsification *(abādhitva)* rather neatly accounted for the two levels of truth (the higher and the ordinary levels) with which the Non-Dualists operated. Thus ordinary knowledge about the world could correctly be called knowledge so long as it remained unfalsified. But falsification could occur in two sorts of ways. On the one hand, within the realm of ordinary knowledge, there could be falsification through the negative instance, or by discovering that a perception was after all illusory, etc. On the other, the whole world-appearance could be seen to be an illusion in the experience of release. Thus ordinary knowledge remains valid, so to say, within its own realm: but upon our achieving a higher insight it is all falsified. On this basis it was argued by the Non-Dualists that one could infer that the whole world-appearance is illusory on the ground of a single instance of empirical illusion. The inference would run as follows: 'Example—this shell is illusory, in that it looks like silver but is not; everything looks other than it really is, viz. the one Power. So everything other than the Power is illusory.'

Such a doctrine of illusionism, together with Mahāyānist Idealism, which more radically denied the existence of an external world, naturally raised questions about the status of perception. Madhva advanced a general argument to show that perception and other recognized bases of knowledge could not be arranged in an order of priority as though one sort of knowledge is 'truer' than another. (It is of course all right to make certain logical distinctions between the bases, as when Rāmānuja distinguished inference from perception on the ground that the application of the former presupposed the use of the latter, though not conversely.) Madhva's target here, of course, is the way in which Non-Dualism effectively raises revelation (as interpreted in a certain way) as a basis above perception, when the whole of ordinary knowledge is seen from the higher level as being invalid. For Śaṅkara the purport of revelation is essentially the experience of non-duality, though he classifies the experience as a sort of perception. It is, however, knowledge without observation. He attempts to show that verbal testimony (i.e. above all revelation) can induce knowledge without observation. For example ten men in a circle each count the number present, leaving out themselves. An outsider who tells one of them 'You are the tenth' induces knowledge not based on observation. It is, incidentally, a complicated example, for a number of reasons. First, the Non-Dualists, like most other schools, explicitly excluded memory as a basis of knowledge. This was because the theory of bases was usually held to be a theory about how new knowledge was acquired, and memory is merely, they held, a recalling of what had previously been known through perception, etc. Secondly, it happens that the term for memory in Sanskrit also refers to the semi-canonical tradition of writings, such as the *Law of Manu*, which were only an adjunct to, and not properly a part of, revelation: thus, just as recognition of testimony involved a recognition of revelation as the 'World', so too recognition of memory was liable to imply recognition as independently valid of the semi-canonical tradition. Third, the example appeals to a person's self-awareness as being part-cause of his recognition that he is the tenth, and this self-awareness is non-observational, even though the knowledge that there are nine others *is* observational. At any rate, Śaṅkara wished to show that the scriptures, in particular the identity- texts—'That art thou' and so on—have the power of arousing the experience of non-duality.

Madhva used two main lines of argument. First, by a basis of knowledge, he held, we meant that which gives us knowledge of things as they are. That is, it provides truths. If this is so, it is absurd to hold that something is a basis of knowledge and yet ultimately is falsified *(bādhit-va)* or transcended in a higher experience. Thus the Non-Dualists are inconsistent in allowing perception as a basis of knowledge. Secondly, Madhva argues that though doubt can be cast upon individual perceptions, there is some perceptual knowledge which is absolutely certain. The trouble is that general prescriptions on the methodology of observation, such as the method of agreement and difference, and the criterion of non-falsification, always leave room for marginal doubt. There must be some court of appeal which is the final arbiter, and which in some cases at least totally eliminates doubt. Madhva found this court of appeal in the inner witness—the self as scrutinizing the material presented to it by the senses, etc. The witness can pass final judgment, and thereby incorrigible truths are known. A number of considerations led the Dualists to posit such an epistemological arbiter. First, the self is aware of such states as pain and pleasure, and there is no room for error in these cases. Second, the apperception of space requires explanation, and it was held that the witness performs this function. (This feature of the witness was useful in explaining perceptual doubts, where the self refuses to pass an incorrigible pro-judgment: for one main cause of indistinctness and doubtfulness in perception is the distance of objects.) Third, the Logic-Atomist appeal to 'external' tests, such as the method of agreement and difference, leads to an infinite regress. For the results have to be tested in the same way...and so on. It is therefore necessary to postulate an arbiter as a limit to the sequence of doubts.

There were other ways of tackling the problem of doubt about perception and inference. Some gave a behaviouristic criterion of doubt. Those who affirmed on philosophical grounds that there was doubt as to whether fire causes smoke. Thus their philosophical doubt is not a real doubt. Somewhat similarly, the Logic-Atomists discussed the problem of how one knew whether the smoke was not caused by some invisible demon, rather than by the fire: and concluded there came a breaking-point beyond which sustaining the doubt was merely frivolous.

Rāmānuja had a rather different approach to the problem of illusion. The thesis that perception, etc., yields valid knowledge was apparently refuted by the existence of perceptual illusions. Thus there did not seem to be an intrinsic connection between cognitive experience and validity. He was therefore at pains to argue that even illusions yield some knowledge—that there is no experience which is totally misleading. He was not alone in arguing this. For instance, some of his predecessors in the tradition that he formulated as Qualified Non-Dualism held the view that sense-qualities arise from the relative preponderance in a given object of material elements themselves possessing sense-qualities. Thus a conch-shell which is mistaken for a piece of silver has more conch-shell matter than silver matter—but it has some at least of the latter. Thus the illusion represents a real perception of silver, but unfortunately the conch-shell side of the object is simply not perceived. Thus essentially illusions are limited apprehensions of the objects which give rise to them. An illusion is a partial—but only a partial—privation of perception. Rāmānuja preferred to describe the situation as mistaking one thing for another. But the mistake still involves a real apprehension of something. Mistaking the conch-shell for a piece of silver involves confusing the past memory of silver with the present object. But one still has an apprehension of something real, viz. silver. Moreover, in so far as something is seen *as* an illusion there is presupposed the concept of genuine knowledge.

However, there were two features of the Non-Dualist thesis about perception which made it particularly slippery to deal with. First, it was not denied by the Non-Dualists that there is a real object of perception, even though from one point of view perceptions are of the illusory world of appearances. For in perception there is an apprehension of substance, of the underlying somewhat, which is ultimate reality: the holy Power conceived as pure being. It is merely that empirical experience projects onto pure being the appearances which constitute the grand illusion. Secondly, the doctrine of illusion could not be simply combated by pointing to the validity of some knowledge, as presupposed in the very use of the concept of illusion (by contrast with genuine perception, etc.). It could not thus be combated simply, since the existential ground of saying that all appearances are illusory was the non-dualistic experience, expressing a higher sort of truth. That is, the use of the principle of contrast to validate most ordinary knowledge was insufficient when a different contrast was brought into play, viz. the contrast between the non-dualistic experience and the experiences of ordinary perception, etc. Because of the analogical sense of illusion that is thereby generated, it has been possible for some followers of Śaṅkara—and notably in recent years—to play down the doctrine of illusion as interpreted to mean that the world is a mere phantasm; for it is only from the higher standpoint that the term illusion can properly be applied to the world. Thus it is not in a literal sense that the expression is used. Thus it is possible to adopt a more 'realistic' interpretation of Non-Dualism. It ought to be mentioned too in this connection that a purely subjectivist interpretation of the world was rejected by most Non-Dualists. It was however a position held by a sub-school within Non-Dualistic Vedānta. This school, the Subjective-Creationists *(dṛṣṭisṛṣṭivādin)* urged that each person's experience was strictly and individually illusory, and from his own experience he 'created' his own world. Like many individuals who agree in seeing a pink rat, so the various individuals happen to have similar illusions. But this did not accord with the orthodox view among the followers of Śaṅkara, namely that the illusion, though not fully real, and so of indefinable character, nevertheless is an objective entity, from the standpoint of ordinary knowledge.

The basis of the Subjective-Creationist position could be said to be the principle that existence consists in being perceived. This principle was given its full application by the Buddhist Idealists (who no doubt strongly influenced this sub-school of Vedānta). Whereas Śaṅkara was opposed to the typically Buddhist doctrine that all events, states, etc., are momentary, the Idealists could find in it support for their subjectivism. If to be is to be perceived, it follows that there are not permanent substances existing in independence of conscious beings, and they do not persist unobserved. (They were indeed delighted to wash their hands of the problem of the 'tree in the quad'.) The Idealists used various arguments against the existence of a non-mental 'external world'.

First, it was argued that the experience of a datum and the datum itself always appear simultaneously together. But two supposedly different events or states occurring together thus cannot be distinguished (thus any reference to the one is always a reference to the other). They should therefore be treated as identical. Consequently one cannot assert the separate existence of the data apart from experiences thereof. In brief, so-called external objects of experience are simply experiences. Secondly, the external world is supposedly made up of a number of separate entities. But the only way of distinguishing between these entities is on the basis of different sorts of experience. But if the experiences are thus distinguishable there is no need to speak further of objects, existing independently of experiences, as distinguishable. Thus the hypothesis of an external world is superfluous. Thirdly, it is supposed that sense-organs are necessary intermediaries between the external world and consciousness. But we have experiences in dreams when the sense-organs are not functioning. It is therefore feasible to explain the existence of sensations as due to the inner determinations of consciousness.

The first and second of these arguments were directly relevant to attempts, in the Buddhist realist schools, to show how it is that we have knowledge of the external world. First, exceptions were made to the principle that the simultaneous concomitance of states implies their identity: in the case of perception, in particular, it was allowed that the relation was of production, not identity. That is, a perception of an object, though simultaneous with it, is produced by the latter. Such a view implies the real apprehension of the object in the outer world, i.e. a direct awareness of it in perception (hence the strict simultaneity). But alternatively, and relevantly to the second Idealist argument, one could retain the principle of the identity of simultaneously concomitant states (and it seemed arbitrary to abandon it, in order to make realism work in a particular instance), by holding that there is no direct apprehension of outer objects: but that these are inferred from our experience. They could be inferred on the ground that there is a variety of different experiences, and these must have different causes. Thus there are outer objects severally corresponding to the various perceptual states. But, as the above Idealist argument indicates, there can be no experiential basis for holding that there are entities distinguishable from experiences—and it is more economical to hold that there are simply experiences.

Nevertheless, the Idealists had to concede (and it was readily made an objection against them) that people *think* that objects are external to consciousness. They certainly distinguish between, say, a pillar and the awareness of that pillar. Now the Idealists, as we saw, held that there is an Absolute, viz. the store-consciousness which comprehends and is the source of individual experiences. The apparent distinction between the subject and the outer world had therefore to be explained as a mode in which the Absolute evolved itself. It evolved itself in such a way that it was as if there were an external world. But the Buddhist saint could, by attaining a realization of pure consciousness and identification with the Absolute, destroy this appearance of an external world (and its twin, a contrasted internal world). Ordinary experience, which falsely suggests that there are non-mental realities, is misleading: but the enlightenment experience is not. Here the Idealists indicate their similarity to the Non-Dualists, in having a double-decker view of truth.

Apart from questions about the general validity of perception and about the external world, there are various theories in the Indian tradition of the particular processes of perception. Of some philosophical interest is the attempt to distinguish betwen two phases or aspects of perception, namely constructive *(savikalpa)* and non-constructive *(nirvikalpa)* perception. This was, roughly, an attempt to distinguish between the bare presentation from those elements 'real into' the presentation by the mind. The construction put upon the datum is chiefly due to memory and language. Thus the Logic-Atomist school held that in non-constructive perception, there is presented the object, its properties, etc. Since the school held that there are real universals, these could be the proper object of perception. But at the constructive stage they emerge, so to say, from their confused and vague condition: they are recognized, through memory, and they are made the object of conceptual judgments. Thus the non-constructive perception of a cow is followed by the constructive judgment 'This is a cow', and thereby the original perception is given clarity and definition. These two phases of perception were sometimes considered as occurring in temporal succession, but later Logic-Atomists took them as aspects which one could abstract from the same event. The arguments in favour of the distinction were really arguments for the non-constructive phase: common-sense finds it difficult, once memory and language are in play, to conceive of 'pure' perception, not overlaid by the constructions put upon it. But since memory, etc., are demonstrably functions of the perceiver, and since conceptual judgments depend on these functions, conceptualized or constructive perception cannot be simply caused by the object, but there must be an intermediary, so to speak, between percipient and object. There must therefore be some pure data given off by the object, but there must be an intermediary, so to speak, between percipient and object. There must therefore be some pure data given off by the object, or constituting an aspect of the object. On the basis of these data, the mind is then enabled to make judgments about the object.

The Buddhist made a somewhat similar distinction between constructive and non-constructive perception. But they used it for a different purpose. They were, of course, opposed to the Logic-Atomist doctrine of substance and real universals, etc. They held, as we have seen, that the illusion of permanent substances is generated, in part at least, by language. Thus, for them, non-constructive perception involved only a pure awareness of data. The categorizing of these data into classes, the reference of them to underlying objects, etc., were due to the process of construction. Thus conceptual judgments are contributed by the individual and do not reflect natural facts. If, therefore, one wishes to consider the external world (we are not here speaking of Buddhist Idealism) in all its purity, one must remove the artificial constructions put upon it by the self. It will then be revealed as an impermanent and insubstantial flow of events.

Generally speaking, the problem of how to describe the process of perception was conceived in the Indian tradition as being the problem: 'How does knowledge arise in the self, as a result of sense-perception?' But the question could be reversed, and one might ask: 'How does the self fail to have knowledge?' For instance, the Jains considered the life-monad essentially omniscient: consequently sense-perception was like the unveiling of pre-existent knowledge. There is an analogy here with the Non-Dualist position. For Śaṅkara, perceptual and other knowledge is the removal of the veil of ignorance. But in ordinary perception this is very partial.

Since Śaṅkara wished to argue that the existence of the veil of ignorance is known in experience, he made use of the further basis of knowledge also employed by Exegesis, viz. negative perception *(anupalabdhi)* One of the puzzles about perception is that we seem able to 'perceive' the absence of something. The Exegetes therefore held that this negative perception was a separate source of information about the world. Śaṅkara argued that 'I am ignorant of such-and-such' and similar locutions express an awareness of the penumbra of nescience that surrounds, so to say, our determinate knowledge. Both the Non-Dualists and two other viewpoints made use also of analogy *(upamāna)* as an extra basis of knowledge, to deal with cases where one recognizes a hitherto unknown object on the basis of its similarity to some known object. This presupposes, of course, that one already knows that the similarity obtains; but it cannot be on the basis of having perceived the unknown object, *ex hypothesi*. Thus the premiss is supplied by testimony (when one is told, e.g. that a yeti is a bit like a gorilla). But in this case, analogy can be subsumed under testimony, and so was found dispensable by most schools as a separate basis of knowledge. Another basis used by both the Non-Dualists and the Exegetes was that of implication *(arthāpatti)* as distinguished from inference. This we shall deal with in a later chapter.

It will be seen from the foregoing that the fundamental bases of knowledge recognized in the Indian tradition were perception, inference and verbal testimony. The first two of these were generally considered adequate sources of knowledge of the empirical world, given that the problem was conceived in terms of arriving at new facts, so that memory could be excluded (except in so far as it was built into the process of constructive perception). The chief importance of testimony was as a source of transcendent truth through revelation. For this reason, it was not, in this sense, recognized by the unorthodox schools.

CHAPTER XIV
CAUSATION

As we have seen, two principal theories of causation were canvassed in the Indian tradition—what we have termed the identity and non-identity theories. The former theory, held by the Distinctionists, and, following them, by some others, consists in the thesis that the effect is identical with the cause: it is a manifestation of what is potential in the cause. This is in line with the Distinctionist picture of the cosmos as the result of a process of evolution or transformation, whereby nature precipitates out from itself the determinate objects of the observable world. Nature as manifested already exists in nature as the indeterminate substratum. The theory not only fitted in with this evolutionist picture, but rested too on the intuitive principle that nothing comes out of nothing. And if it is unacceptable to say 'First nothing, then something' it is equally unacceptable to affirm the converse 'First something, then nothing'. Thus effects must exist after their transformation into the effects. As was pointed out by Logic-Atomist critics, this doctrine seems to abolish the distinction between material and efficient causes (and indeed between these and the so–called accessory *(sahakarī)* causes—e.g. the instrument wherewith the craftsman, considered as efficient cause, shapes the material). Even though from the point of view of observation one might, on the Distinctionist hypothesis, wish to distinguish the efficient from the material causes in nature, taking a larger view the efficient cause would be part of nature as material cause. In effect, the Distinctionist doctrine regards natural changes as due to the internal dynamic of nature through the interplay of the strand-substances in a state of disequilibrium (see above, p. 65).

The support given to the identity theory by these somewhat speculative considerations was reinforced by appeal to examples. For instance, the sesamum-oil must in some way pre-exist in the sesamum seeds, the sculpture in the stone, etc. The agent who produces these effects is merely making manifest the potentialities of the substances with which he is dealing. Furthermore the doctrine made plain that there was a necessary connection between cause and effect, while the Buddhist and Logic-Atomist non-identity theory means that in principle any effect can arise as the result of a given cause. It therefore needs to be explained why there is a regular pattern of causation in nature.

However, some were equally critical of both theories, notably Nāgārjuna and his Voidist followers. They wished to show that the concept of causation itself was contradictory. By applying a dialectical method to all the assumptions of common-sense and all metaphysical speculations they hoped to show the indescribability of reality, its Voidness. There were similar attempts on the part of Non-Dualists, in favour of the illusionist doctrine.

The dialectical arguments do not only attack theories of causation, but the very notion of change itself. Regarding the former, it was argued that in principle one could hold three positions: the identity theory affirming the inner determinations within the cause of the effect; the non-identity view that effects are the result of combinations of conditions which are external to them; or a combination of the views, i.e. that a cause is a determination of a pre-existent cause by an external combination of conditions. Now the first view is nonsense; for a thing is supposed to produce itself. But if it already exists, it is absurd to speak of its being produced. Moreover, on the principle referred to in another chapter (see p. 159) that what is eternal cannot have momentary effects, but must *per impossibile* have eternal effects, then the already-existing (and by analogy eternal) cause must produce changes in itself eternally. This of course would attack the root of the idea of determinate effects as changes occurring at a certain time and for a finite period. Thus the identity-theory cannot be maintained.

But equally the non-identity theory is nonsense. (It should be noted that the dialectical criticism of the Mahāyānists was as much directed against the Lesser Vehicle views as against those of any orthodox school.) If the conditions supposedly giving rise to an effect are totally extraneous to it, then anything can come out of anything. But this would not be a case of causation. Consequently the effect must have some special relation to its causes. This implies that it is in some way reflected in the causes, i.e. already in some way is pre-existent in them. But as has already been argued, the concept of the production of an effect out of a pre-existent cause is absurd. Similarly an application of these arguments will show that the third view of causation, the mixed view, is equally untenable.

In any event, apart from the philosophical theories of causation, it is necessary to examine the concept of change, which is clearly pre-supposed by the concept of causality. Now things can either be regarded as permanent or broken up into sequences of events or states. In particular one could break them up, in the Buddhist manner, into atomic events or states, i.e. they could be analysed into a sequence of momentary events or states. Thus the basic alternatives are: permanent entities or momentary events. But it is clearly absurd to speak of change in regard to what is permanent. It is by definition unchanging. Nor can permanent entities have momentary effects. Thus change must be referred to sequences of momentary events. However, there immediately occurs a different contradiction. Since change involves a process of change, it is necessary to enquire what process occurs among momentary events. Regrettably, there cannot be any. For process involves continuation; but once one momentary event is replaced by another, it has ceased to exist. Nor can it be held that the first momentary event has suffered a change, for it can only do so on condition of somehow becoming the next momentary event. But the two are *ex hypothesi* different. The same sort of argument, moreover, can be generalized to cover all relations, including the temporal one. For two entities to be related, they must exist. But on the hypothesis of momentary events, event A has gone out of existence by the time it is replaced by event B. Thus there can be no relation between A and B. It follows that it is even wrong to say that event A occurs before (or after) event B.

Difficulties of this kind were one motive for the Realist school to insist strongly upon the existence of everything past, present and future: so that events could enter into relations with one another. It is, of course, clear that Nāgārjuna's critique of causality applies to the Buddha's own doctrine of origination (see above, p. 32). Indeed, the Voidists went out of their way explicitly to take that doctrine to bits too. Moreover, the thesis that all events and states are momentary is absurd, if the above arguments are valid. It would seem therefore that Voidism was self-destructive, in so far as it claimed to be an interpretation of Buddhist truth. The difficulty was evaded in various ways. First, the four-cornered negation of the Buddha (see above, p. 20) seemed to point the way to a comprehensive critique of concepts about reality. Second, the Buddha in some sense had, so he said, no views (though it is certain that he enunciated doctrines). Third, the thesis of momentarinesss and the doctrine of origination have a pragmatic value, the first in breaking down preconceptions about the permanence of substances, etc. (such preconceptions tie a man to the world), the second in expressing the truth about existence at the lower level of truth. But they are only pointers towards the non-dual experience: they are ways of hinting at it, and of engineering it. The Buddha in his teachings had a nice sense of diplomacy *(upāyakauśalya)*, and adapted his words to the illusions of his hearers.

The mystical pragmatism of the Voidists made their position a slippery one. Undoubtedly they did speak of the void in Absolutist terms: for reality though insubstantial had, as it were, voidness as its inner nature. This indefinable Absolute was also nirvana. But they claimed to be totally dialectical in their procedure, and to advance no theses. All they were attempting was the destruction of all views about ultimate reality. They were thus criticized in two ways. First, it was urged that in effect they did have a theory. Second, it was argued that in giving proofs of the invalidity of opposing positions, they were implicitly adducing proofs that the negations of such positions were valid. In particular, the slogan that all things are unoriginated (to express the Voidist critique of origination and causation) must be supported by some such proofs. If the Voidist denied this, then there was no reason to accept the slogan, and one could as well assert its contradictory. However, the Voidist reply to such criticisms was simple: their arguments were of the nature of *reductio ad absurdums*. The opponent claimed to prove his position: well, adopting methods of proof, just for the sake of argument, one could show the incoherence of that position. This involved no acceptance of the validity of proofs. (The Voidist method had some influence on Zen Buddhism, with its stress that one should use a sort of spiritual jujitsu on the unenlightened: using their strength to bring about their 'downfall'.)

The Buddhist doctrine of atomic events was bound to raise questions about the continuum. Nāgārjuna himself, in the course of a rather elaborate critique (largely of a verbal kind) of the concept of a goer going through space, remarks that when the goer is actually going, *ex hypothesi* there is then no beginning; but while he is at rest there can be no beginning. So motion is beginningless. It was argued by Logic-Atomist critics that the causal relation between the momentary events postulated by the Buddhists must involve the persistence of the cause's efficacy from one moment till the next—to 'bridge the gap'. This was taken to imply that between cause and effect, some further entity must be inserted. But the same problem arises all over again—and so on. Buddhist defenders of the doctrines of momentariness and causality wished to avoid this implication, since it would constitute a vicious infinite regress. (Such a regress was distinguished from the notion of a non-vicious infinite. Thus, for example, it was reasonable to hold that there is an infinite sequence of causes which has led up to the existence of a tree: it is produced by the seed and that by another tree and so on in an infinite sequence of like causes and effects. But the particular steps in the chain of causes could each be described independently of the infinity of other causes; on the other hand, the trouble with a vicious infinite regress is that each step entails an infinity of sub-steps, so that one can never get round to asserting or explaining what one has in mind to assert or explain.) They therefore held that there is, so to say, a contiguity of causes and effects, such that it is directly through the causal efficacy of the first event that the second event comes into existence.

The Voidist critique of causality was accompanied, of course, by a similar critique of substance. But here the various Buddhist schools were more in agreement. While the attack on causation could scarcely be accepted by more 'orthodox' Buddhists (who rightly saw in it the effective destruction of the Buddha's doctrine of origination), the teaching that all things are impermanent and substanceless was essential to Buddhism, of whatever variety. The prominence assigned to substance by the Logic-Atomists naturally meant that this view-point attracted the fire of the Buddhists. Part of the objection to permanent substances was that they could play no causal role. If a thing naturally produces a determinate effect and is itself a persisting entity, then the effect should be continuous. But the whole point of the Atomist doctrine of atoms is that they are eternal constituents of things, which by their combination account for the changes observed in the world. *Ex hypothesi* the observable states are not permanent, for otherwise there would be no need to postulate more basic entities to account for them. But as we have seen a permanent cause should have a permanent effect. It does not help to reply that atom A only produces effect E in combination with atom B (and this explains why the potency of atom A is not continuously operative) since the actualization of the potency in the atom is itself a change in the atom either attributable to it or to atom B. In either case a permanent entity is having a temporally finite effect.

It was not only the Buddhists who criticized the atomic theory. Śaṅkara and some Qualified Non-Dualists attacked it. The chief arguments were as follows. First, the Atomists laid themselves open to trouble by their doctrine of the combination of atoms to form sub-molecules and molecules (see above, p. 79). For they supposed that out of the combination of infinitesimal atoms there could be generated finite quanta. This was criticized as involving an inexplicable change in type as between the causes and the effect. Whereas atoms had properties which they passed on to the gross combinations, in this case there was a property, that of being infinitesimally small, which was not so passed on. Second, if atoms were to combine, they must have parts: for combination occurs when one part of one object is conjoined to one part of another object. But atoms *ex hypothesi* are partless. Third, the Logic-Atomists (as we saw: p. 83) introduced the category of inherence to explain the way in which atoms combined together to form macroscopic substances. Without this conceptual glue, the notion of macroscopic substances would break down, and with it the claims of Logic-Atomism to express the presuppositions of common-sense knowledge. It was argued by Śaṅkara that the relation of inherence as between atoms was (like other relations, which were mostly classified under the category of property in the Logic-Atomist system, and which were related to substances by the relation of inherence) related by inherence to the atoms. Thus the inherence of atom A with atom B is itself a third entity inhering in them; and so on. Thus there is generated a vicious infinite regress in the atomic theory.

The first of these arguments was useful to Śaṅkara's followers as an *ad homines* objection, in so far as the Atomists and others were critical of the appearance theory of causation as enunciated by the Non-Dualists. This implied that the holy Power, pure and changeless, gives rise (somehow) to the world of appearances which is impure and changeable. That a diverse effect should follow from a diverse cause was already implied in the Atomist doctrine; and therefore there could be no objection in principle to the appearance theory.

To some of these criticisms, by the Buddhists and Non-Dualists, the Atomists were able to reply. Although there might be difficulties in the atomic theory, there were countervailing difficulties in its alternatives. For example, the doctrine of momentariness made it hard to understand how long-term effects could occur: for instance the operation of karma whereby a man's deed in one life affect his situation in the next. Again, the doctrine of momentariness is counter-intuitive, since we are aware of permanent states, and of our self-identity through change. The Non-Dualists argued likewise that many perceptual experiences seem to refute the doctrine: if I am looking at an object over a period of time and my mental state is unchanged, i.e. I am still getting the same visual image, etc., it is absurd, and has no basis in experience, to postulate a succession of different momentary states. The Buddhists on the other hand contended that such experiences, and the fact that I describe a succession of states as though it is a single event, are misleading. First, we induce a false sense of unity in ourselves and in other things, through the operation of our constructive tendencies. Second, we know very well in some cases that something described as a single event is a sequence of momentary states (for example, the flame of a candle is said to burn for five minutes as though this is a single process or event, when we known that it is the rapid replacement of one flame-state by another).

Finally, in connection with the Buddhist critique of causation, there is an interesting argument which seeks to establish the truth of the doctrine of momentariness. It is this. All entities which are produced are destructible (i.e. they will sooner or later be destroyed). But the destructibility of these entities must depend upon their having been produced, and not upon any other condition or conditions. For if it depended on other conditions, a produced entity might go on existing for ever. Consequently, a produced entity must be destroyed as soon as it is produced. (It is clear that a similar argument will apply if we attempt to say that owing to some other conditions a produced entity persists and is not immediately destroyed. For conditions bringing about such persistence will also involve conditions of the eventual demise of the entity.) An entity which is destroyed as soon as it is created is a momentary entity. Thus the doctrine of momentariness must apply to all objects which are effects. We have seen that the Buddhists had different objections which they could bring to bear against permanent unproduced entities, such as atoms.

Although both the Buddhist and the Atomist doctrines of causation are classified together as non-identity theories, it will be clear by now that they have considerable differences. One could put the matter crudely by saying that the Buddhists had a, so to say, two-dimensional notion of a cause, the Atomists a three-dimensional one. That is, the Atomists regarded the cause of something as being a conjunction of properties, etc., possessed by persisting substances, and thereby a conjunction of those substances themselves. The Buddhists on the other hand viewed the cause as a conjunction of short-lived events. Instead of the doctrine of atomic substances, there is the doctrine of atomic events. The notion of brief event-states was developed in two directions. On the one hand the events were fined down until they were quite momentary, and this opened the way for the Voidist critique of all relations between events, including causality. On the other hand, it was developed in the direction of a phenomenalistic account of the world, which ultimately issued in Idealism.

Śaṅkara's appearance theory is sometimes classified as a version of the identity-theory (indeed he referred to it in this way himself), on the grounds that the effect (namely the world of illusion) is identical with the cause (namely, the holy Power). But it is clear that Śaṅkara's doctrine is no ordinary theory of causation, but is limited to the relation between the world and the Power. It is a theory about the causation of the grand illusion; it is not a theory about the particular processes of causation which appear *within* that illusion. Thus it is only an identity theory in so far as the ground of the illusion and the appearance projected upon it are identical, and not properly in the sense that effects pre-exist in their causes. The appearance theory was, of course, a simple consequence of the illusionist position which supposedly had a scriptural basis, though it also borrowed arguments from the Buddhist critique of causation, e.g. that an eternal cause ought to have an eternal effect. But the situation was reversed. Instead of denying an eternal cause or causes by use of this principle, as the Buddhists did (for instance, as we have seen, they criticized Atomism on this basis), the Non-Dualists affirmed the existence of the one eternal Being, and therefore concluded that the effects which are observable in the world, and which are non-eternal, are merely *apparent* effects. But despite the difference of this from a theory of causation proper, the Non-Dualists made use of the categories used elsewhere to describe the causal process. For instance, the holy Power, as pure being, could be said to underlie the appearances, and so in some sense constitutes their material cause.

The Rāmānujists took strong exception both to the concept of pure being as the material cause and to the notion itself as characterizing the divine Power. On the first point, it was argued that it is as useful to call being the material cause of existing things as it is to say that non-being is the underlying stuff from which chimeras are made. In this the qualified Non-Dualists approximated to the Logic-Atomist view of being. For the latter, the attribute of being or existence is simply the most general property which can be ascribed to entities. But it presupposes substances to inhere in. It is therefore senseless to speak of pure being as a self-existent entity.

We have seen earlier (Chapter VIII) that the Qualified Non-Dualist viewpoint denied that anything could be featureless in the way in which the Non-Dualists held that the Power is featureless. Various arguments were used against the latter idea, and therefore against the concept of pure being. First, even if it were true that ultimate reality is featureless, featurelessness is a property distinguishing it from other entities. It is thus itself a feature of God. Second, the Non-Dualist doctrine involved that the scriptures do not describe God in a direct manner, but rather are pointers which indirectly indicate the divine being. This appears to be a strained interpretation of their meaning. It is true that some passages say that the Power is ineffable; but these are only asserting the infinity of God. For this reason, he cannot be fully comprehended by language; but this does not entail that he cannot be described at all. Thirdly, the state of concentration which does not involve ordinary intellectual discriminations is not totally featureless. Not only can it be described as different from ordinary experiences, but it is supposedly the experience of identification with ultimate reality, and this involves a conceptual interpretation. Fourthly, Śaṅkara explicitly affirms that the Power is being, consciousness and bliss. These seem to be different characterizations of the Power, and it is hard to see how Śaṅkara's thesis that they are identical in meaning can be sustained. Fifthly, language itself and in particular the language of revelation, supposed by Śaṅkara to give a superior interpretation of reality overruling the apparent testimony of perception, presupposes the existence of distinctions. For it consists in determinate words, separate from one another. This implies that different words stand for different aspects or features of reality. The language of revelation is no different in this respect from secular language. It follows that the words of scripture would be incabable of referring to a totally featureless reality, and Śaṅkara ought in consistency to say that revelation itself is as misleading and illusion-producing as perception. Of course, Śaṅkara does come very near to saying this: as we have seen, a great deal of scripture was interpreted by him as describing things from the standpoint of lower or ordinary truth, and so not in the last analysis true. But even so, some part of revelation had to express the higher truth, and so Rāmānuja's criticism would still be relevant. Śaṅkara therefore was required by such considerations to introduce a pragmatic account of meaning: what the scriptures wish to express is a realization of non-duality, and even if as plural objects (words) existing in the realm of appearances they are illusory, they can still have the effect of bringing men to the realization in question—just as a terrifying illusion may cause a person to drop down dead.

The concept of pure being was not merely crucial to Śaṅkara's description of the experience of release, etc., but also to his appearance theory. Although as we have said it is not an ordinary theory of causation but in effect is introduced to account for the relation between the world illusion and ultimate reality, Śaṅkara gave it some support from an examination of natural causes. For example, a jug which has been fashioned out of clay and then smashed remains clay all the time, and the shape it acquired and then lost is merely an impermanent form imposed on the continuing clay. Thus if permanence be counted a criterion of reality, and impermanence of unreality, we can extrapolate from the example. For though the clay is a continuing entity, sooner or later it too changes its form and ceases to be recognizable as clay. All the forms of the material causes as ordinarily understood are likewise impermanent. It follows that we should look for some more deep-seated material cause. This can only be something which has none of the forms met with in observational experience. Thus pure being can be said to be the underlying material cause. And it would certainly be wrong to deny its existence on the ground that it is not observed in the ordinary way, since every perception presupposes the contact of the Self with reality. Thus there is an intuitive awareness of being running through all perceptions. Since it does so, it is formless.

However, this argument, if it is meant to show that the effects, i.e. the objects occurring in the world-appearance, are illusory, depends on the doubtful contention (pointed to by Qualified Non-Dualist and Dualist critics of Śaṅkara) that what is impermanent is somehow illusory. There is no reason to suppose, however, argues Rāmānuja, that what is non-eternal is *ipso facto* not real.

One further feature of Śaṅkara's doctrine on these matters is worth mentioning, since it indicates one of the two points of contact between the one reality postulated in the system and the world of ordinary experience. The intuition of the self is, as we have seen, something which according to him is immediate (for this reason, as we have seen, he objected to the Logic-Atomist doctrine that the self is known through inference: for Śaṅkara, the self is implicit in all Experience). Now although it is true that empirical individuals project on to the Self the sense of individuality, and therefore regard themselves as separate selves, the truth of the matter according to Non-Dualism is that the inner witness which is the subject of experiences is indeed the one divine reality. Consequently, there is no question of the self's being caused by the Power. It is identical with it; and the appearance theory does not apply to it. Thus we can see that for Śaṅkara, there were two points of contact, so to say, between ordinary experience and the higher truth—first, in the awareness of being implicit in perception of the 'outer' world; and second, in the intuition of the self as the subject of experience. A proper appreciation of these intuitions exhibits the truth of Non-Dualism. But the power of ignorance (or looking at it from the 'outer' side, illusion) is sufficient to cloud what is given thus in all experience. Only when one attains the mystical realization of the identity of the Self (the third point of contact, one might say) is one in a state of real or existential knowledge of the truth.

We have already seen some of the objections which were raised against the identity theory by the Mahāyāna Buddhist dialecticians. They, however, were equally critical of the alternative theory. It is worth remarking on some of the points which the Logic-Atomists and others made on their own behalf in criticizing the Distinctionist position. One thing was firmly insisted upon, namely that it should not be necessary to have recourse to the idea of an unobservable energy or power relating cause and effect. Such a power was undiscoverable in experience, and it was unnecessary to do more than point to the invariable and unconditional succession of the cause and effect. A like criticism was made by Madhva, namely that the identity theory involved asserting that there was an underlying something, namely nature, which was evolved or transformed into the manifold observable states of the world. But it was complained that this in principle imperceptible entity has no basis in experience: and a licence to introduce such entities was equally a licence to affirm the existence of entities such as the hare's horn (a stock example in the Indian tradition of the absolutely non-existent, i.e. of something which does not merely happen not to exist, but could not exist). Furthermore, the theory that the effect already exists in the cause notoriously runs into the difficulty that it ought then to be produced at an early time. Production means that it comes into existence. If then it already exists at t1 before t2, the time when it is supposedly produced, it should already have been produced at t1. It was therefore a stock Distinctionist reply that the production at t2 is really the *manifestation* of the effect. Madhva criticizes this reply on the ground that the concepts of production and manifestation are quite different. The latter involves that the object manifested is presented to perception. This is not implied in the concept of production. The claim that the effect existed before the time of its manifestation raises the question (similar to that of the first of Madhva's argument above) why it was not perceptible. If the manifestation of an effect is itself a causal change, then, on the theory, the manifestation ought to pre-exist itself. But it is absurd to speak of an unmanifest manifestation.

Finally, it was pointed out by critics of Distinctionism that one feature of the viewpoint marred what otherwise might be conceived as its chief attraction. The latter was the way in which the viewpoint attempted to account for the changes in the world as being due to the internal dynamic of the system of nature. But by attaching eternal souls to nature, the viewpoint was landed with the problem of how it is that these virtually inert entities gained release. And the answer, as we have seen (p. 70) was that nature worked teleologically for the good of the souls. Thus there was some sense in which nature was not merely determined in its evolution by an internal dynamic, but responded teleologcally to the magnetism, so to say, of the souls. Since these were essentially not part of the system of nature—and indeed found their release in the realization of their essential distinctness from nature—there was an incoherence in the Distinctionist attempt at a naturalistic cosmology.

But though the Dualists were critical of the identity theory, for reasons such as those mentioned above, they did not espouse the traditional alternative. As we saw (p. 160) Dualism conceived that the careers of beings were determined inwardly, in accordance with their particular natures. On the other hand, Madhva did not wish to hold that the Lord was identical in any sense with the created world: thus the material cause of the cosmos could not be (as in some other systems) God. Instead, the material cause of the world was thought of as God's energy, which he modified in accordance with the inner determinations of the various selves. Making use of this concept of energy, the Dualists ascribed it to causes as constituting their causal power. Indeed, various types of energy were distinguished—the basic and inconceivable energy *(acintyaśakti)* used by the Lord in his control and formation of the world; the causal energy of natural objects; the sacred energy with which images are implicit; and the energy manifested in language—the power of words to have, through their meanings, determinate effects. It followed from the above doctrines that cause and effect, though distinct, were tightly bound together—and thus the theory could be presented as a synthesis between the identity and the non-identity theories. They were bound together in two ways: first, because the bringing into existence of an effect was part result of the operation of the energy of a substance, and so was an actualization of this implicit energy. Second, the effect was also the evolution of the substance effected by the energy of another substance, and so belonged to an entity which was part-cause or condition of the effect. Thus the effect was argued to be both identical and non-identical with the cause. It may be noted that this theory was held to apply to the material entities in the cosmos, including the material aspects of persons. Selves and the Lord were held to be essentially changeless, and therefore only capable of manifesting themselves, rather than being effects, or undergoing modifications due to other entities. It is also of some interest that something like a principle of causal inertia was enunciated. Something comes into existence when there are sufficient conditions for it to do so; likewise it goes out of existence when there are sufficient conditions for its destruction. Things remain in their *status quo* until something of sufficient energy comes along to disturb them (there is a contrast here with the Buddhist argument for momentariness noticed earlier). The selves are such that there never arise sufficient conditions for their destruction, and they are thus everlasting.

It will be observed from the foregoing discussions that traditional Indian discussions of causation were determined by a tension between different principles. On the one hand, it was felt that an effect is the result of a combination of certain conditions. On the other hand, both on philosophical and protoscientific grounds it was found attractive to postulate permanent substances (e.g. atoms) whose combination would constitute the conditions whereby observable states arise. Yet the notion of permanent substances raised the problem that if they have some causal power, i.e. if there was some invariable association between the permanent entity and its effect, then the effect ought also to be permanent. There was a further tension between the principle that nothing can come out of nothing, so that the effect pre-exists in the cause, and the notion of concomitance of conditions. To explain the emergence of an effect one must postulate some condition outside that of the material cause which is supposedly transformed into the effect, and thus cause and effect are at least partly external to one another and not identical. The first of these tensions had an interesting resolution performed by some of the Realists (who held that entities past, present and future exist). Whereas the Idealists broke up substances into momentary sense-data, etc., the Realists used the concept of momentary atoms. That is, they satisfied two conditions one felt to be essential in a Buddhist analysis of the material and the other alluded to above (the protoscientific urge to get behind observable effects to the underlying causes thereof). The Atomists' everlasting atoms were unacceptable to the Buddhists and in any case created difficulties about causation. But their defect was not their atomicity, but their permanence. The short-lived atoms of the Realist school were not open to this defect, and so avoided some of the classical problems of the Logic-Atomist school. However, this form of atomic theory was confined to the realm of the corporeal. The other groups going to make up individuals were not accounted for through atomic combinations, but were *sui generis* (though, of course, each consisting in a flow of discrete events, and therefore not permanent).

There are some other aspects of traditional Indian discussions of causation which will be left over to the next chapter—i.e. those problems which arise in regard to the discrimination of causal sequences. We have already (in the discussion of epistemological issues) adverted to some of these methodological problems surrounding induction.

CHAPTER XV
INDUCTION AND INFERENCE

There have been left over to this chapter certain epistemological points which are more or less closely associated with logical matters discussed in the Indian tradition. Before going on to theories of inference, about which most of these questions cluster, it is convenient to refer back briefly to that basis of knowledge, which orthodox systems invoked, known as verbal testimony. We observed how the viewpoints built their epistemology on the bases of perception and inference. But the need to incorporate transcendent elements into the viewpoints led to the addition of testimony, chiefly, that is to say, the testimony constituted by revelation. But naturally, the discussion of testimony involved questions about the nature of language. As we have seen, the Buddhists held a conventionalist view about meanings, and the Logic-Atomist viewpoint was halfway to this view. But a recurrent difficulty about saying that meanings are assigned to words by customary usage was the belief, expressed in varying ways, that revelation is eternal. This meant in effect that the words through which it was expressed were eternal, or that underlying them were eternal counterparts in the form of meanings. Since, however, the conventionalist thesis entails that meanings have a non-eternal origin, it was not reconcilable to most orthodoxy. The most conservative statement of the orthodox position was that found in Exegesis, since revelation could not be explained there as the utterance of God, nor could it be held essentially to refer to mystical experience, so that modifications of the fundamentalist position found elsewhere were ruled out.

However, it was of course quite clear to the Exegetes, as to everyone, that language occurs in the form of sounds, etc., and these are temporary and have an occasion for their production. They therefore made use of the distinction (referred to in the last chapter, p. 187-8) between manifestation and production. Words exist eternally, but they only manifest themselves to us through sounds, etc. Reasons for making this claim were (apart from the necessity of it if revelation was to have an everlasting self-validity) the facts that language, so far as is known, has always existed, that the scriptures are not known to have an author, and that meanings are prior to individuals—that is the individual in learning a language apprehends what is already in existence and does not arbitrarily assign the meanings to the words. Such a view of the language of scripture as eternal gives Sanskrit a special place in the scheme of things (other tongues must be degenerations of the fundamental natural language: this feeling lies behind even comparatively recent attempts to show that Sanskrit is the ur-language).

The Exegetes added to these doctrines the further thesis that the language of scriptures is essentially injunctive. It expresses commands on what rituals and duties must be performed. This led to difficulties of interpretation where apparently descriptive statements appeared. However, the Exegetes evaded this trouble by holding that passages must be taken as wholes. It was thereby possible to consider descriptive passages as essentially belonging to wholes whose purport was injunctive.

The Exegete stress on imperatives was supported by a pragmatic theory of the learning of language. The characteristic situation in which a child discovers meanings is one where he is told to bring this or not to do that, etc. Thus language taken in a purely theoretical or descriptive way was detached from its proper roots.

The investigation of the nature of injunctions led to questions about negation. For instance, the negation of 'Let him do X' could be taken as 'Let him not-do X', 'Let him do not-X' and 'Let not-him do X'. The first means that the person is forbidden to perform the action; the second means that he is enjoined to perform an action other than the action in question; the third means that persons other than the person in question are enjoined to perform the action. It was argued that though in the first case of negation, it is impossible that both 'Let him do X' and 'Let him not-do X' should both be operative injunctions, the same impossibility does not hold in regard to the other forms. Thus 'Let him do not-X' does not entail the inoperativeness of 'Let him do X' (i.e. it might be his duty to perform all the actions within a certain genus); nor does 'Let not-him do X' entail the inoperativeness of 'Let him do X' (everybody may have a duty to do X). Thus one cannot tell how the law of contradiction applies until one has determined the locus of the negation. (However, the study of Exegete logic is still in an early stage; and there is doubtless quite a lot of material on injunctive logic to be discovered.)[1]

As we have seen, the Buddha, through his four-cornered negation, appears to have held that the law of contradiction does not, in some sense, apply to a certain class of propositions, namely those involved in the undetermined questions (see p. 20). That is, they do not apply in the sense that given a formulated proposition, one cannot infer from its truth that its negation is false; nor cannot it be inferred that either it or its negation is true. But this did not put the Buddha in the position of implicitly affirming that the law of contradiction, for instance, does not everywhere hold, for there are exceptions to it—namely where a proposition and its contradictory are both true. For this is explicitly denied, in the third arm of the negation, in regard to the propositions in question, i.e. 'It is not the case that both p and not-p'. Thus the Buddha's position amounts to this: that the laws do not *apply* in these cases; but this does not mean that they fail to hold, i.e. that these cases constitute genuine exceptions to the laws. Indeed, from the nature of the examples used to illustrate why these undetermined questions are unanswerable, it seems clear that the Buddha thought them to be so badly formed as to be meaningless. Thus the possibility of affirming any genuine proposition in these cases was excluded.

We have seen too how the Mahāyānist dialecticians used the principle of the Buddha's multiple negations as a slogan to justify their attempt to show that all views about reality are contradictory. But they held that this did not involve *themselves* in contradiction, since they were not (allegedly) affirming any views. Consequently, they recognized the law of contradiction, both negatively (for if it were not valid, they would have nothing against the views which they attacked as contradictory) and positively (for if it were not valid, they would have no motive for silence).

We noted earlier a certain resemblance between the Buddha's negations and the Jain sevenfold classifications of judgments in accordance with its theory of relativism (see p. 56). But again, this is not strictly the doctrine that the law of contradiction fails to hold; since the possibility of affirming both p and not-p depends on interpreting the left-hand p differently from the right-hand one. That is, when we say 'The jug is' and 'The jug is not' the words 'The jug is' are given different interpretations in the two sentences. Thus it is correct to say 'The jug is' in the sense that the jug is; but it is incorrect if it be taken to imply that the jug is identical with being, for being includes flowers and the jug is not identical with flowers—and so on. Thus the theory of relativism is essentially a theory to the effect that a statement must be made in its context; and one can affirm the apparent negation of the same statement, looking at matters in a different context of assertion. But the doctrine also includes, as we saw, the notion that in some sense the nature of the subject of a statement is inexpressible. Thus it is possible to say 'The jug is and is not and is inexpressible'. This, as we saw earlier (p. 55), arises from the fact that determinate judgments involve the concept of the difference between the thing described and other entities; and at least some judgements of difference are inexpressible. It can be said both about the Jain theory and that of the Buddhist undetermined questions that they involve the thesis that there are limitations upon knowledge which are not just contingent. On the Jain view, knowledge required linguistic expression, so that indescribable aspects of reality are in some sense unknowable. But while the Buddhist doctrine of undetermined questions springs from the *particular* nature of certain supposed problems, which involve a sort of category mistake or are ruled out by the structure of Buddhist metaphysics, the Jain position is supported by a *general* theory about language—namely that there is a finite number of basic expressions with determinate senses. Thus although the existence and non-existence of an entity (e.g., its being an orchid and not-being a rainbow) can be asserted consecutively, there is no intermediate expression which will simultaneously express the two aspects referred to. Nevertheless, the bafflement arising from this state of affairs can be indicated by asserting the inexpressibility of the entity in question.

There is an apparent infringement of the law of contradiction in Non-Dualist doctrine. It is true that in so far as the Non-Dualists made use of dialectical methods in the manner of the Voidist, they were in principle exempt from infringing it. But according to the classical Non-Dualist theory of ignorance and illusion, it had to be said that the world of appearance is both real and not real. Its reality is seen in the fact that appearances exist; they are not just a blank. Its unreality is seen in the fact that the ignorance which projects appearances on to pure being is not itself pure being. Thus the world as illusion (i.e. conceived as distinct from the holy Power) is not pure being, but not pure nothing either. Now in principle a contradiction could be avoided here by interpreting the two statements 'It is real' and 'It is not real' differently, and this was indeed sometimes done by the Non-Dualists. The two interpretations can be brought out by saying 'It exists but it is not pure being'. However, the Non-Dualists held that the world-appearance is indefinable precisely on the ground that it still has a contradictory aspect—since being and existence ought to be equivalent. But as a Rāmānujist remarked, if you are going to admit the self-contradictory, why not say that things in ordinary experience are real, and not illusory? It would contradict the doctrine of illusion, to be sure, but what is the trouble with a contradicton?

It will be seen that the above account of the unreality of the world-appearance depends on a contrast with absolute non-existence. This depended on the distinction between qualified and absolute negation or non-existence—a commonplace distinction in the Indian tradition. Thus the son of a barren woman (a stock example) is absolutely non-existent; while the non-existence of dodos is qualified. However, the stock examples are not all cases of the self-contradictory (such as the above one). Indeed the most common other examples are cases of contingent non-existence, such as the hare's horn, the sky-lotus, the water in the mirage. Thus the concept of absolute non-existence is that of entities which cannot exist, i.e. are known never to exist in experience. By contrast, qualified non-existence refers to entities which are known from experience sometimes to exist, but which do not at some time and place exist. It was argued by the Qualified Non-Dualists that all genuine judgments of non-existence are qualified, i.e. that whenever we say such things as 'There are no tigers' this judgment means 'There are no tigers in England now', with the implication that elsewhere and/or elsewhen there are or were or will be tigers. The cases of the horn of the hare, etc., were dealt with by pointing out that hares and horns exist or have existed: thus 'There are no hare's horns' means in effect 'There are no horns in a certain area of time and space, viz. in places and time occupied by hares' (but of course there are horns elsewhere and elsewhen). Consequently, it could not be argued that the illusion of Śaṅkara's system was real in the sense of not being a case of absolute non-existence. Moreover, since the illusion covered the whole of empirical experience, it could never be said that it was unreal in a qualified sense, from Śaṅkara's point of view (i.e. existing elsewhen, but not now, etc.). Thus the only way in which one could talk about illusions, etc., was to say that they exhibited supposed entities which existed elsewhere, but not at the locus of the illusion. Thus, some knowledge must be genuine, and not all perceptions could be cases of illusion.

As we shall see, such discussions had some bearing on theories of inference. The concept of negation or non-existence also created certain problems as to whether perception was a sufficient basis for knowledge of what was given in observation. For in so far as perception was held to be the perception of what exists, or of what is present, there was a difficulty about observations of the absence of something. That is, commonly in ordinary language we are said to notice the absence of something: this seems to imply that there is a special kind of perception, the perception-of-non-existence or the perception-of-absence. This we have dubbed earlier (p. 175) 'negative perception'. Now it might at first be thought that we could get over the trouble if we analysed the situation as being a combination of perception and inference. That is, it could be argued: 'Wherever there exists an object, there is perception; hence, since there is no perception of the object, it does not exist here.' But the premiss can only be established by the method of agreement and difference, i.e. by showing not merely that perception is accompanied by the existence, but that non-perception is accompanied by the non-existence, of the object. But this implies the very awareness of non-perception that is supposed to be explained by this account. Hence negative perception has to be admitted as a separate basis of knowledge.

The Logic-Atomists, without accepting negative perception as a basis of knowledge, nevertheless produced a very similar solution. This consisted in saying that there is perception of non-existence *(abhāva)*.

This forced the later Logic-Atomists to add non-existence to their list of categories. The difference between the two solutions is this—that for the Exegete the perception of non-existence is due to an intuition internal to the perceiver: while for the Logic-Atomists it is the perception of a sort of entity out there in the world. The chief point of criticism against this latter theory is that perception involves sense-contact between the perceiver and the object of perception, but clearly a non-existence cannot be in contact with the sense-organs. It thus seemed better to postulate an intuitive negative perception not involving the ordinary processes of perception. The reply to this was that the thesis that there is contact between outer objects and the sense-organs does not apply, since what is non-existent is not, in any ordinary sense, an object. Only positive substances enter into the relation of contact. It is clear that both accounts meant modifying the straight theory of perception through contact.

Buddhist metaphysics, since it stressed the conventionality of language, was in the position of evading these alternatives, by distinguishing between the manner in which a situation is described (and here negations enter in) and the concrete situation itself. Thus there is no perception of non-existence, but statements like 'There is no jug there' are ways of describing the state of affairs given in perception. The split between perception and linguistically-expressed judgment meant, incidentally, that the Buddhists could not describe what the correctness of a perception consisted in by reference to the truth of the statement describing it. The use of a statement implicitly involves reading concepts into the perception, and this means getting away from the pure presentation. Thus a behaviouristic account of veridicality in perceptions was canvassed: i.e. a correct perception is such that one is not disappointed in one's aims and expectations by acting upon it.

As has been seen, a chief reason for the Logic-Atomist concern about non-existence was its employment of the method of agreement and difference in establishing inductive generalizations. But it would be misleading to suppose that all their inferences were supposed to rest upon premisses describing causal relations. First, we noted earlier that, on their view, a cause had immediately to precede its effect. Thus a causal chain was conceived as a series of causal links: but the relation of causality was not transitive. If A causes B, and B causes C, it does not follow that A can properly be described as the cause of C. Nevertheless, there may be an invariable concomitance between A and C, and this could be the basis of a particular inference (if A accompanies B, then given a B we can infer an A). Buddhist logicians attempted to make a distinction between inferences concerned with production (i.e. with the production of a type of effect by a type of cause) from inferences concerned with identity. For example, 'All cases of smoke are cases of fire' (a premiss that can be used to show that because here is a case of smoke there must be a fire) is distinguished from such instances as 'All pines are trees' (a premiss that can be used to show that because this is a pine it must be a tree). It was objected by the Logic-Atomists that in any event concomitance was a sufficient description of the situation, since there is a concomitance between the universal of treeness and pineness inhering in substances of a certain kind; and that it was wrong to count it a case of identity, since one cannot conversely infer from a thing's being a tree to its being a pine. However, this was largely a verbal point. The Buddhists usually (see above, p. 172) denied that a cause could be simultaneous with its effect. When, therefore, two properties are invariably conjoined in the same locus, but are simultaneous, they must be identical. This was the principle underlying the Idealist argument noticed earlier (p. 172) that a perception and its 'object' must be identical.

The shape of a traditional Indian inference was somewhat complex. Three chief elements were distinguished the sign, locus *(pakṣa)* and inferendum. Thus a typical example of inference was:

(1) The hill (locus) possesses fire (inferendum);
(2) Because of its possessing smoke (sign);
(3) Where there is smoke (sign) there is fire (inferendum)—as in a kitchen.
(4) This hill (locus) possesses smoke (sign);
(5) Therefore it possesses fire (inferendum).

It can be observed that the first statement expresses the thesis to be proved, i.e. one begins with the conclusion. It is odd that (3) includes an example of the sign-inferendum concomitance in a different locus (the kitchen). But a distinction was drawn between the form of an inference designed to persuade others, and the form which it could take if one was inferring something for oneself. This complex form of five propositions, was therefore regarded as reducible to three: namely, (1), (2) and (3), and the example could be dispensed with: its importance was psychological, in reminding the listener or oneself of the kind of observation on which the universal proposition was based.

The weight of Indian concern about inference was directed at making sure that the universal proposition (3) was true, in order to guarantee the inference. In short, it was mainly directed at formulating conditions which would have to be fulfilled before (3) could be asserted. We have already discussed earlier certain arguments about induction closely connected with this concern. It is a principle of the Logic school that (3) must be established by collecting a large number of instances of the sign accompanied by the inferendum. If S stands for the former and I for the latter, we can formulate the matter by saying that instances must be gathered tending to show that all Ss are Is. But if some Ss are non-Is (if for instance some cases of smoke are caused by water and not by fire) the inference will not work. It therefore has to be shown, again by collecting instances, that all non-Is are non-Ss. (This clearly allowed the possibility of a different sort of inference using this as a universal proposition.) The Exegetes were somewhat laxer in their rules of induction: it was sufficient that one had gathered instances to the effect that all Ss are Is, provided one was not aware of counter-instances. The need, according to the Logic-school, for perceptual corroboration implied another methodological rule, viz. that the thesis ('This hill possesses fire') should not be falsified by direct observation. That is, it is itself treated as one of the instances which go to corroborate or falsify the universal proposition. This does not, of course, involve circularity, since it does not entail that the universal proposition is only established when all positive instances have examined, including the inferendum, and since normally there is no perception of the inferendum, and therefore no question of its falsifying the inference.

Although the concomitance of smoke with fire, and like concomitances of the form 'All Ss are Is', were a satisfactory basis for inference, the establishment of causal relations between inferendum and sign required greater stringency. For clearly, though fire immediately precedes smoke and there is no smoke without fire, the fact that there is some fire without smoke means that we should investigate the actual conditions of there being smoke more closely. It is found, say, that it is the association of fire with green wood which causes smoke: and this means that there is an invariable concomitance between the inferendum (green wood plus fire) and the sign (smoke), such that not only is it true that all Ss are Is, but also all Is are Ss. It is therefore important, in establishing causal concomitances, that the antecedent conditions and consequent conditions should be varied as far as is practically possible.

However, the application of the method of agreement and difference could not be applied to all universal propositions. Thus 'All objects of knowledge are describable' cannot be tested by seeing if non-describable things are also non-knowable, since non-knowable things by definition cannot be known. Thus such universal propositions could be established on the basis of the agreement in presence of the two properties, but not by agreement in absence. There was some considerable discussion of this type of inference (which we can dub the no-negative form *kevalānvayī*) among later logicians. Likewise, the Logic school held, and it was denied by some, that there could be the converse of this case, where there are no positive instances, but only negative ones. We can call this the no-positive form *(kevalavyātirekī)*, and it occurs in cases where there is no concomitance between the sign and the inferendum except in the locus which is the subject of the inference: for example 'Immediate intuition is not an object of awareness because it is immediate intuition'. This would expand into the following form:

(1) Immediate intuition is not an object of awareness:
(2) Because it is immediate intuition;
(3) All cases of immediate intuition are not cases of being an object of awareness.

As a form of inference this looks pretty hopeless, since it amounts to saying 'Xs are non-Ys, because they are Xs, and Xs are non-Ys'. However, if we remember the later Logic school held that it could be established negatively, i.e. by the examination of negative instances, the appearance of tautologous groundlessness diminishes. For the real ground of the conclusion, that all Xs are non-Ys, is that all Ys are non-Xs. For instance, you examine all cases of objects of awareness and discover that none of them is an immediate intuition. It was objected, however, to this form of inference that it could lead to fallacious results. For example, the theistic argument 'Omniscience is absent from all entities in the sphere of perceptual experience, so it must belong to an unperceived entity, and such an entity would be God' is no more reasonable than the inference that the horn of the hare is absent from the observable world, so it must belong to an unperceived entity. Thus purely negative instances cannot establish the required conclusion, since it must also be shown that the subject of the inference actually exists.

It should be noted that the above example necessarily involves that there should be no positive instances, since intuition is supposed (and here there is reference to the Śaṅkarite doctrine) to be not an object of awareness and *a fortiori* not an object of perception—upon which generalizations and inferences must be based. But there was a further class of the no-positive form of inference where it was not the case that the subject is by definition unobservable, etc., but there the sign was the defining characteristic of the subject, and where the inferendum expressed the difference of the subject from other entities. For example, 'Earth differs from other elements, because it possesses smell'. Smell is here regarded as the defining characteristic of the earth element, and is that by which the earth element is picked out in perception. Now it was the essence of the earlier Logic account of inference that it was a means of acquiring new knowledge, and so the subject should not be included already in the instances one collected of the sign. Thus in this sort of reasoning, in which the subject can only be picked out through the sign, it was held that there are no genuine positive instances, and so the inference must depend on the negative instances which go to show 'What is not different from the other elements does not possess smell'. But it may then be asked: 'What is the inference supposed to show?' It is simply a way of showing that a definition is adequate, by showing that the defining characteristic does not belong to other entities.

It was objected by some Qualified Non-Dualists that this form of inference is quite unnecessary, and indeed was dangerous where applied in the first way to subjects which are necessarily unobservable. For the definition could be established in the normal manner, through the application of the method of agreement and difference. That is, the basis of a definition is the perception that a certain characteristic belongs to a certain sort of object, and is absent from others. Thus definitions are empirically rooted.

The recognition of no-negative forms of inference raised problems about the definition of concomitance which exhibit ways in which later logicians moved away from an epistemological view of inference to a more formal one. As we saw, the initial concern was with inference as a means of acquiring inductive knowledge, and in particular with the discovery of causal connections. It was thus not surprising that the concomitance of sign and inferendum was regarded as *par excellence* coexistence (i.e. immediate contiguity in space and time throughout the instances). Now since non-causal inferences were allowed, a definition of concomitance in terms of spatio-temporal contiguity was bound to break down. For instance, one could infer from the state of the moon to the state of the tide: and here there was no spatial contiguity (for this very reason, it was not regarded as a case of causal connection). Likewise a chain of causes stretching over a period of time might yield a concomitance between the first and the last, but again it was not regarded as a spatial connection (only the various links in the chain were counted as such) and the criterion of contiguity in time was not satisfied. It was therefore attractive to try to define concomitance as agreement in presence and absence, or as agreement in absence only. But the no-negative type of inference ruined such definitions. Nor was it sufficient to define concomitance as agreement in presence only, since this would not fit the normal inference, which made use of the negative instances.

One way out of these difficulties was discovered by Vedānta logicians, who abandoned, in effect, the inductive and causal flavour of the other attempts at the definition of concomitance. They argued that the principle of inference making use of a universal premiss is the impossibility of denying the inferendum without denying the sign. Admittedly, the way this point was expressed was still epistemological in flavour: namely that a concomitance was such that one could only deny the presence of the inferendum in the subject at the expense of denying the presence of the sign and this latter involves denying an incontrovertible experience. For instance, denying that there is fire on that hill would involve denying the incontrovertible experience of perceiving smoke on the hill. Nevertheless, this was a move in the direction of considering the formal properties of an inference, rather than the methodology required for verifying the universal premiss, etc. It should be noted that the account worked for no-negative inferences; and thus was stimulated by earlier attempts to define concomitance in an epistemological manner. In the current example of a no-negative inference, 'This is describable, because it is an object of knowledge, and objects of knowledge are describable', the impossibility is found in denying the inferendum, i.e. in saying that the subject is indescribable, since this commits one to denying that it is an object of knowledge—and this is plainly false.

Some of the viewpoints, notably the Exegetes and some of the Qualified Non-Dualists and other Vedāntins, added a further basis of knowledge to the usual ones of perception, inference and verbal testimony, namely implication. This was a form of reasoning which could not be subsumed under the forms of inference mentioned above. The stock example was: 'Devadatta is living; but he is perceived not to be in the house; therefore he exists somewhere outside the house.' The principal reason advanced for not subsuming this under inference is as follows. Suppose we attempt to cast it in an inferential form, we have this: 'Devadatta is somewhere outside the house; because he is not in the house; and all existent entities which are not in a given place exist in some other place.' It was argued that the universal proposition was tautologous, since it follows from the meanings of the terms that an existent thing not in one place must be in some other place. (Though we may note that the converse does not apply: because an existent entity is in one place it does not follow that it is not elsewhere—since it might, like the soul according to some viewpoints, be omnipresent.) Hence this premiss does not have the inductive character ascribed to inference as usually understood. However, Madhva and others accepted implication as a form of inference, not wishing to restrict the latter to the typical inductive case.

A further basis of knowledge accepted by Exegesis and Non-Dualism, and by Logic, but not by Atomism, is that of analogy. The stock example is of a person going into the forest who has been told by a forester that a wild ox is rather like a cow. He perceives a wild ox, for the first time, and correctly concludes, on the basis of the similarity with the cow, that it is indeed a wild ox. The reasons for not counting this either as testimony (in a broad sense, not confined to revelation) or as inference are as follows. First, the conclusion 'This is a wild ox' is not asserted by the forester, but depends upon the percipient's awareness of the ox plus its similarity to a cow. Second, it is not an inference of the ordinary kind since it involves perceiving a type of object not previously given in experience, and assigning to it a name. As elsewhere, the notion of a basis of knowledge is interpreted in terms of the acquirement of knowledge; and is indeed individualistically conceived—it exhibits the means whereby the individual gains new knowledge. However, this individualistic emphasis is modified by the use of testimony in a wide sense (i.e., as above, not confined to revelation). This implies the acceptance of the evidence of trustworthy persons; and thus to this extent the acquirement of knowledge is seen as a communal enterprise.

The methodological manner in which mostly inference was treated is also exhibited by discussions of the functions of cogitation *tarka*. Thus according to the Logic school, this is a necessary element in the process of inference, i.e. of establishing a concomitance. It consists in a review of the situation and the attempt to discover conditions which would vitiate the inference. It is thus a method of doubting, whose aim is to eliminate reasonable doubt, by proposing possible ways of falsifying the concomitance, and thereby showing that it survives these tests. It is therefore, in effect, the activity of putting the method of agreement and difference, etc., into operation, by raising fruitful doubts. The concept of cogitation occasioned an ingenious argument from a Vedāntin dialectician—namely, that the method of doubt could not put an end to reasonable doubt; for if, in considering a supposed concomitance, one thinks that maybe there is some vitiating condition, there is only one way in which such a doubt can be removed, namely by the falsification of the concomitance. For example, suppose one is contemplating the thesis 'Wherever, there is green wood plus fire, there is smoke', one uses the method of cogitation by raising the doubt as to whether there is not some hidden condition in the green wood plus fire which gives rise to the fire and which might occur separately from the green wood plus fire. So one tests this doubt, and finds it unfounded. But there can be a host, indeed an indefinite number, of different hidden conditions. So the elimination of one doubt will not eliminate others. Only if one conclusively finds the thesis refuted in experience, through a clear negative instance—a case of green wood plus fire where there is no smoke—are doubts removed. The matter is settled, that the concomitance does *not* hold. Inductive generalizations, then, are never conclusively verifiable, but only falsifiable. (Hence the Non-Dualist doctrine alluded to earlier (p. 167) that the test of knowledge is non-falsification.)

We have discussed various logical issues raised in the Indian tradition from an informal point of view, and in relation to the other points of disagreement, over epistemology, causation, etc. Theories about inference arose from protoscientific concerns (indeed there are interesting connections between early Indian medicine and the Logic school); but the interplay of viewpoints, and the way in which cosmological theories themselves tend to generate philosophical questions, led to an elaboration of inference beyond the sphere of causal concomitances. For example, under the second head the no-negative form of inference in part was necessary because ultimate entities, such as the earth element, possess a simple defining characteristic; and so statements about the difference of earth from other elements cannot be treated on a par with causal inference. Further, though Logic-Atomist inference was closely wedded to perception, both the existence of atoms and, later, the existence of God, required to be proved through inferences by analogy from the perceptible to the unseen. Similarly Exegesis used implication as a way of establishing transcendent truths ('All efforts are rewarded; but sacrifices are not rewarded on earth, so thay must be rewarded in heaven'). As an example of the way in which the interplay of viewpoints generated questions about inference, the no-negative and the no-positive forms arose from a consideration of certain types of metaphysical thesis. For example, as we have seen, the Non-Dualist notion that there is an immediate intuition of the self as the subject of knowledge implied, or was held to imply, that this intuition is itself not an object of knowledge. But being unwilling to accept that the intuited self is not an object of knowledge, the Rāmānujists and others were moved to argue that it is an absurdity to speak of anything which is not in some sense an object of knowledge—and that there could certainly be no awareness or perception of a supposedly unknowable entity. But it followed from this that the thesis 'Intuition is an object of perception' can have no negative instances to examine. Hence the need for the no-negative inference. On the other hand, they were strenuously opposed to the no-positive form, whereby it was sought to establish the negation of the above thesis. It is thus not unreasonable to hold that, generally speaking in the Indian tradition, and more especially up to the time of the later Logic school, when a more formal approach began to come in, discussions about logic were closely bound up with epistemological, and thereby metaphysical, disputes.

The study of Indian logic from a formal point of view is still rather in its infancy; and a great deal of interesting work is to be done there. But formal logic, as such, is fairly remote from the kinds of philosophical issues we have been considering.

POSTSCRIPT ON THE ARGUMENTS

The arguments described in the foregoing chapters are not, needless to say, exhaustive of the discussions in the early and medieval Indian tradition. Nevertheless they represent a fair sample of the more important issues under dispute, although I have understressed one or two. For instance, there is very protracted debate, in all schools or virtually so, about the nature of illusion—under the impact of Śaṅkara's Non-Dualism, and only part of this debate has been alluded to.

If one had to point to a general issue which constituted the major preoccupation of Indian metaphysicians, it would probably be that of the relation between the permanent and the impermanent. This reflected itself in a two-fold way: with regard to things and selves. As to the former, the root problem was perhaps raised by the Buddhist critique of the notion of substance, especially in relation to the part substances or abiding entities are supposed to play in causation. The denial of the concept led to the doctrine of momentariness, and via that ultimately to idealism. In regard to selves, there was a similar problem about causation: but in addition the problem of how they are related to minds and bodies, given the important assumption in the Indian tradition that ordinary mental processes and the apparatus of mental life were held to come under the heading of matter rather than spirit. It was therefore especially tricky to evaluate the monistic thesis of Śaṅkara, that there is but one Self, since the ordinary characteristics associated with an individual's life do not belong, *ex hypothesi*, to the Self. But it is doubtful whether idealism would have proved so powerful, even though some of the philosophical difficulties about the self and causation might already seem to point towards it, had it not been for the religious reasons underlying it. Nor would the sharp division between self and psychophysical organism have been so prominent but for the contemplative quest for a 'transcendent' experience beyond the discriminations of ordinary mental life.

It is perhaps not surprising that many of the arguments we have outlined above are between the Logic-Atomists and the others. Its rather conservative realism, coupled with its concern about the nature of causation, contrasted both with the extreme radicalism of Buddhist analyses of causation and of the ultimate constituents of reality and with the religiously-oriented idealism of the Mahāyāna and Non-Dualism. Yet if our remark above about the major preoccupation of Indian metaphysics is correct, it was the Buddhists who posed the key questions, both by their denial of the self and their phenomenalistic tendencies.

It is to be hoped that the foregoing chapters have given some insight into Indian argumentations in the early and medieval period. But I am not concerned with the question of how these argumentations tie up with those of Western philosophy. No doubt they can speak for themselves. Where similarities occur, it is interesting that they should thus occur in independent traditions. Perhaps, though, dissimilarities are more suggestive. But that is as may be.

NOTES

CHAPTER I

1. The remark requires a double elucidation. First, much depends on what is meant by 'creator'. As we see (p. 92) the Indian concept does not involve that of creation out of nothing (as in the Christian tradition), but rather it means that God orders pre-existent matter, e.g. atoms *aṇu*, or that he evolves the cosmos out of his own substance. Moreover the 'pulsating' universe of nearly all Indian mythological cosmology implies that creation is not a single, but a recurrent event. But even though the Indian concept is not as drastic as the Christian one, and so one could say that, e.g., Logic *(Nyāya)*-Atomism *(Vaiśeṣika)* does not hold to a doctrine of creation 'in a full sense' (assuming that the Christian doctrine has the 'full sense'), the classical Yoga doctrine falls short of that of the Logic-Atomists. For the Lord, in Yoga, is simply a soul which has never been entangled in nature. Meditation, by the Yoga adept, on the Lord creates a *rapport* which helps the soul towards release. However, by the late medieval period the concept of God in Yoga became increasingly assimilated to that of Logic-Atomism. To quote Mircea Eliade: 'All in all Īśvara is only the archetype of the yogin—a macro-yogin; very probably a patron of certain yogic sects.' (*Yoga, Immortality and Freedom*, p. 75.)

2. In varying ways, such an interpretation has been attempted by Mrs C.A.F. Rhys Davids (*What was the Original Gospel?* I, p. 79 ff., and *Sakya*, p. 112 ff.); Ananda Coomaraswamy (see his Introduction to *The Living Thoughts of the Buddha*); Miss I. B. Horner in R.C. Zaehner (editor), *The Concise Encyclopedia of Living Faiths;* G. Appleton, *The Eightfold Path*, pp. 126-7. Professor Zaehner is another, and highly distinguished, representative of this trend.

In *At Sundry Times* (p. 98), he writes: 'If there is such as deathlessness, peace and an unchanging state, must there not be someone or something that is conscious of this state?' He then proceeds to quote a number of texts collected by Miss Horner, suggesting a belief in a permanent Self (p. 99ff.), principally from the *Dhammapada* (even though he concedes that this work shows much more evident signs of Upaniṣadic influence than does the bulk of the Pāli canon). He quotes the passage 'If one knows the Self as precious (*piyam*, "dear"), he should guard it well-guarded' (*Dhammapada*, 157, Miss Horner's translation). Note the use of the question-begging capital. He claims that *atta* cannot here refer to the empirical ego, which is the source of evil, referring us to *Dhammapada* 161 and 165, and which is therefore scarcely likely to be referred to as 'precious' or 'dear'. But this argument is in no way conclusive, and for the following reasons. First, the passages afford no real support. For instance: 'The evil is done by one's self, one suffers by one's self; by one's self evil is left undone; by one's self one is made pure. The pure and the impure stand and fall by themselves; no one can purify another.' The whole point of this passage is that one must be self-reliant; and it would be straining it considerably to translate 'The evil is done by one's self... by one's Self one is made pure.' If such a distinction is being made, it could certainly have been put more perspicuously.

Secondly, the Buddha's repeated emphasis on individual effort indicates that one is capable of good as well as evil. The individual is capable of *kusaladhammā (Sutta-nipāta,* 1039, 1078, etc.). Are we to argue by parity of reasoning, with Zaehner, that good dispositions, and conscience, belong to the Self? (*At Sundry Times:* 'It is a moral entity, manifesting itself as conscience.') This would run contrary to the whole spirit of Buddhist psychology. Not only is there no distinct entity recognized as conscience, but more importantly, the elaborate analysis of the personality into elements or groups, which are impermanent *(khandha), anicca* would break down. It may perchance be replied that the doctrine of *khandhas* etc., is a later accretion (as according to Mrs Rhys Davids, *Indian Psychology*, pp. 192-203); but the central image to illustrate the Buddhist theory of the self, the chariot simile, is not. Moreover, if a self is postulated as different from the body, feelings, etc., it would surely approximate to the Distinctionist notion: and to suggest that good dispositions or conscience belong to *this* would be absurd.

Moreoever, if Hindu and Western commentators are right in ascribing a Self or selves to early Buddhism, it is surely remarkable that the Buddhist schools never dared to propound it. The *pudgalavādins* came near to it, of course; but it is highly significant that they did not dare use *ātman* as their key expression. Nowhere in all the proliferations of the Mahāyāna (in other respects not unwilling to introduce doctrinal novelties and reinterpretations) is there an explicit *ātmavāda*.

Another passage cited by Zaehner is *Sutta-nipāta*, 778: 'Desire he should curb for either course,/Committing nothing that the Self would blame.' The key word here, *attagarahī*—'self-censuring', need hardly be strained in this way. And it readily becomes apparent that one can always find examples to suit the *ātmavāda* thesis because (naturally) the simple reflexive *atta* is so common (about as common as the English 'self'). One can imagine how entertaining it would be to translate David Hume as follows (in his *Essay of Miracles*): 'I flatter my Self that I have discovered an argument of a like nature, which, if just, will, with the wise and learned, be an everlasting check to all kinds of superstitious delusion...'

There are two other main points adduced by Zaehner which merit attention. First, he draws attention to the famous words 'Go along, having Self as lamp', etc. (*Dīgha-nikāya*, ii, 100). He comments (*op. cit.*, p. 101): 'The Self than which one should have none other refuge, then, would appear to be identical, in some mysterious way, with the *dhamma.*' Also: 'We do, however, read elsewhere (*Dhammapada* 151) that the *Dhamma* of good men never ages, and in all its connotations *dhamma* would seem to mean an unchanging something, usually an unchanging law, either of Nature, or of the Buddha.' Now inasmuch as the Mahāyānist doctrine of the *dharmakāya* has any justification in the Pāli texts, it is in this notion of assimilating the *dhamma* to oneself; and if *dhamma* is interpreted metaphysically as Truth rather than as truth or truths, then in some sense one becomes united with ultimate reality through this assimilation or appropriation. But certainly such an interpretation is foreign to the Theravādin tradition. Moreover, it can hardly assist the Zaehner thesis, since he is wishing to argue, not the Coomaraswamy doctrine that Buddhism involves belief in one Self or Absolute, identical for all, but rather the doctrine that each person has an 'eternal element' (*op. cit.* p. 98).

The other main point in his argument is that his thesis is 'amply confirmed by the passages illustrating what the Self is not' (p. 101). For instance, it is not the body, feelings, dispositions, etc. But this, far from confirming the Zaehner *ātmavāda,* is clearly explained in the famous passage in the *Milindapañha* (40-45), where a Humean analysis of the self is propounded. Moreover, the Buddha himself is reported to have remarked that though the self is not to be identified with the body, it would be better for the ordinary uninstructed man to make this identification than to fall into the opposite error of eternalism (*Saṃyutta-nikāya,* ii, 95).

It is a pity that so distinguished a commentator as Zaehner has fallen thus into the eternalist *(sassatavāda)* interpretation of the Buddha's doctrine; and quite unnecessarily, for his evaluation of the patterns of Indian mysticism could be made more convincing still if it were accompanied by a lively application of the distinction between experience and interpretation. It does not follow that because Yoga and the Theravāda, for instance, interpret their goals very differently (in some respects at any rate) that therefore we are dealing with radically diverse kinds of mystical or contemplative experience.

3. As will be seen (p. 37), I use 'Absolute' to mean the ground or inner nature of the world, and thus it has here a narrower sense than that given to it by E. Conze in his *Buddhist Thought in India,* where it is used as an equivalent of 'Unconditioned' or of that which is not in relation to anything else. This allows him to speak of Theravādin nirvana as the Absolute. I wish, however, to avoid this: since (roughly) the Theravadin concept is of a transcendent *state,* not a unitary substance or quasi-substance, as in Mahāyāna conceptions of *Tathatā,* etc. But my usage may be criticized on the ground that the Mādhyamika doctrine of the Void, for example, is not that of a *substance* which is the inner nature of reality. Is not the whole point of the Mādhyamika a critique of substance (*dravya*)? Nevertheless, I am here in the excellent company of T. R.V. Murti. Moreover, the identification of *Śūnyatā* with the *dharmakāya* of

the Buddha is neither fortuitous nor unimportant. To quote Conze: 'The Dharma-body is eternal, immutable and omnipresent' (*op. cit.* p. 233). Nor can this doctrine be regarded as a later superimposition on the Mādhyamika position—as Conze himself remarks, 'The originality of the Buddhology of the Mahāyāna has often been overestimated. The three 'bodies' of the Buddha had already been distinguished quite clearly by the Sarvāstivādins'. Thus, although of course the Mādhyamika dialectic steers between speaking of the Void as real or unreal, the flavour of Mādhyamika talk about the Void is the flavour of talk about an invisible underlying substance which, so to say, permeates the world. It is this which makes it possible to see the close connection between Advaita and Nāgārjuna. Admittedly, it might be answered that the Absolute is indescribable, and the dialectic is a means of silencing the enquirer and ridding him of all views *(diṭṭhi)* or theories, even a theory about the Void. But still, though this element in the Mādhyamika is often emphasized, one can pose the following dilemma. Either the higher truth is absolutely unspeakable, in which case one cannot even begin to characterize the Mādhyamika position; or it has at least a certain atomsphere, such that one can describe the position, at least in a provisional way. In the latter case, it is quite natural and appropriate to place Nāgārjuna and his followers in the milieu to which they have been traditionally assigned —namely that of a form of Buddhism, represented by the *Prajñāpāramitā* literature, and which was excogitated in the context of a growth of devotionalism, requiring a synthesis between this type of religion and the more traditional Buddhist yoga. (On this, one may note a significant point made by Murti about Śantideva, sometimes credited with introducing popular doctrines into the Mādhyamika tradition: 'One is invariably reminded of the *Imitation of Christ* in reading the *Bodhicaryāvatāra,* which is the stronger in appeal, as it is born of deep philosophical insight. Devotion (*bhakti*) to the Buddhas and Bodhisattvas, and confession of one's transgressions (*pāpadesanā*) before them are enjoined as part of spiritual purification. This is by no means an innovation; Nāgārjuna's *Catuḥstava* is in the same strain.' (*Central Philosophy of Buddhism,* p. 101.) Thus there is some reason to use 'Absolute' in my sense to refer to the doctrines of *Tathatā*, *Śunyatā* and (of course) *Ālayavijñāna*.

CHAPTER II

1. See Paul Tillich, *Christianity and the Encounter of the World Religions*, p. 5 ff. On the question of the definition of religion, especially in relation to Thervāda Buddhism, see my 'Nirvana and the Definition of Religion', *Church Quarterly Review*, January—March 1958, p. 216 ff.

CHAPTER III

1. I am influenced here by Henrich Zimmer. He coined the word 'transtheistic' to describe systems of belief such as Buddhism and Jainism. He wrote, for instance (*Philosophies of India*, pp. 181-82): '...the supreme objects of Jaina contemplation, the Tīrthankaras, have passed beyond the godly governors of the natural order. Jainism, that is to say, is not atheistic; it is transtheistic.' Others have adopted the expression: thus Dr. E.G. Parrinder, in his excellent *Worship in the World's Religions*, says that it is wrong to count Jainism and Buddhism as atheistic, and refers to Zimmer's concept (p. 99 n.). Undoubtedly the term is meant to perform a useful classificatory task. But as it stands it could be misleading (that is why I use 'transpolytheistic').

Both Buddhism and Jainism allow gods (though not God) to exist, i.e. it is polytheism rather than theism that they transcend (except in certain phases of the Mahāyāna). But in what sense is 'transcend' used here? One can view this transcendence as being constituted by the superior value attached to the Buddhas and Tīrthaṃkaras as compared with the gods. Or again one can view it in relation to the concept of liberation employed in these faiths: for both Jainism and Buddhism transcend the worship of the gods in positing a mystical or contemplative goal which has an immensely superior significance to that of the popular cults. Thus we can state the idea that these faiths transcend polytheism in these two ways:

> (i) They do not deny that polytheistic worship has some value, but place a much greater value on their super-saints, the Tīrthaṃkaras and Buddhas than on the gods;

(ii) They do not deny that polytheistic worship has some value, but place a much greater value on contemplation leading to release than on the worship of the gods.

It is interesting to compare this kind of transcendence of popular religion with that which is found in some forms of Hinduism. Śaṅkara's doctrines, e.g. imply that though belief in an Īśvara has a certain value for ordinary people who have not attained the higher mystical insight that Brahman alone is real, it nevertheless has ultimately to be discarded. Thus Śaṅkara allows for theism, but represents it as a 'lower level' of religious insight. Corresponding to (ii) above, we may formulate Śaṅkara's position as follows:

(iii) It is not denied that theistic worship has some value, but a much greater value is placed on the contemplative's insight that Brahman alone exists.

However, the position is further complicated by the fact that polytheistic cults are never excluded in Hinduism, and by the further fact that they can be regarded in different ways. In line with the famous verse in *Ṛg-veda* i, 164, 46, the gods are regarded as so many fragmentations of the one divine reality. Thus Dr Radhakrishnan writes, regarding the gods: 'They are useful symbols which serve as the bearers of the divine power or mystery' (*The Brahma Sūtra,* 134). But the more classical view has been to see them as beings inhabiting the cosmos, and subordinate to the supreme Lord: thus in *Brahma-Sūtra,* i, 3, 26, the gods are shown to have this inferior ontological and religious status. But both these ways of regarding the gods have the same practical result: namely that polytheism is integrated into the structure of higher religion. Thus theistic Hinduism (as represented by Rāmānuja and Madhva, for example) transcends polytheism while not excluding it. This position can be formulated as follows:

(iv) It is not denied that polytheistic worship has some value, but a much greater value is placed upon theistic worship and insight.

How can we arrive at a terminology to express these different positions? The answer is simple, if the prefix 'trans-' is taken to be a shorthand way of referring to such kinds of transcendence. Thus (i), (ii) and (iv) represent aspects of religious systems which transcend polytheism. These systems then can be conveniently labelled 'transpolytheistic'. We now have a *new* use for Zimmer's neologism 'transtheistic', viz. to express (iii) above. Thus in this new sense of the term the Advaita and analogous doctrines can be classified as 'transtheistic'.

It would perhaps be of interest to draw up a chart of various doctrines—which in turn reflect differing ways of practising religion. Roughly, the fundamental forms of various systems of doctrine can be listed as follows: theism, absolutism, polytheism and atheism (or agnosticism). Each of the ultimate principles might in theory transcend any other, but in practice it is impossible to find polytheism as an ultimate belief transcending any of the other types of doctrine. Further, it must be remembered that atheism and agnosticism are here to be taken as religious in nature (i.e. they are atheism, as in the text, p. 23). It must also be remembered that some religions do not transcend, but exclude, polytheism: thus Judaism, Christianity and Islam are strongly antipolytheistic. Hence they are to be distinguished from Indian forms of theism.

Thus we have the following categories:

I. Antipolytheistic theism (Judaism, Christianity, Islam);

II. Transpolytheistic theism (Madhva, Rāmānuja, Śaiva Siddhānta, Caitanya, etc.).

III. Antipolytheistic transtheistic absolutism (Eckhart, some Ṣūfis).

IV. Transpolytheistic transtheistic absolutism (Advaita, some forms of the Mahāyāna—though the Tathāgata is not creator, but corresponds nevertheless to the Advaitin *Īśvara*).

V. Transpolytheistic atheism (Jainism, Sāṃkhya and Theravāda Buddhism).

VI. Polytheism, animism, etc.

Needless to say, there are elements in actual religious practice which blur the above distinctions. For example, the cult of saints in some Christian countries is not so very far removed from polytheism. Again, the reverence paid to the Buddha in Theravādin countries is sometimes hard to distinguish from worship, as though the Buddha were a god. Nevertheless, the concepts of religion are important as well as the practices and indeed serve as a norm for guiding practice. Thus it would be grossly misleading for an observer, on the basis of what he has seen in temples, to describe the Theravāda as a form of theism: just as it would equally be wrong to say that Christianity really incorporates, through the cult of saints, a kind of polytheism. To understand the teachings of a faith it is necessary to go beyond the outward and visible and to heed what an educated and perceptive adherent of the faith would regard as the real import of practices. The above classification thus attempts, roughly, to show the ontological presuppositions of various religions and systems of doctrine. There are, moreover, some subtle variations not mentioned above. For instance:

> VII. Transabsolutistic theism (for Rāmānuja and the *Gītā* recognize the impersonal Brahman as comprehended within the personal Lord).

In the sphere of religion, the kinds of entities believed to exist transcend one another in varying ways.

CHAPTER VII

1. Of course, for Śaṅkara, the pursuit of *karma,* as the fulfilment of religious duties, and the attitude of *bhakti,* on the one hand, and the path of spiritual knowledge (*jñāna*) on the other hand are for different classes of persons. They are distinctively different approaches and the former is subordinated to the latter—works and faith lead to the *brahmaloka,* not to ultimate release. Nevertheless, three significant points should be noted. First, *brahmaloka* is, so to say, on the way to release; although works and faith do not themselves bring release, they give adherents a more favourable vantage point in the round of rebirth for attaining the non-dualistic experience. Second, Śaṅkara's whole system is predicated on the assumption that the Veda is revelation: in other words, the higher truth has to be seen as transcending a certain prior context, without which Śaṅkara's system would neither be orthodox nor properly intelligible. Thus the performance of Vedic duties, and the attitude of devotion to a personal Lord, are the necessary context of Non-Dualism. Third, though in principle the way of knowledge and the way of devotion are for different persons, yet Śaṅkara himself was a devotional poet of some power. As Radhakrishnan has remarked (*The Brahma Sūtra,* p. 37): 'While Śaṅkara is an absolute non-dualist in his metaphysics, he had great faith in *bhakti* or devotion to a personal God.' Radhakrishnan goes on to

cite some verses from Śaṅkara's hymns. A good collection of these is translated in the Appendix to Swami Nikhilananda's *Self-Knowledge* (an edition of the *Ātmabodha*). Thus it is a cause of no surprise *bhakti* should have expression in the Non- Dualistic tradition, and it is odd for Dasgupta to remark, about Madhusūdana (*History of Indian Philosophy*, ii, p. 226): 'It is...interesting to note that, though he was such a confirmed monist in his philosophy, he was a theist in his religion and followed the path of *bhakti* creed. These works, however, have *nothing to do with the philosophy of the Vedānta*' (my italics). As we shall see (p.), it was precisely the religion of worship which, injected into mysticism, gave rise to Absolutistic doctrines (where such a religion of worship was taken account of, but also, so to say, tamed). However, of course, Dasgupta was concerned with the exposition of philosophical arguments, and certainly in this sense he was right to neglect the *bhakti* literature of the Vedānta. But without an understanding of the religious milieu of the rise of Non-Dualism, there can be no appreciation of its spiritual roots.

CHAPTER X

1. In treating the *Tathāgata* as equivalent to *Īśvara*, I am in effect following the example of Murti's *The Central Philosophy of Buddhism* (see his excellent discussion in ch. xii of that book). The situation is a little more complicated than the proposed identification of the Lord with the Buddha as a celestial being accessible to the eye of the faithful. The celestial Buddhas are numerous: but they are united in the *dharmakāya*, but it is something of an oversimplification to construct the equivalence: *Brahman* is to *Īśvara* as *dharmakāya* is to *sambhogāya*. For in Mahāyāna metaphysics we have to do with an extra concept, viz. that of the Absolute as the Void or as 'Suchness', etc. Now though the *dharmakāya* is commonly identified with the Absolute, it is yet somewhat different in *concept* (just as *Brahman* and *Ātman*, though identified, are different in concept). The *dharmakāya*, as we saw in note I.3, has the flavour of an omnipresent, immanent reality (and not just of an indescribable X). Thus, though celestial Buddhas are the objects of Buddhist devotionalism, they have to be seen against the background of their unity in the *dharmakāya*. In short, the concept of the *dharmakāya* forms a bridge (as it were) between the indescribable Absolute and the objects of devotion. Thus we

could amend the above equivalence to: *Brahman* is to *Īśvara* as the Absolute is to celestial Buddhas as united in their *dharmakāya*. In this sense it is fair to compare *Īśvara* with the Tathāgata. Moreover, though there is no doctrine of creation in Buddhism, the capacity of the great Buddhas to bring paradises, etc., in to being (the concept of the *Buddhakṣetra*), assimilate them in some degree to the creative gods of Hinduism.

There is a further point. It might be replied to the above account that the flavour of immancence attaching to the *dharmakāya* makes it unsuitable as part-factor in the concept of a Lord who is object of worship. For does not devotionalism imply a difference between God and the devotee, while complete immanence would suggest the non-duality of Reality and the individual? (The point is put in a curious way by Śankara: 'O Lord, even after realizing that there is no real difference between the individual soul and *Brahman*, I beg to state that I am yours and not that you are mine. The wave belongs to the ocean and not the ocean to the wave'—trans. Radhakrishnan, The *Brahma Sūtra*, p. 38). One of the difficulties here is that in some respects it is hard to distinguish between the concepts of transcendence and immanence: for 'transcendence' only means that the divine Being is 'beyond' the cosmos, and this is a spatial analogy; while 'immanence' means that God is 'within' all things—but again not literally (by cutting open a tree you do not find the divine Being). Since neither 'beyond' nor 'within' is used literally it is hard to see how the two concepts differ, save pictorially. (This is why pantheism and theism are not as easy to distinguish as some Christian apologists like to imagine.) Thus in principle there is no reason why the immanentist flavour of the *dharmakāya* should rule out its being the support, so to say, of objects of worship conceived as distinct from the worshipper. But, of course, the worshipper ultimately becomes identified with the Absolute, and the distinctness is only provisional. It is therefore useful that the *dharmakāya* should have an immanentist flavour—it means that it can serve as a bridge between the Absolute and the *sambhogakāya*.

On questions of the identification of different entities in religion, see the discussion in my *Reasons and Faiths*, especially ch. iii.

2. There is an interresting discussion of such a bifurcation in the context of Buddhism in Eliade's *Yoga, Immortality and Freedom*, pp. 174-76. He refers to the trend to distinguish between the 'experimentalists' (*jhāins*) and the 'speculatives' (*dhammayogins*). But the distinction ought ul-

timately to be unrealistic: as Eliade remarks, 'There is sufficient evidence to prove that the Buddha always closely connected knowledge with a meditational experience of the yogic type.' The two sides—the contemplative, existential impact of the doctrines, and the doctrines themselves, must always be held together. This arises because concepts such as *vidyā, jñāna* and *prajñā,* are used, in the spiritual context, not just of theoretical knowledge or insight; but involve a kind of 'knowledge by acquaintance'.

CHAPTER XV

1. The remarks in this paragraph are largely based on the interesting researches of J. F. Staal. See, for instance, his 'Negation and the law of contradiction in Indian thought: a comparative study', *Bulletin of the School of Oriental and African Studies,* 25 (1962), 52-71.

GLOSSARY

Abbreviations: S. for Sanskrit, P. for Pāli.

accessory (S. *sahakārī*): the accessory cause whereby an effect is brought about, as distinguished from the efficient and material causes—e.g. the craftsman's tools are accessory to his bringing an object into existence.

active tendencies (S. *samskāra;* P. *saṅkhāra*): one of the groups making up the individual, according to Buddhist doctrine. The problem of translation is discussed in the text (p. 30).

analogy (S. *upamāna*): in some schools held to be a separate basis of knowledge. Its difference from verbal testimony and inference is discussed in the text (p. 198).

appearance theory (S. *vivartavāda*): *vivarta* literally means 'turning round', and hence 'transformation'. More particularly, it is used in Non-Dualism to refer to the changing appearances of the empirical world: see p. 75, 221.

atom (S. *aṇu*): literally 'minute' or 'minute thing'. This expression is used in various schools for the smallest unit of matter, notably Atomism, for the smallest unit of matter (though in distinctionism, infra-atoms, the potentials, underlie the atoms). According to Atomism, they are without magnitude and eternal, and for these reasons do not strictly correspond to the modern concept. Further, some psychic entities, such as the mind-organ, and sometimes the self, are regarded by some viewpoints as atomic.

atomic: see atom.

Atomism (S. *Vaiśeṣika*): because of its doctrine of atoms, the *Vaiśeṣika* view-point is here called Atomism. The term *vaiśeṣika* is built up from *visesa*, one of the categories posited by the viewpoint. I have used atomism with a small *a* to refer to atomic theory in the Indian tradition, as distinguished from the doctrines of Atomism considered as a complete system.

atheism (S. *anīśvaravāda*): literally the Sanskrit means the 'non-Lord-doctrine', i.e. the denial of a personal Lord. As pointed out in the text, atheism in this sense does not imply an anti-religious attitude (see p. 11), nor does it imply denial of intra-cosmic deities.

attachment (P.S. *upādāna*): literally the material or fuel supporting continued life (conceived as like a flame or fire), in Buddhist doctrine. It thus means the tendency to cling to worldly existence.

attributive intelligence (S. *dharmabhūtajñāna*): I follow here M. Hiriyanna's translation (*Essentials of Indian Philosophy*, p. 180), a substance postulated in Qualified Non-Dualism as a bridge between matter and spirit; it depends upon God and selves as a kind of spiritual body which is capable of expansion and contraction (selves being regarded as atomic are incapable of this). In the state of release, attributive intelligence is all-pervading, as too in the case of the Lord. It expresses itself in the form of feelings, passions and volitions, which are immediately known to the self and do not depend on external data, as in the case of perceptions.

awareness (P. *sati*, S. *smṛti*): the stage in the Noble Eightfold Path enjoining a certain a kind of self-discipline. Literally 'memory' the term refers to the way in which the Buddhist aspirant is supposed to be at all times clear about his psychical and physical states—e.g. aware of his motives, etc. It should be noted that the Sanskrit equivalent also means the semi-canonical Hindu tradition regarded as an appendage to revelation (i.e. those writings which are 'remembered' by contrast with 'what is heard', i.e. revelation). Also, in its primary sense, the term literally means memory. This is not usually considered a separate basis of knowledge in the Indian tradition, since the doctrine of bases is intended to account for the acquisition of *new* information.

basis of knowledge (S. *pramāṇa*): from the root *mā* 'to measure', i.e. measuring the correctness of knowledge. More precisely, it refers to the source or means of acquiring new knowledge (see p. 180), and there is a multiple distinction between *pramātā*, and knower or investigator, *prameya*, the object of investigation, *pramā*, the correct conclusion the investigator reaches about the object of knowledge, *prāmāṇya*, the validity of his conclusion, and *pramāṇa*, the basis on which he founds his conclusion (e.g. perception, inference, etc.). The sources or bases of knowledge are held to count as such if they are independently necessary to account for the kind of results men get in their investigation of the world, and thus different schools and viewpoints canvass different lists of fundamental bases of knowledge. The different views can be set out in the following table:

	Mat'ism	Bud-dhism	Logic-	Atomism	Dist.-Yoga	Exeg.	Non-D.	Other Vedāntins
perc'n:	X	X	X	X	X	X	X	X
infer.:		X	X	X	X	X	X	X
testim.:			X		X	X	X	X
analogy			X			X	X	X
implic.:						X	X	
neg. perc'n:						X	X	

body (S. *śarīra*): (see p. 99) It should be noted that I also translate *kāya* as 'body', in connection with the Three-Body doctrine of Mahayana Buddhism.

brightness (sattva): from the root *sat* 'being' (cp. identity theory). In the context of the doctrine of strands (p. 66) it refers to the most refined of the three forms of elementary substance, which has the properties of brightness and intelligence. 'Brightness', given also the colloquial sense of the term, meaning cleverness, seems an adequate translation.

category (S. *padārtha*): literally 'the meaning or reference of words'. It is thus closely analogous to the expression *category* in its original sense.

cogitation (S. *tarka*): deliberation about some object to consider the reasons for or against some thesis about it (see p. 204). Regarded as a necessary accompaniment of the process of framing an inference, since the latter's validity usually depends on applying the method of agreement and difference, etc.

cognition (P. *saññā*, S. *samjñā*): see text, p. 29.

concentration (S.P. *samādhi*): the attainment of a unified and rapt state of consciousness in Buddhist and Hindu yoga. The principal means of attaining this is through the stages of meditation. It constitutes the eighth stage in the Noble Eightfold Path: thus the Buddhist life culminates in the reaching of mystical insight.

condition: see *limiting condition.*

conjunction (S. *saṃyoga*): literally 'yoking together'—the adventitious concomitance of two dntities, as contrasted with inherence (see p. 81).

connective understanding (S. *apekṣābuddhi*): the mental process whereby entities are seen in conjunction, as countable (see p. 79).

consciousness (S. *vijñāna*, P. *vinnana*): There are a number of terms in Sanskrit corresponding to the English 'consciousness'—e.g. *vijñāna*, cit, caitanya. These have normally been translated in the text as 'consciousness'. Though literally, or in ordinary usage, *vijñāna* means 'intelligence', 'discrimination', etc., in philosophical usage it has the sense of pure consciousness as that which lies behind or illuminates other mental states (similar remarks can be made about *cit* and about the self as conceived in most schools). But in Buddhism, consciousness is not regarded in any sense as either a unitary or transcendent entity like the self. However, the term translated 'Idealism' in the text is in Sanskrit *vijñanavāda*, literally 'doctrine of consciousness', i.e. the view that all entities are really of the nature of experiences or mental events, derived from the transformations of Absolute consciousness, viz. the store-consciousness.

constructive (S. *savikalpa*): the epithet for that aspect of perception which involves the application of concepts and of past experience to what is given immediately in sensation. Literally, it means 'with imagination', i.e. the imagination, etc., put a construction upon sense-data. See *non-constructive*.

corporeal (S.P. *rūpa*): literally 'form'—here the reference is to the *rūpaloka* or plane of 'form' or bodily events which is, in Buddhist doctrine, held to constitute the realm of gods who are visible and audible, but not tangible (as distinguished from the *sensual* and *incorporeal* planes).

craving (P. *taṇha*, S. *tṛṣṇa*): literally 'burning thirst'. In Buddhism it signifies the craving for satisfactions, and is opposed to the peace of mind attainable by the true saint. Moreover, it is considered the primary factor in rebirth. Those who die still under the influence of craving are reborn, and so on. Consequently the gaining of tranquillity—the tranquillity of empirical nirvana (p. 34)—entails the cessation of rebirth.

creation (S. *sṛṣṭi*): from the root *sṛj* 'to let go', i.e. to bring forth or allow to emanate. Indian doctrines of creation differ from that of the Judaeo-Christian tradition in two main ways: first, the cosmos is held to be a 'pulsating' one—a period of creation is followed by a period of dissolution, then one of creation, and so on; and secondly, the concept of creation out of nothing is not known (the nearest equivalent being that the Power transforms himself or itself into the cosmos). See also note I.1.

creator: see *creation*.

creative substance (S. *māyā*) : see p. 100 and *illusion* (p. 91).

cycle (S.P. *saṃsāra*): the cycle of rebirth, and more generally the process of empirical existence.

dependence (S. *paratantra, asvatantra*): *tantra* literally means a loom, and hence the essential part or feature or framework of a thing. *Para-* means 'other'. Thus something which has as its framework some other thing is 'dependent' on it. See p. 118. *Asvatantra* means 'not providing its own framework', and so is equivalent in meaning.

devotion (S. *bhakti*): from the root *bhaj*, 'to allot'. Thus one who is *bhakta* is allotted, i.e. to God. It thus comes to mean 'devoted to', and the noun *bhakti* means the attitude expressed by a person in this condition. It has a strong element of love, and thus 'loving adoration' would well express the attitude, though I prefer here the shorter 'devotion'. The attitude is not absent in the Veda, but gradually acquires greater intensity from the time of the *Gītā* onwards. It thus comes to invest, and sometimes even to replace, the activity of formal worship and ritual: but it can only be understood as arising out of such activity, and thus there is a contrast between this attitude of loving dependence and the typically yogic attitude of self-training and self-reliance. It thus connects with grace.

devotionalism (S. *bhaktimārga*): The *mārga* or path of *bhakti*, sometimes contrasted with the path of *karma* or works, and that of *jñāna* or mystical knowledge. It contrasts with the former because it is by grace, not ritual, that release occurs, according to devotionalistic doctrine (as in the *Gītā:* though works performed in the spirit of *bhakti* do not implicate one in rebirth). It contrasts the way of knowledge for the reason mentioned under the head of *devotion* above. I use 'devotionalism' to refer in particular to the Indian manifestation of the attitude of loving adoration of a personal God, and in addition I use the word to refer more generally to this attitude in religions other than and including the Indian traditional faiths.

diplomacy (S. *upāyakauśalya*): 'skilfulness in means' characterizes the Buddha, according to the Mahāyāna, as he adapts his teachings and methods to the state of the recipients (with this concept goes that of a developing revelation, for the Buddha, having first raised men towards spirituality in the Lesser Vehicle, now leads them on to the Greater Vehicle teachings, etc.). I here use Edgerton's fine suggestion 'diplomacy'—for the Buddha is careful to respect those whom he addresses, and yet artfully gets them to follow the path he has in mind.

directional space (S. *dik*): one of the three concepts of space in Indian thought, the others being local space and the medium of motion (motion-medium). In addition one of the terms used, *ākāśa,* is often used for a fine ether-like substance, serving, among other things, for the propagation of sound. *Dik* incorporates the notion that directions (upwards, downwards, etc.) are absolute. See p. 82 .

discrimination (S.*viveka*): the ability to see the essential difference between nature and souls, in the Sāṃkhya system.

disjunction (S. *vibhāga*): the converse of *conjunction,* and one of the types of property in the Logic-Atomist collection of categories.

dissolution (S. *praḷaya*): see *creation.*

Distinctionism (S. *Sāṃkhya*): the term used here for the Samkhya viewpoint.

Dualism (S. *Dvaita*): the term used here for Madhva's school.

Elder Doctrine (P. *Theravāda,* S. *Sthaviravāda*): the term used here for the school of Lesser Vehicle Buddhism, known as the 'doctrine of the elders': see p. 28.

energy (S. *śakti*): 'power', 'energy', a term with extensive overtones in the Indian tradition. As the Lord's energy, it is sometimes treated as a power semi-independent of God, and symbolized mythologically as his consort (the expression being feminine). See, in regard to Śaivite Doctrine, p. 115.

enjoyment (S. *saṃbhoga*): literally 'bliss', 'ease', 'enjoyment', this term is used to characterize one of the aspects under which the Buddha is conceived in developed Mahayana doctrine. The *saṃbhogakāya,* or Enjoyment-Body, is that aspect whereby Buddhas appear as celestial beings, roughly equivalent to the gods and Lord of Hinduism. Compare *transformation* and *truth.*

enlightened one (P.S. *buddha*): the title of anyone who has reached enlightenment—in particular, of the historical Buddha.

enlightenment (P.S. *bodhi*): the state of transcendental insight reached by a Buddha, involving the discovery of the truth about reality through the attainment of an inner mystical experience.

eternalism (P. *sāssatavāda*, S. *śāsvatavāda*): the doctrine that the self is eternal, and condemned severely by the Buddha. Compare *non-self.*

evolution (S. *pariṇāma*): the 'transformation' or 'evolution' of something already existing into a state where new properties are manifested. It is a key concept in Distinctionist cosmology, and ties in with the identity theory of causation. It does not, of course, have the sense in which 'evolution' is used in modern biology, etc. Cosmologically, Distinctionist evolution is more like the precipitation of determinate forms in nature as a result of the disturbance of an initial equilibrium, than the linear evolution of new species, etc.

Exegesis (S. *Mīṃāmsā*): the name here given to the Mīmāṃsā viewpoint: see p. 26.

existence (P. *bhava*): one of the stages in the doctrine of origination in Buddhism. From the verb *bhavati*, 'to be', 'to come into existence', the concept has the flavour of the process of becoming, rather than that of static existence.

falsification (S. *bādhitva*): see *non-falsification.*

featureless (S. *nirviśeṣa*): without *viśeṣas*, an expression used in Non-Dualism to refer to the Power as without characteristics or differentiating properties. See also *qualityless*. The term *viśeṣa* is used also in special ways by Madhva (see *relative particulars*) and by the Logic-Atomists (see *particularity*).

feelings (P.S. *vedanā*): one of the groups in Buddhist doctrine.

Fordmakers (Tīrthamkara): title of the Jain teachers, such as Mahāvīra, Pārśva, etc. They show the faithful the way across the stream of existence.

force (S. *rajas*): the second of the three strands in the Distinctionist and other cosmologies—the substance which imparts energy and motion to the entities composed by it; it is also psychologically identified with pain (brightness with pleasure and mass with dullness).

four-cornered negation (S. *catuṣkoṭi*): the multiple denial, by the Buddha, of possible answers to the undetermined questions. Thus it involves denying 'S is P', 'S is not P', 'S both is and is not P' and 'S is neither P nor not P'.

grace (S. *prasāda*): 'clearness' and hence 'brightness of countenance'. Thus it comes to mean 'graciousness' and 'favour'—and more technically the help given by the Lord to his devotees; it is therefore roughly equivalent to the Christian concept of grace.

gross (S. *mahat*): literally 'great': the second quantum described in the Logic-Atomist doctrine of the generation of macroscopic entities out of infinitesimal atoms. See p. 79, and *minute*.

group (P. *khandha*, S. *skandha*): the original meaning of the term was the trunk of a tree (sometimes the branches); it thus came to mean a mass or aggregate of things. 'Aggregates' is a common translation for its Buddhist sense, viz. the various types of mental and physical states which go to make up the individual. See p. 28. I have preferred 'groups' as it perhaps brings out more clearly that the five groups do not refer to five different constituents of the individual, but to complexes and series of states falling under the various headings. Thus consciousness is a series of states of consciousness.

heaven (P. *sagga*, S. *svarga*): Indian mythology, whether atheist or not, tended to proliferate heavens and purgatories. Except in some cases (e.g. Rāmānuja's concept of heaven), beings who attain heaven are thought of as liable to rebirth in lower states. Thus release is normally conceived as a state beyond heaven, because beyond rebirth. Heavens, like the rest of the cosmos, are usually considered to disappear during the state of dissolution, to reappear again at the next time of creation.

higher truth (S. *paramārtha*): literally 'highest reference' or 'truth in the highest meaning'. Both Non-Dualism and Voidism (see p. 43, 87 and p. 93) make use of the notion of a higher truth distinguished from common-sense or ordinary knowledge (see *ordinary*), i.e. it is what is apprehensible in the higher mystical state, etc., and constitutes the essential import of revelation or of the Buddhist religion.

Idealism (S. *Vijñānavāda*): literally 'doctrine of consciousness', and the name used here for the Vijñānavāda school of the Mahāyāna, also sometimes dubbed the *Yogācāra* (see Yoga-Practitioners; consciousness and store-consciousness).

identity theory (S. *satkāryavāda*): literally 'the being-effect-doctrine', viz. the theory that the effect pre-exists in the causes, as distinguished from the non-identity theory. Śaṅkara's *vivartavāda* (appearance theory) is sometimes misleadingly classified as the identity theory also, but the latter term should properly refer to the Distinctionist doctrine of causation, and its analogues in those Vedāntin schools which have made use of Distinctionist concepts.

ignorance (S. *avidyā*, P. *avijjā*; also S. *ajñāna*): these concepts have to be understood by contrast with knowledge in the sense of an existential, spiritual insight into the nature of reality. Thus ignorance is the spiritual ignorance which obstructs the individual from gaining the release that true insight would bring. Hence, commonly in the Indian tradition, it is original ignorance rather than original sin which lies at the root of men's troubles. In particular, the Non-Dualistic concept of ignorance is illusion seen from the side of the Self, and is thus virtually a cosmic principle clouding the one Reality, viz. the Power. See knowledge.

illusion (māyā): from the root *ma*, 'measure', 'make', the term *māyā* underwent a long evolution in the Indian tradition. It is used of God's creative power, or of the substance from which he creates the world. But it came to have a strong flavour of the magical, and hence the sense of 'magical transformation' or 'illusion' (like that produced by the conjuror). Consequently, 'illusion' is here used as a translation of *māyā* in its sense as cosmic conjuring trick: but see also *creative substance*.

impermanence (P. *anicca*, S. *anitya*): 'impermanent', 'non-eternal'. One of the three epithets used in Buddhist doctrine about empirical entities (viz. that they are full of suffering, without self or non-self-ish, and impermanent). With the notion of impermanence there went the doctrine that there are no substances, i.e., no permanet entities. See *permanent*.

implication (S. *arthāpatti*): see p. 175.

impurities (S. *mala*): the expression used in Śaivite Doctrine for that which keeps the soul from release. See *obscuring substance*.

incarnation (S. *avatāra*): literally 'descent', i.e. of the God into human form or animal form. This concept differs from the Christian one in at least two ways: first, the manifestation of the Lord is not unique (i.e. Viṣṇu is incarnate in different forms at different times); and second, *avatāras* in animal forms are believed in.

inconceivable energy (S. *acintyaśakti*): *acintya* means 'unthinkable', 'inconceivable', and here in an epithet of God's creative energy, according to Dualist doctrine (see p. 188). Likewise in Non-Dualism, illusion is so characterized, as inconceivable or indefinable, because it is both real and not real.

incorporeal (P.S. *arūpa*): together with the sensual and the corporeal, one of the three planes of existence in Buddhism.

indefinable (S. *anirvacanīya*): or *inconceivable,* an epithet used in Non-Dualism of the world-appearance or illusion. As well as being both real and not real, it is not possible to explain its origin

independence (S. *svatantra*): see *dependence.*

individuating factor (S. *ahaṃkāra*): literally the 'I-maker', it is one of the stages of nature's evolution in Distinctionism. It is also a concept used by other schools, e.g. in Non-Dualism, for that which gives a person his sense of individuality.

inference (S. *anumāna*): used for the five- proposition or three-proposition form of syllogistic inference (see ch. XV) usually of an inductive sort. It is counted by all schools except the early Materialists as a basis of knowledge. It is normally distinguished from implication and analogy, which invove inference (in a wider sense).

inferendum (S. *sādhya*): the term which figures as the predicated in the first proposition of an inference, and which is ascribed to the subject on the basis of the sign.

inherence (S. *samavāya*): a category used in the Logic-Atomist referring to the relation between property and substance, and between atoms in combination, as well as between cause and effect. This intimate relation differs from mere conjunction, which is the contingent association between two entities, properties, etc.

inner controller (S. *antaryāmin*): the Lord's aspect, in Qualified Non-Dualism, as immanent director of the self, and as controller of matter.

Through this immanent operation, the Lord may induce virtuous and vicious deeds in those who love or hate him markedly, and give grace to the faithful.

inseparability (S. *apṛthaksiddhi*): the necessary relation between substance and attribute, and between self and body (see p. 83), in Qualified Non-Dualism. N.P.

sight (P. *paññā*, S. *prajñā*): sometimes translated 'wisdom', this refers to an element in the attainment of nirvana. In that state, the saint sees the truth, existentially, of Buddhist teaching about the world (or in the case of the Voidist school, of the voidness of things). I have preferred the term 'insight', since 'wisdom' in English tends to mean sagacity as a result of long experience of men and affairs; while 'insight' indicates that an existential, contemplative apprehension of the truth is involved.

insubstantiality (S. *adravyatā*): a characteristic of the world, according to Buddhist teaching, since permanent substances are denied. See *substance*.

intellect (S. *buddhi*): this comes from the same root as enlightenment. It is that faculty whereby a person understands what is given in sense-experience and through the mind-organ; and figures as one of the stages in the evolution of nature in Distinctionism. The object of Yoga is so to still the operations of the intellect, that the soul is seen through it (as it were) in its purity, and is thus clearly seen as distinct from the psychophysical organism. See *discrimination*.

intuition (S. *anubhūti*): an immediate awareness of the existence of the Self, in Non-Dualist doctrine; the Self is thereby recognized as being implicit in all experience, though it cannot be an *object* of experience, but only the subject. Hence this immediate intuition is distinguished from all cognitive experiences, which involve a subject-object distinction.

isolation (S. *kaivalya*): literally 'wholeness', 'completeness' and hence 'self-completeness'—the state of release aimed at in Yoga, where the soul is isolated from the psychophysical organism, from the rest of the world, from other souls and even from God.

knowledge (S. *vidyā*, *jñāna*): by contrast with ignorance, knowledge is used of spiritual insight, the content of which varies with differing schools. The *jñāna-mārga* or 'way of knowledge' is thus one of the recognized paths to release (see *devotionalism*).

law (S. *dharma*, P. *dhamma*): the expression *dharma* has a number of meanings—law (in particular the 'everlasting law', namely orthodox Hindu religion); truth (see *Truth-Body*); teaching or doctrine (in particular the teaching of the Buddha); state (in particular the short-lived states into which entities are analysed in Buddhist doctrine); and, rather eccentrically in Jainism, the medium of motion (see *motion-medium*).

limiting condition (S. *upādhi*): the empirical conditions through which, in Non-Dualism, the one Self appears as many individuals.

life-monad (S. *jīva*): one of the three main terms for the eternal element in living beings (see *soul* and *self*). In particular, it is the term used in Jainism, which conceives of the *life-monads* as liable to expansion and contraction. It is also used of the transmigrating individual in Non-Dualism.

living release (S. *jīvanmukti*): the state of one who has attained saintliness in this life, and is assured of no more rebirth, i.e. of final release upon death. The *jīvanmukta* or living released one is conceived as having destroyed the karma which would lead to rebirth, but some still remains to be used up, and he goes on living therefore a while. Most viewpoints accept the notion, though Qualified Non-Dualism is a notable exception. The Buddhist concept of empirical nirvana (see p. 34) corresponds to it, since this too involves the notion that one who has attained it will not be reborn.

local space (S. *ākāśa*): space considered as a system of locations rather than as a medium of motion (see *motion-medium*). See also *space*.

locus (S. *pakṣa*): that in which the sign and inferendum inhere, i.e. the subject of an inference, or the denotation of the terms expressing the sign and inferendum. See p. 198.

Logic (S. *nyāya*): the term used here for the *Nyāya* viewpoint. See p. 29.

Lord (S. *īśvara*, P. *issara*): literally 'prince', 'lord', this term came to be used of God as a personal being and supreme object of worship (whether or not he was conceived as creator). See also *theism* and *atheism.* In Non-Dualism, the Power is featureless in higher truth, but considered from the ordinary point of view, it is a personal Lord with qualities.

mass (S. *tamas*): in the doctrine of strand-substances (see *strands, brightness* and *force*), this is the dark, inert and dull factor in natural objects.

Materialism (S. *Cārvāka, lokāyata*): the name used for the school of philosophy supposedly instituted by *Cārvāka* (hence one of the names for the school in Sanskrit). It is sometimes also referred to as *lokāyata* or as naturalism (see below). The former term means, probably (there is a good deal of uncertainty and discussion on the topic), 'world-basis', i.e. a doctrine concerned with this world, but not with another sphere of existence, and the adherents of this school are supposed to have produced sophistical arguments of various kinds, partly no doubt to discredit belief in the transcendent. In so far as one can refer to a system of metaphysics represented by anti-religious movements, I refer to it as Materialism; but in a broader sense, I use 'materialism' (with a small *m*) for anything falling under such movements.

meditation (S. *dhyāna,* P. *jhāna*): for a discussion of Buddhist stages of meditation, or meditations, see p. 37. (Incidentally, the Sanskrit *dhyāna* was transliterated into Chinese as *ch'ān* and into Japanese as *Zen*—hence the name of that school of Buddhism). More generally, I use the term meditation for all methods of inner contemplation in the Indian tradition, whether Buddhist or not. See also *knowledge.*

meditative knowledge: see *knowledge,* and p. 127.

mind-organ (S. *manas*): frequently *manas* is translated (partly in accordance with etymology) as 'mind' in English, and I have conformed to this: but since the entity referred to by *manas* is a kind of internal organ, often regarded as a 'sixth' sense which coordinates the material presented by the other senses, I use the phrase 'mind-organ'. It is certainly not to be equated with the concept of mind in English. N.P.

minute (S. *hrasva*): the first quantum formed by the combination of atoms in Logic-Atomism: see *gross,* and p. 79.

momentary (P. *khaṇika,* S. *ksaṇika*): strictly the Sanskrit term means 'having the property of perishing as soon as it is produced', but following

Dasgupta and others I translate it by 'momentary'. Compare the argument on p. 38.

motion-medium (S. *dharma*): whereas elsewhere *dharma* means 'law', 'truth', 'teaching' or 'state' (see under these headings), in Jain metaphysics it is given a special meaning, and refers to the medium of motion, as distinguished from local space, i.e. space conceived as a system of locations. See p. 52.

naturalism (S. *svabhāvavāda*): literally the 'doctrine of self-being', i.e. the coming into existence of things of their own accord and not through some supernatural agency. It is one of the terms used of the early materialist schools.

nature (S. *prakṛti*): the Sanskrit literally means 'making before', i.e. what constitutes the primary nature of whatever is under consideration. It thus comes to mean 'character', 'disposition', 'root' (in linguistics), etc. More metaphysically, it signifies the underlying stuff of the material world, which, according to Distinctionism, evolves into the varied forms we perceive, etc. This stuff is considered as a unitary whole, in which are blended the three strands.

negative perception (S. *anupalabdhi*): the perception of the absence of something, regarded by Exegesis and Non-Dualism as a separate basis of knowledge: see p.175.

no-negative inference (S. *kevalānvayī*): an inference where negative instances cannot be collected, e.g. 'This is describable, because it is an object of knowledge'. The premiss 'All objects of knowledge are describable' cannot be checked by seeing if non-objects of knowledge are indescribable for they cannot be investigated, by definition. See p. 200.

no-positive inference (S. *kevalavyātirekī*): the converse of no-negative inference. See p. 200.

Noble Eightfold Path (P. *ariya*, S. *ārya;* P. *aṭṭhaṅgika magga*): the words *ariya* and *ārya* mean 'noble': a term also applied by the Aryan invaders to themselves—hence the word 'Aryan'.

Noble Truths: see *Noble Eightfold Path.*

non-constructive (S. *nirvikalpa*): that aspect of perception where the latter is considered as 'pure' or 'neat', without the addition to the experience of imaginative and conceptual elements, i.e. without 'reading into' the perception the name of the object, and memories associated with it. It is contrasted to constructive perception.

non-dual (S. *advaya*): an epithet for the mystical experience of identification with the Absolute in Mahāyāna Buddhism, e.g. in Voidism.

Non-Dualism (S. *Advaita*): the name here used for the Advaita Vedānta school of metaphysics.

non-dualistic (S. *advaita*): used equivalently to *non-dual*, of the experience of the identity of the Self with the Power in Non-Dualism.

non-existence (S. *abhāva*); see p. 191.

non-falsification (S. *abādhitva*): see p. 167. The root *bādh* literally means 'to drive away', 'harass'—hence to annul or invalidate. It is sometimes translated 'sublate', but this is scarcely English, and I prefer the more straightforward 'falsify'. It can also mean 'contradict', but owing to the epistemological flavour of most Indian treatments of logic and inference (so that perception can be said to 'contradict'), 'falsify' is better.

non-identity theory (S. *asatkāryavāda*): by contrast with the identity theory, the non-identity theory (literally 'non-being-effect-doctrine') denies the pre-existence of the effect in the cause. It is held by the Logic-Atomist and Buddhist schools.

non-injury (S. *ahiṃsā*): 'non-injury', i.e. the duty not to take life, whether animal or human.

non-intelligent (S. *acit*): the term *cit* is one of those used for consciousness in Sanskrit, and is one of the three cheif epithets of the Power (being, consciousness and bliss: *saccidānanda*). The 'non-conscious' or 'non-intelligent' is the world of material substances, e.g. in Dualism: see p. 108. Compare *non-living*.

non-living (*ajīva*): the material aspect of nature in contrast with the *jīvas* or life-monads in Jain cosmology. See p. 51.

non-self (P. *anattā*, S. *anātman*): the denial in Buddhism of a permanent self or soul or life-monad, or of a unitary Self in the style of Non-Dualism.

obscuring substance (S. *āṇava*): a concept used in Śaivite Doctrine which refers to the original obscuring principle which implicates souls in the empirical world. Literally it means the 'atomizer' (see *atom*). It 'shrinks' souls: only in release can they 'expand'. As fundamental form of the impurities which cling to the unreleased soul, it corresponds to ignorance in the Non-Dualistic school.

ordinary (S. *vyāvahārika*): literally 'what is customary, conventional, ordinarily accepted'. In both the Mahāyāna and Non-Dualism a contrast was-drawn between higher knowledge, centering on mystical experience, and ordinary or common-sense knowledge. E.g. that the sun is larger than the moon is an ordinary truth, but both sun and moon are part of the grand illusion seen from the standpoint of higher truth. See *higher*.

origination (S. *pratītyasamutpāda*, P. *paticca- samuppāda*): the Buddha's doctrine of the causes of 'suffering, etc. See p. 32. Literally 'after getting, arising', i.e. one thing is produced after something else, its cause. Sometimes it is translated 'dependent origination', though I have preferred a shorter form.

orthodox (S. *āstika*): belonging to the tradition which recognizes revelation, i.e. the Veda. See *unorthodox*, and p. 7ff. *Āstika* is built up from *asti* 'it is' or 'there is'. Though the term sometimes means 'one who believes there is a God', and so also 'pious', the primary sense is that explained in the text.

particularity (S. *viśeṣa*): one of the Logic-Atomist categories: see p. 10, and also *relative particulars* and *featureless*.

peace (P. *santi*, S. *śānti*): there are a number of epithets used about nirvana to signify its peacefulness: thus nirvana involves *upasama* or self-pacification, through the destruction of craving and thereby the passions. The state of peace or *santi* thereby gained is a common expression for the serenity of the saint.

perception (S. *pratyakṣa*): perception has a somewhat wider sense in Sanskrit than in English, since it includes, as well as ordinary perceptions, the supersensual cognitions of the yogi, etc. It is univesally counted as one of the bases of knowledge.

permanent (P. *nicca,* S. *nītya*): permanent, everlasting or eternal—an epithet used of nirvana in Buddhism, though permanence is denied to substances and selves. On the other hand, selves, for instance, are regarded by the orthodox viewpoints as permanent. See also *impermanence.*

person (S. *pudgala,* P. *puggala*): the term used by the Personalists to refer to the individual who lies behind the groups and supports them. It may be noted that the same word was used in Jainism in quite a different sense, to refer to material entities.

personalists (S. *pudgalavādin*): the school who posited a person and who came nearer than any other Buddhist school to the doctrine of a plurality of selves.

perspective (naya): see p. 44.

planes (loka): literally 'worlds'—the three forms of existence according to Buddhism (see p. 36) discoverable in the cosmos, i.e. this side of nirvana. See *sensual, corporeal, incorporeal.*

potentials (S. *tanmātra*): colloquially 'only a bit', 'a trifle'. Hence it is used of the micro-elements (or 'infra-atoms' as Dasgupta translates it) of the Distinctionist systems. I use 'potentials' to bring out the fact that they are meant to have sensible qualities implicit in them, but these only become actualized when they combine into atoms.

Power (S. *Brahman*): the supreme principle in Upanisadic thought, sometimes conceived personally, sometimes impersonally. Its fundamental sense was the power implicit in the sacrificial ritual, and the root from which it derives, *brh,* means 'to increase'. Thus Brahman is the implicit power of growth, the capacity to bring about effects, conceived as residing within sacred actions and objects, and indeed persons (the *Brāhmana* or priestly class). By a generalization it came to mean the sacred Power sustaining the cosmos. I have used 'Power' as translation not only for this reason, but because it has, if necessary, a suitable impersonal air. I have preferred not to use 'Absolute'—using this in a wider sense—partly because 'Power' may more easily suggest the ritual and religious origin of the concept.

projection (S. *adhyāsa*): commonly this is translated 'superimposition', i.e. the way in which, according to Non-Dualism, illusory appearances are projected on to reality. It is thus through ignorance that the one Power is obscured by this projection.

property (S. *guṇa*): the term *guṇa* has two important senses: a rope or strand (see *strands*); and quality of attribute—here translated property. This is one of the categories of the Logic-Atomism school. Since universal is also a category, one can see that properties here refer, not to the universals, but to the *qualia* or particular qualities, etc., inhering in substances. Since relations, etc., are included under *guṇa,* I have used the term 'property' rather than 'quality'. It may be noted that when the Power is said, in Non-Dualism, to be qualityless, the term *guṇa* is used. See also *qualitied.*

psychophysical complex (P.S. *nāmarūpa*): literally 'name and form', and sometimes translated thus (though it does not mean much). The 'form' element here stands for what is corporeal (see *corporeal,* where the same term *rupa* is used); 'name' for the mental side (this connects up with the Buddhist doctrine of language as enshrining ways in which the mind projects ideas on to reality). *Nāmarūpa* thus means the psychophysical organism as an individual entity, in the Buddhist doctrine of origination. Thus, in order that there should be sense-contacts, etc., it was held that a unified organism is presupposed, and this in turn presupposes consciousness, etc. See p. 32.

purgatory (*niraya*): an evil state of suffering described in Buddist and Hindu texts, but one which is usually thought as non-external. After a long time, an individual will leave the purgatory. It is often translated 'hell'.

Qualified Non-Dualism (S. *Viśiṣṭādvaita*): the name here used for Rāmānuja's system. See p. 12.

qualitied (S. *saguṇa*): the Lord, in Non-Dualism, is described as the Power in its aspect of having qualities. This qualitied Power is differentiated from Brahman considered from the level of higher truth, which is qualityless and featureless. It may be noted that the term *guṇa* which constitutes part of the Sanskrit expression (*sa-*: 'with') is also used of the strands, but these are not considered to be substance in Sankara's system, but primordial qualities of *māyā* or illusion.

qualityless (S. *nirguṇa*): see *qualitied.*

Realists (S. *sarvā*stivādin, P. *sabbatthivādin*): literally 'those who hold the doctrine that everything is': a Buddhist school (see p.). In particular they held that past events exist, as otherwise they would have no causal efficacy, see p. 39f.

reflection (S. *pratibimba*): 'reflection' is an analogy used to describe the way the one Power remains single and unaffected although manifesting itself in many selves. See p. 93.

relative particulars (S. *viśeṣa*): a doctrine of Madhva's described on p. 107. It may be noted that the Sanskrit term is used in Logic-Atomism for the category of particularity (see *particularity* and also *featureless*).

relativism (S. *syādvāda)*: literally the 'doctrine that maybe' or 'could-be-ism' (see p. 54), held by the Jains.

release (S. *mokṣa, mukti, nirvāṇa*, etc.): a number of expressions are used in Sanskrit for the state of release from the round of rebirth, the most common being *mokṣa* and *mukti,* from a root meaning 'to liberate'. *Nirvāṇa* is used in Hindu contexts as well as in Buddhism, but is here used for Buddhist release only. See also *isolation* and *living release.* Conceptions of what the state consists in, apart from release from rebirth, differ according to the various systems.

rest-medium (S. *adharma*): i.e. non-*dharma,* used in its special Jain sense of the motion-medium. To account for rest, Jainism postulated a complementary medium corresponding to that of motion. See p. 52, and *motion-medium.*

revelation (S. *śruti*): literally 'what is heard', i.e. the Vedic revelation as apprehended by the early seers.

saint (S. *arahat*): literally 'worthy one', i.e. one who has attained empirical nirvana, i.e. the Buddhist state of living release (see p. 33). The ideal of the saint is sometimes contrasted by Mahayanists with that of the Buddha-to-be or Bodhisattva, as being narrow, while the latter is compassionate—for the Bodhisattva puts off his nirvana in order to serve others.

Saivite Doctrine (S. *Śaivasiddhānta*): the name here used of the school of Śaivite metaphysicians described on pp. 115ff.

seer (S. *ṛṣi*): those early figures to whom are ascribed the apprehension of the Vedic revelation.

Self (S. *ātman*, P. *atta*): together with soul and life-monad one of the main terms for the eternal element in living beings. The Sanskrit *ātman* and the Pali *atta* is often used reflexively, like the English 'self' and in such ordinary usage has no metaphysical reference. It is probably derived from a root meaning 'to breathe', and in this respect compares with the English 'spirit'. It is used metaphysically to refer to the eternal self underlying the psychophysical organism. Likewise it is sometimes used for the World-Spirit, the single self animating the whole cosmos. In Non-Dualistic Vedanta, the *ātman* is identified with *Brahman*, the Power; and so there is only one self underlying the illusory psychophysical individuals. In this sense, I use 'Self' (with a capital S). See also *non-self.*

Self-luminous (S. *svaprakāśa*): the Self, in Non-Dualistic doctrine, is held to be self-luminous, i.e. it shows itself in all experiences, though it is not an object of knowledge and is known by immediate intuition (see *intuition*).

sense-contact (P. *phassa*): one of the elements in the chain of origination (q.v.). Literally 'touch', it means the combination of sense-organ, outer object and sensation in perception, and gives rise to feelings.

sense-fields (P. *āyatana*): literally 'fields of operation', i.e. those aspects of things accessible to the six senses (i.e. including the *mind-organ* as sixth).

sensual (P.S. *kāmaloka*): the world of sensual pleasure (*kama*), i.e. one of the three planes of existence in Buddhist doctrine (see *corporeal* and *incorporeal*); it is the realm of beings, such as humans and animals, which are in a full sense corporeal, i.e. constituted by elements perceptible by the five senses.

separateness (S. *prthakatva*): one of the Logic- Atomist categories: see p. 81.

sign (S. *liṅgam*, hetu): two terms are used of the middle term in traditional inference, lingam or 'sign' and *hetu*, 'cause' or 'reason'. I have preferred the first of these alternatives. See p. 167.

soul (S. *puruṣa*): one of the three main expressions for the eternal element in living beings, *purusa* is that used by the Distinctionist and Yoga schools. It means literally 'person' or 'man'.

space (S. *ākāśa*): this word is used both of pure space and more commonly of a sort of ether, which serves as the medium of sound (see *directional space*, *local space* and *motion-medium*).

state (P. *dhamma*, S. *dharma*): the word *dharma* in the singular principally means law or teaching, and here is not meaningfully used in the plural. But it is also used in Buddhist doctrine, in a way in which it is sensible to use the plural, of the states or events which compose the shifting things observable in the cosmos. The states are short-lived (eventually they were considered as momentary), and they are not properly states *of* anything (in the sense of inhering in substances, etc.). Generally I have translated the term 'states', though also at times as 'events'.

store-consciousness (S. *ālayavijñāna*): the Absolute in Buddhist Idealism, the transformations of which result in the conscious states of which we are ordinarily aware.

strands (S. *guṇa*): the three types of substance in Distinctionism, the interplay of which brings about the evolution of nature (see p. 77). The same term is also used by the Logic-Atomists for one of the categories (see *property*). Compare also *qualitied* and *qualityless*.

Subjective-Creationists (S. *dṛṣṭisṛṣṭivādin*): a school of Advaita Vedānta holding that the illusion is simply the product of our perceptions: hence the name 'perception-creationism'. The congruence between different individuals' perceptions is, so to say, a coincidence, and not due to a common external world. It could be said to be the doctrine of illusion applied at the level of ordinary truth.

substance (S. *dravya*): that which is the (at least relatively) permanent bearer of properties, etc.; one of the categories in Logic-Atomism.

substratum (S.*bhūtādi*): one of the evolutes of nature in the Distinctionist system. See p. 67.

Suchness (S. *tathatā*): a name for the empty or absolute in Mahāyāna Buddhism - it connects with the title.

suffering (P. *dukkha*, S. *duḥkha*): the opposite of *sukha*, 'well-fare', 'unhappiness'. It thus covers pain, sorrow, dissatisfaction, trouble. 'Illfare', were it not a barbarous expression, would serve well as a translation, but I have retained the customary 'suffering' as the translation of this term.

testimony (S. *śabda*): literally 'sound', the expression is used for one of the bases of knowledge recognized by some schools. It is sometimes taken to include all the verbal testimony of trustworthy persons, and sometimes more narrowly to refer to the testimony constituted by revelation.

theism (S. *īśvaravāda*): belief in a personal supreme Being or 'Lord'. See *atheism*. It does not exclude belief in other gods as manifesting or as subordinate to the one Lord.

Three-Body (S. *trikāya*): the doctrine of the three bodies or aspects of the Buddha in Mahayana Buddhism; see p. 15. Also see *transformation*, *enjoyment* and *truth*.

Transcendentalists (S. *lokottaravādin*): a school of Buddhism, at the time of the early development of Mahayana Buddhism, which affirmed that the Buddha is 'beyond the world' (*lokottara*), i.e. a transcendent being existing even after his nirvana.

transformation (S. *nirmāṇa*): 'transformation' here has a magical flavour about it: the implication being that the Buddha, in adopting his Transformation-Body and appearing on earth, uses skilful means or diplomacy in adapting himself to the requirements of mortal beings. This is in line, too, with docetic tendencies in the Mahayana.

transphenomenal (S. *sāmānyatodṛṣṭa*): 'by likeness to the unseen'—a use of inference to come to conclusions about the transcendent or unseen world, or more generaly about unobservable entities; see p. 80.

truth (S. *dharma*): the Truth-Body of the Buddha is the Absolute (see p. 55). The Buddha's teaching (for dharma also means 'teaching' and in particular the Buddha's) ultimately points to the realization in inner experience of identity with the Absolute. Hence the Buddha's most fundamental aspect could be called his 'teaching body'—but in English this would cause some confusion with the Buddha's transformation body (i.e. that with which he manifests himself on earth to teach men). Hence I translate, in a conventional way, 'Truth-Body'. See *transformation* and *enjoyment.*

undetermined (P. *avyākatāni,* S . *avākṛtāni*): 'unexplained', or 'undetermined', i.e. those questions (see p. 19) which the Buddha refrained from answering because they were wrongly posed or inapplicable.

universal (S. *sāmānya*): 'like' or 'similar', i.e. the common aspect in virtue of which different substances, etc., are described by the same term. It is one of the Logic-Atomist categories (see p. 82).

unorthodox (S. *nāstika*): an adjective built up on *nāsti,* i.e. *na asti* 'it is not' or 'there is not', describing those who do not accept the Brahmanical revelation. It can also, secondarily, mean 'impious' and 'atheistic'. See *orthodox.*

unseen force (S. *adṛṣṭa*): sometimes used as the equivalent of karma, that unseen foce which controls men's destinies through their actions. But see p. 92.

view (P. *diṭṭhi,* S. *dṛṣṭi*): the right view or outlook required of the faithful Buddhist constitutes the first stage of the Noble Eightfold Path: this is right *diṭṭhi*. But the Buddha at the same time claimed to repudiate all *diṭṭhis*, all views or theories (on the basis of this the Voidists justified their comprehensive dialectical destruction of all theories about reality, including even what appeared to be orthodox Buddhist teachings). See *views*. *Diṭṭhi* and *dṛṣṭi* also more literally mean 'seeing', 'perception', etc. (see *Subjective-Creationasts*). Probably the Buddha's meaning was that while the aspirant must have the right vision or view of the world, he must eschew all opinions which are not based on experience.

views (P. *diṭṭhi*, S. *dṛṣṭi*): see *view*.

viewpoint (S. *darśana*): from the same root as *dṛṣṭi*, viz. *dṛś* 'to see', this term came to be used of the different visions of the world enshrined in the various orthodox metaphysical systems. The English 'viewpoint' serves to bring out both the notions of vision and metaphysical standpoint implicit in the Sanskrit.

Void (S. *śūnya*): the 'empty' or 'void' is the characterization of reality by the Voidist school (see p. 42), and hence the term used for the Absolute.

Voidism (S. *Mādhyamika*, *śūnyavāda*): the name here used for the Mādhyamika school; see p. 15.

voidness (S. *śūnyatā*), the emptiness of all phenomena in virtue of the insubstantiality and contradictoriness, as argued by the Voidist school.

without author (S. *apauruṣeya*): literally 'non-personal' (sc. in origin), a characterization by some schools of the Veda. But we may note that the Logic-Atomist view, that revelation proceeds from God, counts as a doctrine of the personal origin of scriptures, by contrast with the *apauruṣeya* view, upheld notably by Exegesis. See p. 112.

witness (S. *sākṣi*): pure consciousness as the subject of experience in finite conditions, in Non-Dualist doctrine. For the special Dualist use of the concept, see p. 119.

works (S. *karma*): as well as meaning 'action' and the law which controls rebirth, *karma* also means the ritual and ethical works enjoined by revelation. See p. 92. The *karmayoga* or method of works is often distinguished from the *jñānayoga*, or method of mystical knowledge, and that of *bhaktiyoga*, method of devotion. In some degree therefore the distinction between *Karma* and *bhakti* corresponds to that between works and grace in Christian theology.

Yoga (S. *Yoga*): literally 'yoking' or 'harnessing' (one's faculties). The name here used for the viewpoint is written with a capital *Y*: with a small *y* it refers more generally to methods of contemplation in the Indian tradition. See p. 9.

Yoga-Practitioners (S. *Yogācārin*): an alternative name for the Idealist school of Buddhism, in virtue of their concentration on yoga as the means of enlightenment. See p. 15.

BRIEF HISTORIES OF THE SCHOOLS

ATOMISM (*Vaiśeṣika*). Though Atomism has roots going back to a very early period (perhaps as far as the sixth century B.C.E. or before), it took shape as a system about 100 C.E. The *Vaiśeṣika-sūtra* ('Atomism-aphorisms') probably date from this time and are attributed to the legendary Kaṇāda. After this (third to fifth centuries C.E.) there was composed the *bhāṣya* or commentary of Prasastapada. From the fifth century to the tenth the school coalesced with that of Logic and acquired a theistic (or perhaps one could say more properly a *deistic*) character—though traditional commentators try to read theism into the 'Aphorisms', projecting the later theism into the earlier period. It is probable that the superimposition of theism upon the originally naturalistic doctrines had three main causes: first, the coalescence with Logic; second, the need to reply to Buddhist and other critics (who by pointing to certain theoretical defects in Atomist cosmology stimulated the Atomists to bring in the hypothesis of a Lord who keeps the cosmos organized); and third, the general drift towards theism in the medieval period. See also LOGIC.

DISTINCTIONISM (Sāṃkhya). The origins of the Distinctionist viewpoint are somewhat obscure. It has been argued by Dasgupta that its earliest form was theistic and that it was reinterpreted in an atheistic sense by Pañcaśikha (some time before 200 C.E.). It is true that Distinctionist elements are incorporated in the Upaniṣads and more clearly in the *Gītā* (? 200 B.C.E.or later); and in the medieval period Distinctionism was used as a basis for the Vaiṣṇavite schools and of Śaivite Doctrine. Nevertheless, it has been powerfully argued by Zimmer that Distinctionism has close historical affinities with Buddhism and Jainism; and it is hard to understand how, if Distinctionism was originally theistic, it lost this character. It is more reasonable to hold that, just as non-Aryan yoga came to be incorporated in the Upaniṣads, so atheistic Distinctionism was blended with theism in the course of the synthesis between the various elements of Indian religious culture. But as a distinctive viewpoint, Distinctionism preserved its originally atheistic character. Unfortunately this thesis cannot be directly confirmed, since the works of Kapila (the supposed founder of the school) and of Pañcaśikha are lost. The first extant work of the school is Īśvarakṛṣṇa's *Sāṃkhya-kārikā* ('Concise Verses on Distinctionism'), perhaps of the third century C.E. or later. Other important works of the school are *Tattva-kaumudī* ('Elucidation of Principles') of the ninth century C.E., and commentary of Vijñanā Bhikṣu (sixteenth century C.E.). Since Yoga made use of Distinctionist categories from an early period (e.g. in the *Yoga-sūtra* of Patañjali, perhaps of the second century C.E.), the two viewpoints are virtually identical. See further YOGA below.

DUALISM (*Dvaita*). For the founder to the school see MADHVA in the section of Biographical Information. Among his successors who headed the Madhva sect the most important philosophical writer was Jayatīrtha (thirteenth century C.E.), whose *Nyāya-sudhā* ('Nectar of Logic') is a commentary on Madhva's *Anuvyākhyāna* ('Exposition').

ELDER DOCTRINE (*Theravāda*). The doctrines of Lesser Vehicle Buddhism probably reached their main shape by the time of Aśoka (third century B.C.E.); and the school known as the Elders, introduced into Ceylon at that time, and basing its teachings on the Pāli canon, has continued this conservative tradition. The Pāli language, a form of Middle Indic, indicates that those who brought Buddhism to Ceylon were from Western India. In due course the Pāli canon, and Elder doctrines, became established in Burma and South-East Asia. The chief figure of Elder Buddhism was Buddhaghosa (fifth century C.E.), whose commentaries and above all his *Visuddhimagga* ('Path of Purity') are classical expositions of the Elder doctrines. The Pāli canon (committed to writing in the first century C.E.) contains primitive elements, considerably overlaid by scholastic elaborations. It is divided (as other Buddhist canons) into three sections or 'baskets'—hence its name of 'Three Baskets' (P. *Tipiṭaka;* S. *Tripiṭaka*): the *Suttapiṭaka* (S. *Sūtrapiṭaka*), 'Basket of Discourses', i.e. of the Buddha); *Vinayapiṭaka,* 'Basket of the Discipline', i.e. of the Sangha or Buddhist Order; and *Abhidhammapiṭaka* (S. *Abhidharmapiṭaka*), 'Basket of Doctrinal Analysis', containing attempts at a systematic exposition of doctrines. With the demise of other Lesser Vehicle schools, the Elder school remains the sole living representative of this wing of Buddhism today.

EXEGESIS (*Mīmāṃsā*). The earliest exposition of Mīmāṃsā ritualism is the *Mī māṃsā-sūtra* ('Aphorisms of Exegesis') ascribed to Jaimini, which acquired their present form between 300 B.C.E. and 200 C E. Although other numerous commentaries of an early period were lost, there remains that of Śabara (? fifth century C.E.). This was commented on in turn by Kumārila Bhaṭṭa (eighth century C.E.) in *Ślokavārttika* ('Verse glosses'), dealing with the philosophical aspects of Exegesis. Prabhākara, a younger contemporary, though remaining loyal to the main features of Exegesis, differed from Kumārila over various matters—e.g. the latter accepted negative perception as a basis of knowledge. Thus two sub-schools of Exegesis were formed. This period also saw the substitution of the classical doctrine of release for that of the attainment of heaven as the goal of ritual endeavour. In the later medieval period, Exegesis was influenced by the new Logic school. This phase is summed up in the sixteenth century Nārāyaṇa's work, but remains largely unexplored.

IDEALISM (Vijñānavāda). The rise of Buddhist Idealism can be traced to a number of sources. First, earlier developments gave a phenomenalistic character to Buddhist speculation. For instance, the Sautrāntika school had argued that perception is representative and reflects outside objects, which are only known by inference. This suggested the Idealist thesis that there is no experiential evidence for an external world independent of consciousness. Second, the Voidist dialectic created a reaction against its rather intellectualist approach and stimulated the Idealists to stress yoga. This discipline would result in the purification of consciousness and suggested that ultimate reality itself is of the nature of pure consciousness. Third, docetic doctrines of the historical Buddha contributed to an illusionist account of the empirical world. The first great systematizer of Idealism was Maitreyanatha (? 270-350 B.C.E) known now chiefly through the work of his disciples the brothers Asanga and Vasubandhu (since there are differences of viewpoint in the works ascribed to the latter, it has been argued by Frauwallner that there are two persons of this name who have become conflated in the tradition: but see P.S. Jaini 'The Theory of Two Vasubandhus' in the *Bulletin of the School of Oriental and African Studies* (Vol. 21). The Idealist school remained in close liaison with the Voidists, though the Voidist Candrakīrti seventh century C.E.) criticized the Idealist position. Chief among later philosophers were Dignāga and Dharmakīrti, whose interests were mainly logical (fifth century onwards). The chief religious text of Idealism is the *Lankāvatāra-sūtra* ('Discourse of the Descent on Lanka'). Other important texts are the *Mahāyānasaṃgraha* ('Summary of the Greater Vehicle') of Asanga and the *Viṃśaka* and *Triṃśaka* ('Twenty Verses' and 'Thirty Verses') of Vasubandhu.

JAINISM (*Jaina* school). It is probable that Mahāvīra or Vardhamāna (see Biographical Information), at one time considered to be the 'founder' of Jainism, was merely the reformer of a tradition dating back to Pārśva (eighth century B.C.E) and beyond. The Jain tradition has carried on in a highly conservative way to the present day, though in the first century C.E. it became divided into two sects, the *Digambara* ('Sky-clad') and the *Śvetambara* ('White-clad'), the doctrinal differences between them being slight—they centre chiefly on the validity of the extant canon and on the issue of whether nudism for monks is necessary (nudism being a symbol of the complete renunciation of worldly goods and values). After flourishing considerably in the medieval period, especially in west and south India, Jainism now numbers probably less than two million adherents. During the period from the ninth to the fourteenth centuries, Jain writers took a considerable interest in logical matters, but the main shape of Jain doctrine was not affected. The chief authoritative expositions of Jain doctrine, apart from the canon (called the *Siddhānta* or *Āgama*) are the *Pravacanasāra* ('Essence of Exposition') of Kundakunda and the *Tattvārthādhigama sūtra* ('Aphorisms penetrating to fundamental principles') of Umāsvāti (some time after the third century C.E.).

LOGIC (*Nyāya*). The Logic viewpoint probably had its origin in the attempt to formulate rules of argument for use in disputations (a feature of the theological and philosophical life of India over a long period), and it probably existed as early as the fourth century B.C.E. The *Nyāya-sūtra* ('Logic aphorisms'), however, probably date from the second century C.E. and already include some elements from the Atomist aphorisms. This marks the beginning of the syncretism between the two schools. The *Nyāya-sūtra* was commented on by Vātsyāyaṇa (fifth century C.E.), Vācaspati (ninth century), Jayanta (tenth century) and others. By the time of Udayana (see Biographical Information) the two viewpoints were fully merged. However, about 200 C.E. the school of *Navyanyāya* (New Logic) was formed—mainly through the work of the logician Gaṅgeśa, and this

wing of Nyāya engaged in an interesting formalizaton of previous logic, which had mainly been oriented towards epistemology.
MATERIALISM (*Cārvāka*). The period from the sixth century (or earlier) saw an elaboration of sceptical and anti-religious ideas, known as Materialism or Cārvāka, after its legendary founder, naturalism, and *Lokāyata* (i.e. the doctrine that there is no world beyond the empirical cosmos). However, the original texts of the schools, or schools, are lost: and indeed there remains merely the seventh-century C.E. *Tattvopaplasimha* ('Lion assaulting all philosophical principles'). But there is a fair amount of information on the Materialist arguments from orthodox and Buddhist works which attempt to refute them. But there is a great deal of fluidity in the way in which Materialists are described, since there entered into this unorthodox, anti-religious tradition both genuinely materialistic views and sceptical ones (represented by the above-mentioned text). There remains therefore a lot of work to be done in disentangling the various strands of thought in the heterodox tradition, and this is made more difficult by its virtual demise by the late medieval period.

NON-DUALISM (*Advaita*). This school owes its main shape to Śaṅkara (see Biographical Information) in whose writings there is a confluence of Upaniṣadic and Mahāyāna ideas. He commented on the *Brahmasūtra* ('The Power aphorisms') of Bādarāyana (sometimes entitled *Vyāsa* or 'arranger', 'composer'), perhaps of the fourth century C.E. These writings were mediated to Śaṅkara by the orthodox Gauḍapāda (early eighth century C.E). Śaṅkara's powerful idealistic interpretation of the *Brahmasūtra* had an immediate impact, and his school was carried on by Maṇḍana Miśra, Sureśvara, Vācaspati Miśra (ninth century C E) and others. In the twelfth century, Śrīharṣa and others made use of dialectical methods to defend Non-Dualism, somewhat in the style of Voidist methods. The last two important figures of the traditional school of Non-Dualism (as opposed to modern interpretations) were Madhusudana and Appaya Dīkṣita (sixteenth century C.E.), both of whom wrote extensive religious, as well as metaphysical, works.

PERSONALISM. The circumstances of the arising of the Personalist school are not altogether clear, but by the second and first centuries different forms of the doctrine were in existence, as an offshoot from the Elders. They reacted against the break-up of the individual into groups of states which are essentially impersonal, and postulated a person behind the groups, to form a continuous personal entity which could persist into nirvana (this helped to establish the continued existence of the Buddha in line with transcendentalist views—see Glossary). By the seventh century they acquired considerable influence, but were under continual fire from other schools as covertly reintroducing the doctrine of a self, and later vanished from the Buddhist tradition, with the demise of Indian Buddhism. Only a handful of manuscripts explaining their position survive, and their main doctrines have been discovered through the recorded criticisms of their rivals.

QUALIFIED NON-DUALISM (*Viśiṣṭādvaita*). For the founder see RĀMĀNUJA in the section on Biographical Information; and for one of the principal exponents see VEṄKAṬANĀTHA. After Rāmānuja the school became divided into two sub-schools, which differed mainly on the nature of grace. The *Vaḍa-galai* school holds the 'cat-principle', viz. that the Lord transports the self to release just as the mother cat transports its kitten, without effort on the part of the latter. Thus once one is committed in devotional love to the Lord, he does the rest. On the other hand the *Ten-galai* adopted the 'monkey-principle'—the mother monkey leads her young along by the hand, and so the individual has to be active in co-operation with the Lord if he is to attain release. Latter religious developments were considerably influenced by the Qualified Non-Dualist doctrines, which became the most widespread basis (though modified often) for devotional religion.

REALISM (*Sarvāstivāda*). The *Sarvāstivāda* school is as old as that of the Elders, and the fairly close affinities between the two are notable; while the differences can be explained partly through the operation of geographical separation upon an oral tradition. The canon of the Realists was in Sanskrit, and the school had its principal influence in north-west India. The *Abhidharma* ('Doctrinal analysis') of the Realists is preserved in Chinese and Tibetan translations. By the early second century great commentaries (*Vibhāṣa*) were composed, and thus the school is often referred to as the *Vaibhāṣikas.* The chief exposition of Realist doctrines is to be found in the *Abhidharma-koṣa* of Vasubandhu (see IDEALISM).

ŚAIVITE DOCTRINE (*Śaiva Siddhānta*). Southern Śaivism probably had quite ancient roots, and there grew up a corpus of sacred literature, the *Śivāgamas* ('Scriptures of Śiva'). Added to these were Tamil texts, the *Tevaram*, including poems by three great teachers, Appar, Tirujñāna-Saṃbandhar and Sundaramūrti; they carried on a tradition of doctrine started by Tirumular (first century C.E.), and lived probably in the eighth century. At a slightly later period, there was the fourth and greatest of the Tamil-speaking poets and teachers, Mānikkavāchakar, whose *Tiru-vāchaka* is an extraordinarily fine devotional poem of some length. The theology implicit in this literature was expounded in the *Śiva-jñana-bodham* of MEYKAṆḌA (q.v). The most important other philosophical exponent of Śaivism, Śrikantha possibly belonged also to the thirteenth century. As well as in the south, forms of Śaivism flourished particularly in Gujrat and Kashmir.

VOIDISM (*Śūnyavāda*). Although it has been said that the Mādhyamika doctrines were the creation of NĀGĀRJUNA (q.v.), his approach is essentially a development of ideas found in the so-called 'Wisdom literature', the *Prajñāpāramitā* texts, the oldest of which, the *Astasāhasrikā* ('Eight thousand verses'), dates from the first century B.C.E. or earlier. It is probable that Nāgārjuna was acquainted with the famous *Saddharmapuṇḍarīka* ('Lotus of the Good Law'). But there is no doubt that it was Nāgārjuna who gave definitive shape to the dialectical method, and he was clearly a thinker of considerable brilliance and originality. His work was carried on by his pupil Aryadeva (late second century). During the fifth century there was a division within the Voidist school, between those (headed by Buddhapālita) who held strictly to the method of *reductio ad absurdum*, i.e. of convicting all theories of being contradictory—and thus establishing Voidism negatively; and those (headed by Bhāvaviveka), who employed positive apologetic arguments for Absolutism. with Candrakirti (sixth century C.E.) we get the reaffirmation of the dialectical method, and he and Sāntideva (seventh century) were highly influential. Candrakīrti's most penetrating work is his *Prasannapadā* ('Clear-worded'), an exposition of the *Mādhyamikā-karikā* of Nāgārjuna, Śāntideva's *Bodhicaryāvatāra* ('Manifestation of the practice of enlightenment') is a very popular Greater Vehicle text. Candrakirti, though criticizing the Idealists, recognized Idealism as valid at the ordinary level of truth, and this prepared the way for a full syncretism between the two schools. It was this form of Voidism that became the dominant philosophy of Tibetan Buddhism.

BIOGRAPHICAL INFORMATION

BUDDHA, THE. The title 'Buddha' is ascribed to Gautama (Pali: Gotama) (family name) or Siddhārtha (P. Siddhattha) (personal name) of the Sakya clan (hence he is known as Śākyamuṇi or 'sage of the Sakyas'). Another common title ascribed to him is Tathāgata (the meaning of which is debatable: but it probably means 'One who has gone thus', i.e. disappeared into a state that can only be indicated, not described). Probably born in 563 B.C.E. at Kapilavastu, near the borders of modern Nepal, he was son of a local prince, Suddhodana, and of Mahāmāyā (or Māyā). According to scriptural accounts he was brought up in some luxury and shielded from the painful features of worldly existence. But after growing up, he became acquainted with the facts of disease, old age and death, and with the fact that there were recluses who withdrew from the world in order to attain a higher peace and insight than the tribulations of ordinary life could bring. At the age of twenty-nine he therefore left his young wife (Yasodharā) and new-born child (Rahula), in order to go out as a wandering recluse in search of the solution to the problem of suffering. For some six years he, sometimes in company with five other ascetics, experimented with methods of self-mortification and austerity in the hope of achieving illumination; but concluded that such extremes are not helpful. Finally, under the Bo-tree at Bodh Gaya he achieved enlightenment, while seated in meditation. He thereafter went to Sarnath, just outside Banaras, and preached his first sermon to the five ascetics, who had in the meantime deserted him because of his repudiation of self-mortification. He spent the next forty or more years of his life in continuing his teaching, and founding an order of recluses, the Sangha, including both monks and nuns. He died, of a digestive illness, at Kusinara, not far from his birthplace, aged 80. Thus he achieved final nirvana.

CARAKA. One of the principal Indian writers on *Āyurveda* (literally 'science of life', i.e. traditional medicine). According to a Chinese source he was court physician to the emperor Kaniṣka (first century C.E.). At all events, he was probably a contemporary. He wrote the *Carakasamhita*, but left it unfinished, and it was completed by someone else, probably Dradhabala (ninth century C. E.).

CĀRVĀKA. The legendary founder of the Materialist school, sometimes called Cārvāka after him. Little or nothing is known of him, or whether indeed he was an historical personage at all.

KUMĀRILA. Kumārila Bhaṭṭa was, together with Prabhākara, one of the two great commentators on the *Mīmāṃsā-sutra* (i.e. 'Exegesis aphorisms') of Jaimini (third or second century B.C.E.) The philosophical portion of the commentary is the *Ślokavārttika* ('verse glosses'). He probably lived in the late eighth century C.E. The followers of Kumarila are referred to as the Bhattas.

LAKṢMĪ . Lakṣmi, or Śrī, is the divine consort of Viṣṇu, and is goddess of beauty and good fortune.

MADHVA. Born in 1197, Madhva came from Udipi, near Mangalore in South Canara, on the west coast of India south of Bombay. He was deeply opposed to the Non-Dualism of Śaṅkara, partly because of his Vaiṣṇavite affiliation. As a young man, he toured South India, establishing a powerful reputation for ability in doctrinal debate, chiefly against Non-Dualists. A tour in the north followed, and he seems later to have suffered some persecution from his opponents. However, little is known for sure of his biography, since the accounts of his life have a largely legendary character. These have led some to see Christian influence: e.g. he is supposed to have walked on water, etc., and to be the manifestation of Vāyu (*q.v.*), the god of wind or 'holy spirit'. He died at the age of 79 in 1276. His principal works were commentaries on the *Brahma-sūtra* (the holy Power aphorisms of Bāḍarāyana), on various Upanisads and on the *Gītā*, as well as a work called the *Tattvoddyota* ('Light on Principles').

MAHĀVĪRA. This is the title ascribed to Vardhamāna, the Jain teacher: literally it means 'Great Hero'. Other titles given to him (and to other great teachers in the tradition) are *Jina* or 'Victorious One' and *Tīrthaṃkara* or 'Fordmaker'. He was, like the Buddha, a *kṣatriya* or member of the warrior or noble class, not a Brahmin, and was born in Vaisali, north of Patna in Bihar, son of a prince, Siddhārtha, and of Triśālā. He married Yaśodā, and became father of a daughter. But at the age of thirty, after the death of his parents, he became a wandering ascetic (thus like the Buddha he too left his wife and child). After twelve years, he attained the experience of liberation and omniscience. He spent the rest of his life (forty-two years) preaching, and died of self-starvation in 477 or 467 B.C.E.

MEYKAṆḌA. The author of the *Śivajñānabodham* ('Explaining the knowledge of Śiva'), the principal text of southern Śaivism, i.e. of Saivite Doctrine as here expounded. He probably lived in the early part of the thirteenth century C. E.

NĀGĀRJUNA. Probably he was a Brahmin of South India. The details of his life, however, have become obscured by legend. Thus Tibetan sources describe him not merely as a metaphysician but as an alchemist. It is possible that an alchemist of the same name and roughly the same date has been confused with the philosopher. There is evidence connecting the philosophical Nāgārjuna with the great Buddhist centre of Nāgārjunikonda in Andhra Pradesh, and he had relations with a king of that area. However, the main scene of his philosophical activity was at the Buddhist university of Nālandā in North India. His main work is the *Mādhyamika-kārikā* ('Middle school verses'), the basic text of the Voidist school. He wrote five other larger treatises, some minor works and the *Catuḥ-stava* ('Four hymns'), which is of a devotional character.

PURANDARA. A later Materialist writer, probably of the seventh century.

RĀMĀNUJA. Born in 1017, according to tradition, though possibly up to a century later, in Bhūtapurī, in South India, Rāmānuja was married at sixteen, and shortly thereafter went to Kāñcī (Conjeevaram) to study. After a difference with his teacher, he set out for Śrīrangam (near Trichinopoly) to sit at the feet of Yamuna, whose doctrines corresponded to what Rāmānuja later formulated as his system of Qualified Non-Dualism but Yamuna died before Rāmānuja reached there. Rāmānuja, however, carried on Yamuna's work. About the age of thirty, or shortly thereafter, he renounced domestic life, and set up as a *sannyāsin* and thereafter, he renounced domestic life, and set up as a *sannyāsin* and religious teacher. Tours in South and North India, including Banaras, and Puri, where he established a monastery, were followed 1096, according to the traditional dating) by persecution by Rajendracola, a Śaivite king. He fled to the Hoysala country, where he succeeded in converting a Jain king. Later he was able to return to Śrīrangam, and died there at an advanced age (allegedly in 1137, which would make him 120 years old). His principal works are a commentary on the *Brahma-sūtras* (the holy Power aphorisms of Bāḍārāyana), the *Vedāntadīpa* ('Lamp of Vedanta'), *Vedāntasaṃgraha* ('Epitome of Vedanta') and *Vedāntasāra* ('Essence of Vedanta'), and a commentary on the *Gītā*.

ŚAṄKARA. Probably born in 788, at Kaladi in Kerala, Śaṅkara was a Śaivite Brahmin. Taking a vow of celibacy at an early age, he devoted himself with great energy not only to the composition of philosophical and religious treatises, but also to travel and the reform of religion. In the course of his travels, he founded monasteries at four points in west, north, south and east India. He made numerous converts, and in a short life of thirty-two years succeeded in leaving a lasting imprint on Indian theology. His teacher Govinda followed Gaudapada, who formulated a version of Non-Dualism; but it was Śaṅkara who gave the system definitive shape. His principal work is the commentary on the *Brahma-sūtra* ('The Power aphorisms'); and he also wrote important commentaries on the principal Upaniṣads and on the *Gītā*. Other writings include hymns of a devotional character.

ŚIVA. Literally 'Auspicious One', a name ascribed to Śiva because of his awesomeness, to ward off the terrible power of the God. Śiva ranks as one of the two great Gods of later Hinduism: he and Viṣṇu being regarded by their respective followers as Supreme Being. The cult of Śiva goes back to prehistoric times, judging from evidence found in excavations of the Indus Valley civilization. He combines opposing characteristics—he is the great ascetic, the *mahāyogī;* but also closely associated with fertility, the *liṅgam* or sacred phallus being his emblem. His consort Kali is usually depicted as peculiarly fierce and destructive—for the divine Being is both creator and dissolver or destroyer of the cosmos. Brahmā (the personal form of *Brahman* the holy Power), Viṣṇu and Śiva are regarded as the three forms of the Supreme Being, though Brahmā is not normally the object of a cult: thus later Hinduism represented Śiva and Viṣṇu as alternative manifestations of the one underlying Power.

UDAYANA. The Logic-Atomist writer of the tenth century C.E., whose chief work, the *Kusumāñjali* ('Handful of Flowers') is regarded as the principal text-book of natural theology in the Indian tradition: therein he collects together the arguments for the existence of a Lord.

VARDHAMĀNA. See MAHĀVĪRA.

VĀYU. The Vedic wind-god: conceived by Madhva as an important intermediary between the Lord and men.

VEṄKAṬANĀTHA. One of the principal Qualified Non-Dualists, Veṅkaṭanātha was born at Mañcī (Conjeevaram) in 1268. He was early recognized as showing promise of being one of the pillars of the Rāmānuja school, and spent his life in composing philosophical religious works, and in pilgrimages to the north. In 1326, Śrīraṅgam, where he then was, was pillaged by the Muslims, but he escaped by hiding among the corpses, and then fled to Mysore; when the temple at Śrīrangam was restored, he returned there. He died in 1369. His principal works are a commentary on Rāmānuja's *Brahma-sūtra* commentary, and an extensive logical work, the *Nyāyaparisuddhi* ('Classification of Logical Method'). In addition to philosophical and theological works, he wrote a number of poems, and drama based on the life of Kṛṣṇa.

VIṢṆU. One of the two great gods of Hinduism (see ŚIVA), though only a minor deity in the Vedic writings. His consort is LAKṢMĪ (*q.v.*). A gentler figure than his great rival, Viṣṇu is associated with the doctrine of incarnations, in which he descends to earth in various forms. His seventh and eighth incarnations are as the heroes Rama and Kṛṣṇa. By the medieval period the Buddha was counted a ninth incarnation; and Vaiṣṇavites look forward to a tenth, as Kalkī, who in the distant future will come to earth to rid it of evil.

SELECTED BIBLIOGRAPHY

1. GENERAL WORKS ON INDIAN PHILOSOPHY

DASGUPTA, Surendranath. *A History of Indian Philosophy,* 5 vols. (Cambridge, 1922- 1955).

FRAUWALLNER, E. *Geschichte der indischen Philosophie,* 2 vols. (Salzburg, 1953-56).

HIRIYANNA, Mysore. *The Essentials of Indian Philosophy* (2nd impression, London, 1951).

Outlines of Indian Philosophy (4th impression, London, 1958).

RADHAKRISHNAN, Sarvepalli. *Indian Philosophy,* 2 vols. (London, 1923-27).

RADHAKRISHNAN, S. and MOORE, C.A. *A Source Book in Indian Philosophy* (Princeton, 1957).

RADHAKRISHNAN, S. and others. *History of Philosophy Eastern and Western,* vol. I (London, 1952).

TUCCI, Giuseppe. *Storia della filosofia indiana* (Bari, 1957).

WARDER, A.K. *Outline of Indian Philosophy* (Delhi, 1971).

ZIMMER, Heinrich. *Philosophies of India* (ed. Joseph Campbell, New York, 1957).

2. BUDDHISM

BRANDON, S.G.F. *The Saviour God* (Manchester, 1963).

CONZE, E. *Buddhism: Its Essence and Development* (London, 1954).

Buddhist Thought in India (reprint, Ann Arbor, 1970).

The Prajñāpāramitā. (The Hague, 1990).

COOMARASWAMY, Ananda. *Buddha and the Gospel of Buddhism* (London, 1928).

DUTT, Sukumar. *Buddhist Monks and Monasteries of India* (London, 1962).

DAVIDS, C.A.F. Rhys. *The Birth of Indian Psychology and its Development in Buddhism* (London, 1935).

Sakya or Buddhist Origins (London, 1931).

GOMBRICH, Richard. *Precept and Practice* (Oxford, 1971).

Theravada Buddhism (London, 1988).

KALUPAHANA, David J. *Buddhist Philosophy: A Historical Analysis* (Honolulu, 1976).

KEITH, A.B. *Buddhist Philosophy in India and Ceylon* (Oxford, 1923).

LING, Trevor. *Buddhism and the Mythology of Evil* (London, 1961).

LUBAC, H. de. *La Rencontre du Bouddhisme et l'Occident* (Paris, 1952).

MURTI, T.R.V. *The Central Philosophy of Buddhism* (London, 1955).

PANDE, G.C. *Studies in the Origins of Buddhism* (Allahabad, 1957).

SILBURN, Lilian. *Instant et Cause* (Paris, 1955).

STCHERBATSKY, Th. *The Central Conception of Buddhism and meaning of the word 'dharma'* (London, 1924).

Buddhist Logic, 2 vols. (Leningrad, 1932).

STRENG, Frederick J. *Emptiness: A Study in Religious Meaning* (New York, 1967).

SUZUKI, D.T. *Studies in the Lankāvatāra Sūtra* (London, 1932).

THOMAS, E.J. *History of Buddhist Thought* (London, 1933).

WARDER, A.K. *Indian Buddhism* (Delhi, 1970).

WILLIAMS, Paul. *Mahayana Buddhism* (London, 1989).

3. JAINISM

DELLA CASA, Carlo. *Il giainismo* (Torino, 1962).

JAINI, Jagmandar. L. *Outlines of Jainism* (Cambridge, 1940).

JAINI, Padmanabh. *The Jaina Path of Purification* (Berkeley, 1979).

GLASENAPP, H. von. *Der Jainismus* (Berlin, 1925).

STEVENSON, MRS. S.T. *The Heart of Jainism* (London, 1915).

4. OTHER UNORTHODOX SCHOOLS

BASHAM, A.L. *History and Doctrines of the Ājīvikas, a vanished Indian religion (London, 1951).*

MITTAL, Keval Krsna. *Materialism in Indian Thought* (Delhi, 1974)

RIEPE, Dale. *The Naturalistic Tradition in Indian Thought* (Seattle, 1961).

TUCCI, Giuseppe. *Linee di una storia del materialismo indiano* (Rome, 1924).

5. EXEGESIS

JHA, Ganganatha. *Pūrva Mīmāṃsā in Its Sources* (BHU, Varanasi, 1964.)

KEITH, A.B. *The Karma Mīmāṃsā* (London, 1921).

MAZUMDAR, P.K. *The Philosophy of Language in the Light of Pāṇinian and Mīmāṃsaka Schools of Indian Philosophy* (Calcutta, 1977).

THADANI, N.V. *The Mīmāmsā; the Sect of the Sacred Doctrines of the Hindus* (New Delhi, 1952).

6. DISTINCTIONISM AND YOGA

DANIÉLOU, A. *Yoga: The Method of Reintegration* (London, 1949).

ELIADE, M. *Yoga: Immortality and Freedom* (London, 1958).

KEITH, A.B. *The Sāṃkhya System,* 2nd edn. (London, 1924).

LARSON, G.J. *Classical Sāṃkhya,* 2nd edn. (Delhi, 1979).

LARSON, G.J. and BHATTACHARYA, R.S. (eds.) *Sāṁkhya: A Dualist Tradition in Indian Philosophy* (Princeton, 1988).

WERNER, Karel. *Yoga and Indian Philosophy* (Delhi, 1977).

7. LOGIC AND ATOMISM

BHATTACHARYYA, Gopikamohan. *Studies in Nyāya-Vaiseṣika Theism* (Calcutta, 1961).

INGALLS, D.H.H. *Materials for the Study of Navya-Nyāya Logic* (Cambridge, Mass., 1951).

KEITH, A.B. *Indian Logic and Atomism* (Oxford, 1921).

MATILAL, B.K. *Nyāya-Vaiśeṣika* (Wiesbaden, 1977).

MOHANTY, J. N. *Gaṅgeśa's Theory of Truth* (Delhi, 1989).

POTTER, Karl H. *Indian Metaphysics and Epistemology* (Princeton, 1978).

RANDLE, H.N. *Indian Logic of the Early Schools* (Oxford, 1930).

SEAL, B. *The Positive Sciences of the Ancient Hindus* (London, 1915).

VIDYABHUSANA, S.C. *A History of Indian Logic* (Calcutta, 1921).

8. NON-DUALISM

BHATTACHARYA, Asutosh. *Studies in Post-Sankara Dialectics* (Calcutta, 1936).

BHATTACHARYA, Kalidas. *A Modern Understanding of Advaita Vedanta* (Ahmedabad, 1975).

DEUTSCH, Eliot. *Advaita Vedānta: A Philosophical Reconstruction* (Honolulu, 1969)

DEVANANDAN, Paul. *The Concept of Māyā* (London, 1950).

GOVINDAGOPAL, Mukhopadhyaya. *Studies in the Upaniṣads* (Calcutta, 1960).

LACOMBE, O. *L'Absolu selon le Vedānta* (Paris, 1937).

NIKHILANANDA, Swami. *Self-Knowledge (Ātmabodha)* (New York, 1936).

OTTO, R. *Mysticism East and West* (New York, 1932).

URQUHART, W.S. *The Vedanta and Modern Thought* (Oxford, 1928).

9. QUALIFIED NON-DUALISM

CARMAN, John B. *The Theology of Rāmānuja* (New Haven, 1974).

CARPENTER, J. Estlin. *Theism in Medieval India* (London, 1921).

LOTT, Eric J. *God and the Universe in the Vedantic Theology of Rāmānuja* (Madras, 1976).

SRINIVASACHARI, P.N. *The Philosophy of Bhedābheda*, 2nd edn., revised and enlarged (Adyar, 1950).

SRINIVASACHARI, S.M. *Advaita and Visiṣṭā*dvaita (London, 1961).

10. DUALISM

GLASENAPP, H. von. *Madhvas Philosophie des Vishnu Glaubens, mit einer Einleitung über Madhva und seine Schule* (Bonn, 1923).

KRISHNASWAMI AIYAR. *Srī Madhwa and Madhwaism* (Madras, 1907).

RAGHAVACHAR, S.S. *Dvaita Vedanta* (Madras, 1977).

RAGHAVENDRACHAR, H.N. *The Dvaita Philosophy and its Place in the Vedanta* (Mysore, 1941).

SHARMA, B. N. K. *Madhva's Teachings in his own Words* (Bombay, 1963).

A History of Dvaita School of Vedānta and its Literature, 2 vols., 2nd edn. (Bombay, 1981).

11. ŚAIVITE DOCTRINE

DHAVAMONY, Mariasusai. *Love of God according to Saiva Siddhānta*, (Oxford, 1971)

MAHADEVAN, T.M.P. *The Idea of God in Saiva Siddhānta* (Annamalai, 1955).

PARANJOTI, V. *Śaiva Siddhānta* (London, 1954).

12. MISCELLANEOUS

BILIMORIA, Puruṣottama. *Śabdapramāṇa: Word and Knowledge, A Doctrine in Nyāya-Mīṃāmsā Philosophy.* (Dordrech 1988).

CHENNAKESAVAN, S. *The Concept of Mind in Indian Philosophy* (London, 1960).

ELIOT, Charles. *Hinduism and Buddhism, an historical sketch,* 3 vols. (London, 1921).

MAHADEVAN, T.M.P. *Invitation to Indian Philosophy* (New Delhi, 1974).

MATILAL, B.K. *Perception : An Essay on the Theories of Knowledge in Classical Indian Philosophy* (Oxford, 1986).

RADHAKRISHNAN, S. *The Brahma Sūtra* (London, 1960).

SMART, N. *Reasons and Faiths* (London, 1958).

STACE, W.T. *Mysticism and Philosophy* (London, 1960).

ZAEHNER, R.C. *At Sundry Times* (London, 1958).

(ed.) *Concise Encyclopedia of Living Faiths* (London, 1959).

INDEX OF SUBJECTS

See also the Glossary; and the major schools are also found in the Brief Histories of the Schools.

INDEX OF NAMES

INDIAN THOUGHT

ISSN 0924-8986

1. MOHANTY, J.N. (ed.), Ganeśwar Miśra. Language, Reality, and Analysis. Essays on Indian Philosophy. 1990.
   ISBN 90 04 09305 2
2. JACKSON, W.J. (ed.), J.L. Mehta on Heidegger, Hermeneutics and Indian Tradition. 1992.
   ISBN 90 04 09488 1
3. CHATTOPADHYAY, R., A Vaiṣṇava Interpretation of the *Brahmasūtras*. Vedānta and Theism. Translated by KANTI CHATTOPADHYAY. Preface by BIMAL K. MATILAL. 1992.
   ISBN 90 04 09570 5
4. SMART, N., Doctrine and Argument in Indian Philosophy. (Second revised edition). 1992.
   ISBN 90 04 09479 2